IMAGINING THE ACADEMY

IMAGINING THE ACADEMY

higher education and popular culture

EDITED BY

Susan Edgerton, Gunilla Holm, Toby Daspit, and Paul Farber

RoutledgeFalmer

NEW YORK AND LONDON

Published in 2005 by
RoutledgeFalmer
270 Madison Avenue
New York, NY 10016
www.routledge-ny.com

Published in Great Britain by
RoutledgeFalmer
2 Park Square
Milton Park, Abingdon,
Oxon, OX14   4RN
www.routledgefalmer.com

Printed in the United States of America on acid-free paper.

10 9 8 7 6 5 4 3 2 1

Library of Congress Cataloging-in-Publication Data

Imagining the academy: higher education and popular culture/edited by
Susan Edgerton . . . [et al.].—1st ed.
     p. cm.
   Includes bibliographical references and index.
   ISBN 0-415-92936-9 (alk. paper) — ISBN 0-415-92937-7 (pb : alk. paper)
1. Education in popular culture—United States. 2. Education, Higher—
Social aspects—United States. 3. Education, Higher—United States—
Marketing. 4. Education, Higher—United States—Public opinion. 5. Public
opinion—United States. I. Edgerton, Susan Huddleston, 1955–
   LC191.94.I53 2004
   306.43'2—dc22
                                                        2004009275

To

Mary Beth
Matilda
Toni, Terry, and Tracy

Contents

Acknowledgments

We are especially grateful to our contributors for their immense patience as we struggled to complete this manuscript through a variety of obstacles. We want to thank our colleagues at Western Michigan University and at Massachusetts College of Liberal Arts for their continuous support. Thanks go to the editors at Routledge: Karita Dos Santos, Seema Shah, Paul Johnson, and Catherine Bernard, who shepherded us through the various phases of this project as well as through changes at Routledge. Special thanks to Elizabeth Ellsworth, Peter Taubman, and an anonymous reviewer for useful suggestions and encouragement. We are grateful to Stephanie Higdon for her assistance with some technical matters. Deep gratitude goes to Stacy Alatalo and to Ellen Barber for their willingness to read works in progress and to offer helpful commentary.

Introduction
Dreaming the Academy

SUSAN EDGERTON AND PAUL FARBER

As I (Susan) pass through my living room where the television is on for the day's weather forecast, I hear for the umpteenth time the commercial for Olympia Career Training Institute: A bank teller asks her customer, who is making a deposit, "And did you win the lottery?" Customer replies, "No, but I got a really great job" (after graduating from OCTI). I get my coffee and return minutes later. It's on again, but this time the happy OCTI student peeps, "Four years of college is not for everyone—especially not me. I needed a REAL career, and I needed it fast!" The emphasis on the word *real* seems to imply something negative about the careers that result from traditional nonprofit, four-year college educations. "Maybe that's what's wrong with me," I mutter, "I need a REAL career." Later, at the university where I work, I attend meetings about new kinds of "outreach" that are clearly entrepreneurial, hear complaints about a part-time faculty member in a new regional center program, and listen to arguments about theory versus practice. There are discussions about the "dumbing down" of teacher education classes and American Association of University Professors (AAUP) contract negotiation issues. There are discussions with colleagues jealous over promotions, publications, and privileges. I work behind a computer in my tiny (but larger than most others on the floor) office in a run-down 1960s building that has been scheduled for renovation for the past ten years but has once again been placed on a back burner.

Still, whatever the frustrations, I know that life as a professor is a privileged life in so many ways. Many of us enjoy flexibility of schedules, much

1

work that can be done at home, work that can challenge and reward one's creative spirit, and more. But it also offers a disturbing standpoint from which to observe some of the worst trends in social and cultural change, as well as the best. Such a standpoint carries with it the responsibility of speaking one's "truth to power."

Finally, home for the day, I spend a seductive hour with *The Education of Max Bickford*, a short-lived television series about a history professor at a private elite college. There are scenes amidst masses of ivy, hardwood floors and trim, and big wooden desks in big messy offices. The professor, played by Richard Dreyfuss, is wise though flawed. The issues he faces look like few of mine as a professor in a large Midwestern state university. The next day begins with news of students at my university who have rioted for the second time this year as the culmination of a drunken party. It was "to relieve stress," one student explained to the news reporter. At work, our dean suggests that the only research that counts for us now is funded research. We are shown slick, expensive new recruitment brochures meant to convey images of a serious learning community that is also full of fun and images of a world of work after college that is exciting and rewarding, leaving everyone in smiles.

Many times I've heard colleagues and myself utter the phrase, "This is not what I thought it would be like to be an academic—to be a *professor*." Why was our image of the academy so different from the reality? How was it different? What is the broader public image of the academy, and how does that differ from "reality?" How have those images and that reality changed over the years? What expectations of the academy resonate within contemporary society? Based on the variety and often-contradictory nature of comments we get from student evaluations of our classes, one could argue that expectations are complex and multiple. In an institution that is increasingly operating as a corporation, we are continually striving to "please the customer," as if we know what the customer wants. It would be important, if for no other reason than that, to explore the multifarious ways in which academia is perceived and fantasized in order to expose the fallacies of such a pursuit. But the reasons run deeper.

The nature and direction of higher education in American society are matters widely pondered. What transpires in higher education directly and profoundly affects the well-being of the society as a whole. This is so in part because of the kinds of expertise and leadership that higher education is expected to foster. But more than this, higher education represents a crossroads of our social and political landscape, the nearest thing we have to a laboratory for addressing the promise and challenges of our contentious, culturally diverse, and fundamentally incomplete democracy.

A great deal is said and written about the role and tendencies of higher education. The debates and discussions are earnest, as they should be, and often illuminating. Scholarly works, high-level policy studies, and journalism each in their own way confront issues in higher education and contribute to public understanding and debate. Within particular colleges and universities, vigorous internal debates over priorities and initiatives are commonplace. Both kinds of discussion are important and welcome, a sign of health in the institution of higher education.

This book was written to place such efforts in a seldom-acknowledged context. What higher education is, what it means, and where it is (or should be) heading are not matters for specialists and experts alone to judge. The questions have meaning and carry consequences for broad segments of the population in an open, democratic society. And in any event, whatever any elite panel of commentators might believe or wish for, the policies and practices of higher education depend upon forms of public support and a workable convergence of views, as, for example, when the expectations of entering students encounter the demands of their professors. The question, then, is how the broader public understands the institution of higher education. By what means do notions about the academy and its role in society circulate and crystallize in people's minds? The question points to the diverse phenomena and ubiquitous media of popular culture.

The book is intended to draw together diverse studies of the relationship of higher education and popular culture. In these pages, we examine representations of higher education in various forms of popular culture, both historical and contemporary. The meanings of "cultural studies" and "popular culture" and approaches toward their study are embedded in an academic history of contestation with analyses that range between the structuralist and the post-structuralist or post-modernist. Contributions to this volume represent a variety of methodological approaches to cultural studies as well as a variety of points of view toward the concept of popular culture. It is our hope that the reader will find a balanced offering in this set of stories around the relationship of popular culture and higher education. These works, taken together, ground and extend inquiry, exploring ways in which debates about the status and purpose of higher education are shaped and constrained by notions circulating in the wider culture through the media of popular culture.

The book is organized around three matters central to the evolving landscape and mission of higher education, in sections entitled: *Constructing and Contesting the Image of the Ivory Tower*, *The New Vocationalism and the Marketing of Higher Education*, and *Exploring Identity and Difference in the Context of Higher Education*. Before introducing the work in these sections, however, it should be understood that within these three categories there are different but overlapping approaches to the study of relationships between higher education and popular culture. Some chapters, through the analysis of movies, novels, television, and/or music, examine popular representations of higher education in those venues. A second approach involves exploring the impact of larger (popular) cultural movements on the university. For example, it can be argued that the ways market forces have educated us to a shopping mentality influence our approaches to selecting and dealing with a university as consumers in a shopping mall. In such a world, *credentials* take precedence over traditional notions of what it means to become an educated person (see, e.g., Labaree, 1997). University administrators feel compelled to respond to these pressures, at times, by situating students as customers. Hence, a third approach of study must be to view higher education as a conveyer of, and conduit for, popular cultural forms through, for example, advertisements for universities and hidden curricula validating anti-intellectual and entrepreneurial tendencies.

Constructing and Contesting the Image of the Ivory Tower

To what extent and in what ways is the popular notion of academia as the ivory tower accurate and desirable? In what ways does it serve to marginalize the work and limit the effectiveness of scholars in academia to have an impact on urgent social and political issues and debates of their time? Alternatively, to what extent does intellectual freedom, and much that is good emerging from it, depend upon academic insulation from the everyday affairs, interests, and pressures of the "real world?" Academic scholars have a vital interest in how the traditional notion of the ivory tower evolves because it colors public perceptions of the worth, relevance, and meaning of their work. And because such perceptions in turn condition the possibilities for academics in addressing vital issues of the day from their place in the academy, others with an interest in such matters also have a stake in how the image of the ivory tower changes over time. Contesting notions abound about the distance there is, or should be, between the academic and everyday worlds. Part I of this book explores how popular culture reflects and informs such notions and the debates in which they are entangled.

Susan Talburt and Paula M. Salvio's chapter, "The Personal Professor and the Excellent University," "explore[s] the effects of consumerist and technocratic ideologies and practices on the work of faculty and on the ways academics' responses do and do not challenge the privatization of the university's purposes." They examine both the concept of institutional "excellence," developed by Bill Readings, and the personal writing by "academic stars" that emerges from this notion of excellence. Some such writing, they argue, becomes tangled up in a complex matrix of ego, the erotics of teaching, and the commodification of the educational process. Indeed, for certain popular types of academic personal or autobiographical writing, the work serves to further commodify ourselves and our work. Instead, Salvio and Talburt suggest that we "engage in sustained conversations about the ways in which the personal can be used to address how academics and students are complicit in sustaining a logic of excellence that fosters a profound sense of displacement and isolation."

In "Picturing Institutions: Intellectual Work as Gift and Commodity in *Good Will Hunting*," Jo Keroes presents a detailed study of *Good Will Hunting*, a film centered on the story of young man of hidden mathematical genius who, coming to the attention of a distinguished MIT professor, grapples with conflicts of class, loyalty to his friends, and the potential uses of his gifts. Keroes's treatment of this film explores its portrayal of deep American ambivalence about the nature and value of intellectual activity, the way that extraordinary talents are converted to a commodity in higher education, and the longing for a kind of authentic teaching that functions instead as an exchange of gifts (as exemplified in Will Hunting's relationship with a community college teacher unencumbered by ambition). The analysis in this chapter presents a range of questions, attitudes, and tensions about the intersection of higher education and the life of the mind.

Susan Ikenberry, in "Education for Fun and Profit," examines the history of popular college fiction as it has represented—and often romanticized—university life, professors, students, and the college classroom. In so doing, she more accurately describes the intellectual self-image of American society and culture. This essay provides evidence of some of the historical roots of the American conflation of education and democracy with credentialism, social mobility, and vocational training as opposed to the idealized notion of the university as a center of ideas and a humanizing and democratizing force.

Michelle Byers, in "Those Happy Golden Years," critiques the cultural spaces of television and education as sites of performance using one of the more comprehensive television portrayals of college life, the popular *Beverly Hills, 90210* (1990–2000). Byers explores the production of California University as it performs educators and education, and the way it reflects the representations of these in popular culture more generally. By focusing on *90210* thematically through teacher/student relations, university politics, and issues of gender and race, she investigates the discursive and ideological structures of *90210*. What Byers reveals is how these performances and discourses allow for a positive reading of (mis)education.

Toby Daspit and John A. Weaver, in "Rap (in) the Academy," raise the question, "*What*, now, is the academy?" Just as Peter Kramer (*Listening to Prozac*) asked us to revisit our definitions of "self" and "personality," and N. Katherine Hayles and Donna Haraway report to us the extent to which our "selves" are integrally connected to our machines, Daspit and Weaver wonder at the new nature of the academy in such a techno-culture. How does the academy manage to constrain meanings and thereby guard itself from "lo-tek" hackers (rappers), and yet simultaneously commodify, or support commodification of and by, the same?

The New Vocationalism and the Marketing of Higher Education

A second issue revolves around public perceptions of the role of universities. How universities garner and maintain support for their mission has changed over time. The older notion of a kind of higher calling closely linked to the roots of higher education as a training ground for clerics has given way to a new kind of vocationalism. Universities are now geared to and marketed in terms of their role as credentialing agencies and sites for the development of marketable skills and expertise. Although, as David Kirp (2003) reminds us, the university has *always* been driven by the pursuit of funds, "what *is* new, and troubling, is the raw power that money directly exerts over so many aspects of higher education." (p. 3) In some situations, Kirp notes, market forces within and upon the university have had positive effects. It is good news, too, that lively debates rage within academia about the soul of higher education. The future of such debates and their practical possibilities are greatly influenced and constrained by the public's perception of what higher education provides. Hence, popular perceptions of the university's "cash value"—the personal and social economic interests it is believed to enhance—have a distinct bearing on internal struggles to shape and define the mission and values of academia.

Paul Farber and Gunilla Holm examine the self-presentation of universities in 30-second promotional films made for television, typically shown during broadcasts of college athletic events, in their chapter, "Selling the Dream of Higher Education." University promos are analyzed in terms of the principal slogans they present, the most common images they incorporate, the major interest groups to whom they are addressed, and the thematic tensions they embody. These unifying elements are examined against the contrasting backdrop of prevailing conflicts, tensions, and uncertainties that characterize contemporary higher education.

Karen Anijar, in "In Just Six Short Weeks, You Too Can Be a Truck Driver, a Teacher, or a Preacher . . . a Doctor, Lawyer, . . . or Engineer," offers a provocative suggestion that proprietary institutions, many of which have been built on fraudulent claims, may have led the way toward greater corporatization for traditional higher educational institutions in recent years. Through various political and marketing strategies that could have included "infiltration" of government regulating agencies, proprietary institutions of higher learning now occupy a prominent position in the higher education marketplace. The Higher Education Act of 1998 "afforded proprietary schools closer to equal status with 'traditional' colleges and universities," Anijar writes, enabling money to flow for student loans and otherwise from the government to these institutions at a more vigorous rate than ever before. Now, traditional universities must compete for students with schools that advertise almost instant gratification and superior practicality. No effort is expended attempting to disguise disdain for "ivory tower eggheads"—that is, traditional notions of the intellectual and the calling of the university.

In "Meritocracy at Middle Age: Skewed Views and Selective Admissions," John G. Ramsay examines longstanding issues concerning the way valued places in higher education are allocated in the competitive context of selective admissions. In particular, he attends to debates and perspectives concerning the question of how meritocratic such a process is or ought to be. Given the inherent complexity of the social phenomena in question, a central role in public understanding of the issues is played by popular and journalistic accounts of aspects of the competitive testing and admissions system. These include cartoons, newspaper stories, magazine articles centered both on public affairs and personal anecdotes, as well as book-length studies. Ramsay's discussion provides an overview of and context for such accounts. In doing so, he frames current issues that warrant consideration as the more or less meritocratic selection process unfolds in higher education.

Glenn M. Hudak, in "On Publicity, Poverty, and Transformation," employs psychoanalytic and interpretive approaches to examining the motives behind publicity as well as to explain how it is received—why it works. Closely examining a slick brochure promoting a teacher education program in the competitive New York City market, he uncovers elements of our deepest and least acknowledged desires, fears, and illusions. Hudak concludes, with interpretive readings from theological and spiritual literature, that the movement of educational institutions into more and more consumerist appeals and promises undermines our very deepest desires to "be all that we can be."

Exploring Identity and Difference in the Context of Higher Education

Finally, universities have long provided a context both for individual self-exploration and for the examination of and struggles over the meaning of group identity and difference, centered on categories such as race, social class, gender, ethnicity, and sexual orientation. The opportunities provided for such exploration in connection with exposure to multiple perspectives, intellectual exchange, and cultural alterity are manifest. But popular images and ideas about the nature and promise of such engagements vary greatly. Suggestive notions about the value of the personal encounters in higher education shape and constrain what ultimately is possible. The issue then is how popular culture conditions the way participants in higher education, and in particular professors and students, think about and enter into the patterns of interaction that the institution supports.

In "'Should I Stay or Should I Go?' Lesbian Professors in Popular Culture," Allison J. Kelaher Young focuses on themes depicted in *Desert Hearts* (1985) and *When Night is Falling* (1995), which relate stories of lesbian professors reconciling their professional and personal-sexual identities. *Desert Hearts* and *When Night is Falling* focus on the transformation of the professor from a rigid academic to a more open and multidimensional person. However, this transformation may have a professional cost, which is an issue explored more clearly in *When Night Is Falling*. Situating herself as a white middle-class lesbian professor, Young explores how these depictions of lesbian professors leave us with many questions involving issues of identity, visibility, fear, and freedom within and outside the academy as well as the role that the institutional environment plays in coming to terms with one's personal-sexual identity. She analyzes the models these films create for gays and lesbians in higher education and how these films serve to expose the silencing conservatism of institutions of higher education, which exists in stark contrast to the popular perception of academia as liberal.

"Mamet's *Oleanna* in Context: Performance, Personal, Pedagogy" by Lee Papa is a personal, anecdotal look at three performances of David Mamet's *Oleanna* and how interpretation of the play shifted due to directorial interpretation, place of performance, and circumstances around the performances. The play's initial run on Broadway caused controversy and debate that spilled into the popular press. Because of *Oleanna*'s ambiguous take on political correctness and sexual harassment, the performative environment has always influenced its performance and reception. Papa discusses these intersections between performance, culture, and academia. He examines the power issues that both deconstruct and reify the power of professor in the classroom as well as how *Oleanna* creates a discursive paradox for teachers of drama.

In "Vampires on Campus: Reflections on (Un)Death, Transformation, and Blood Knowledges in *The Addiction*," Morna McDermott and Toby Daspit explore possible meanings in Abel Ferrara's 1995 film *The Addiction*. The film centers on Kathleen, a New York City doctoral student in philosophy, who while completing her dissertation also struggles with the transition from being human to becoming a vampire. The authors, a tenure track assistant professor and a recent PhD graduate, use autobiographical reflections from their educational and life histories, including their past romantic relationship, to investigate poststructural implications for the way knowledge is represented in Ferrara's film. They suggest, using a post–avant-garde framework, that Kathleen's "annihilation of the self" gestures toward new ways that the academy might respond to the uncertainty and fluidity of "knowledge" in poststructural contexts.

"Black Higher Learnin': Black Popular Culture and the Politics of Higher Education," centers on two popular films exploring facets of contemporary black experience in higher education. Here Linwood M. Cousins examines the works of Spike Lee (*School Daze*) and John Singleton (*Higher Learning*) in the context of current debates about the educational achievements and aspirations of African Americans in American society. The films display something of the complex interplay of race- and class-based themes and issues in higher education. Lee's film attends closely to issues arising among blacks in the setting of a distinguished black college. Singleton evokes the interplay of both intraracial and interracial tensions in higher education. The chapter centers on an analysis of specific scenes and dialogue that are revealing with regard to the issues in question. This highlights important features of the contested meanings of higher education for the characters displayed. Taken together, the films suggest how black popular culture has lifted into view significant ideas about and considerations affecting the expression of black aspirations in higher education.

The Context of Academia: Emerging Imperatives and the Popular Imagination

As organized in these three sections, we see a range of tensions and possibilities generating discussion and exploration as higher education evolves. Should the walls of the ivory tower be bolstered or dismantled, and in either case, how? What is the place of the new vocationalism in higher education, and how should academia market itself? What are the most desirable ways to conceptualize the role of higher education as a site of self-discovery and a meeting ground of multiple perspectives and cultures? Popular culture is not silent on any of this. The popular imagination is stoked and stimulated on all of these fronts as popular media circulate images and ideas that the discussion cannot help but reflect and ought, in fact, to address. The studies in this volume provide some starting points for inquiry into how this is so and why it matters.

Although this division of the collection is a convenient way to organize and differentiate among the various perspectives and approaches in contributions, it should be understood that several chapters touch on issues within more than one of these categories. We have identified an additional theme that cuts across many of the chapters in this volume and therefore warrants mention at this time. It concerns the variety of ways in which popular cultural forms are now taken up as well as employed and extended by institutions of higher education. To see this, and in order to understand this book as fulfilling the title's promise, it seems important that we attempt to clarify our use of the phrase "popular culture." But it must be understood that, as with any terminology that matters to people, this phrase has a history of contested connotations and denotations.

Raymond Williams, upon returning to Cambridge after World War II, found that key terms in academic humanities and social sciences seemed to be taking on new significances and alluding to new contexts. In 1956 he wrote his well-known *Culture and Society* and included an appendix in which he had begun to trace the history and evolution of terms such as *culture*, *art*, and *democracy*. The publisher forced removal of the appendix for reasons of space, and so Williams began to develop a book dedicated to the concept and process of that appendix. It was completed in 1976 and became an influential title for years thereafter. *Keywords* (1976) begins the entry for *culture* with an extended history of the word's usage. Williams notes that hostility toward the term began to build as early as the late nineteenth and early twentieth centuries. He writes:

> It is significant that virtually all the hostility (with sole exception of the temporary anti-German association) has been connected with uses involving claims to superior knowledge, refinement (*culchah*) and distinctions between 'high' (**culture**) and popular art and entertainment. It thus records a real social history and a very difficult and confused phase of social and cultural development. It is interesting that the steadily extending social and anthropological use of **culture** and **cultural** and such formations as **sub-culture**, has, except in certain areas (notably *popular entertainment*), either bypassed or effectively diminished the hostility and its associated unease and embarrassment (pp. 92–3).

Popular culture has also inspired hostility through the years, though for largely different reasons. Prior to the nineteenth century, the term *popular* generally implied a kind of political manipulation, as in "courting the favour of the people by undue practices." (Collier, 1697, cited in Williams, 1976, p. 237) Though it gradually turned to a meaning of those things decided upon or made by "the people" for themselves, it has continued to maintain the pejorative sense in its association with "inferior kinds of work (cf. **popular literature, popular press** as distinguished from *quality press*); and work deliberately setting out to win favour (**popular journalism** as distinguished from *democratic journalism*, or **popular entertainment**) ... The sense of **popular culture** as the culture actually made by the people for themselves is different from all these." (Williams, 1976, p. 237) Williams' analysis continues to inform scholars of cultural studies and popular culture; however, new developments in the university since the book's 1976 publication have made it sensible to expand and redefine somewhat our conceptions of the popular with respect to academia.

In *Academic Keywords: A Devil's Dictionary for Higher Education* (1999), a title play on Williams' classic (as well as Ambrose Bierce's *Devil's Dictionary*), Cary Nelson and Stephen Watt extend the lexicon for cultural studies to include "corporate university" and "distance learning," to name two entries related to our collection. For example, increasing emphasis on funded research as the "only real research" by public institutions that are increasingly dependent on private funds moves university culture deeper into the world of commodification and compromise, as several chapters here attest. Nelson and Watt write of the corporatized university department,

> When the profit available from contract research becomes a department's main priority, then prestige and rewards flow to the department members bringing in the money. As institutions become more broadly addicted to the corporate profit pipeline, their whole raison d'etre begins to shift. Profit-making departments become the first priority for institutional resources, and the profit-making function within those departments begins to dominate their other activities, from student recruitment to faculty hiring to curriculum design. 'Excellence,' that ambiguous, hyperbolic concept aptly analyzed by Bill Readings, gradually becomes conflated with profitability. . . . *Those departments that reach the nadir of corporatization abandon all their intellectual function* (1999, p. 86).

We might add that as corporate needs and functions become less and less distinguishable from state needs and functions, so goes the influence of government-funded research in the university as well. Funded research, whether by corporation or government, has become an increasingly important financial resource and motivator for universities over the past three decades, and this tendency has been dramatically exacerbated by the higher education budget crisis of the same time. This crisis has never been more acute than it is as we write in 2004. The potential ramifications are many and ominous. For example, as Robert F. Kennedy, Jr. writes, the marriage of the federal government to corporate interests in funding of scientific research is catapulting the nation (and, indeed, the world) into an alarming environmental descent (Kennedy, 2004). Similarly, Richard Horton, in a review of Sheldon Krimsky's *Science in the Private Interest*, examines how the profit motive in biomedical research threatens to corrupt longstanding traditions of scientific inquiry in the academy (Horton, 2004).

Ramifications of the economic crisis in higher education are not limited to selected domains of inquiry. As Nelson and Watt (1999) comment,

"Although the effects of the crisis have been differential, that is, selective, unequal, and ideologically targeted, the crisis has also transformed university culture as a whole." (p. 90) University governance becomes budget driven. It seems natural that values of materialism that have dominated modern Western popular culture can find reinforcement only from the experience of university life in which profit and budgets become bottom lines. The university, an institution that in its traditional role (or image) might direct the larger culture toward a more reflective, critical, and democratic way of being, is instead cranking up the volume on our most self-destructive cultural tendencies. Even though it seems highly unlikely that the university can (or should) ever divorce itself completely from market forces, "there is a place for the market, but the market must be kept in its place." (economist Arthur Okun as cited by Kirp, 2003, p. 7)

> Still, embedded in the very idea of the university—not the storybook idea, but the university at its truest and best—are values that the market does not honor: the belief in a community of scholars and not a confederacy of self-seekers; in the idea of openness and not ownership; in the professor as a pursuer of truth and not an entrepreneur; in the student as an acolyte whose preferences are to be formed, not a consumer whose preferences are to be satisfied (Kirp, 2003, p. 7).

Had *The Education of Max Bickford* remained on the air a little longer might these issues have surfaced? Seems doubtful. Besides *Max Bickford*, a number of recent novels carry on with compelling tales of intense, sometimes comical, and often destructive relations in the halls of academia: Roth's *The Human Stain*, Russo's *Straight Man*, Coetzee's *Disgrace*, Prose's *Blue Angel*, Franzen's *The Corrections,* and so on. But as with *Max Bickford*, these stories zero in on the personal—academia as a greenhouse of rare types. Although there are academic publications and a few novels that analyze or at least broach the subject, there is little evidence that this cultural shift has been critically represented in any broad popular cultural form. We believe that such a cultural shift in the university is significant to the movement of social and cultural life more broadly. Hence, one might hope for the advent of more popular cultural artifacts or forms that can represent with greater complexity, and perhaps a measure of sympathy, the institution that we believe still stands as one of the pillars of our democratic aspirations as a nation. In the shadow of that deficiency, we offer this collection of critical essays and reports about the state of the relationships between higher education and popular culture. For those who share our interest in the public promise of building a better, more equitable, and stronger academy, there is a great deal at stake in the way such relationships unfold.

References

Bierce, A. *The Devil's Dictionary*. Owings Mills, MD: Stemmer House, 1978.

Coetzee, J. M. *Disgrace*. New York: Viking, 1999.

Deitch, D. (Director). *Desert Hearts* [Motion picture], 1985.

Franzen, J. *The Corrections*. New York: Farrar, Straus and Giroux, 2001.

Hann, D. (Producer), and Ferrara, A. (Director). *The Addiction*. [Motion picture], 1995. (Available from USA Home Video).

Holcomb, R. (Executive Producer). *The Education of Max Bickford* [Television series]. New York: CBS, 2001.

Horton, R. "The Dawn of McScience." *The New York Review of Books*, v.51, n. 4 (March 11, 2004).

Kennedy, R. F., Jr. "Bush's Junk Science: It's More Fiction than Fact." *The Nation*, v. 278, n. 6 (March 8, 2004).

Kirp, D. L. *Shakespeare, Einstein, and the Bottom Line: The Marketing of Higher Education*. Cambridge, MA: Harvard University Press, 2003.

Kramer, P. *Listening to Prozac*. New York: Viking, 1993.

Labaroee, D. F. *How to Succeed in School without Really Learning: The Credentials Race in American Education*. New Haven, CT: Yale University Press, 1997.

Lee, S. (Director). *School Daze* [Motion picture], 1988 (Available from Columbia Tristar Home Entertainment).

Mamet, D. *Oleanna*. New York: Vintage, 1993.

Nelson, C., & Watt, S. *Academic Keywords: A Devil's Dictionary for Higher Education*. New York: Routledge, 1999.

Prose, F. *Blue Angel*. New York: Harper Collins Publishers, 2000.

Roth, P. *The Human Stain*. Boston: Houghton Mifflin, 2000.

Rouzema, P. (Director). *When Night Is Falling* [Motion picture]. Canada. October Films, 1995.

Russo, R. *Straight Man*. New York: Random House, 1997.

Williams, R. *Keywords*. New York: Oxford University Press, 1976.

———. *Culture and Society*. New York: Columbia University Press, 1958.

Van Sant, G. (Director). *Good Will Hunting* [Motion picture]. United States: Miramax, 1997.

1

Constructing and Contesting
the Image of the Ivory Tower

1

The Personal Professor and the Excellent University

SUSAN TALBURT AND PAULA M. SALVIO[1]

Nearly a decade ago (1995), a widely discussed collection of essays edited by Michael Bérubé and Cary Nelson, Higher Education Under Fire, painted a portrait of a legitimation crisis for the academy in the popular imagination. The text took up the topic of the culture wars of the 1980s, during which conservatives portrayed an academic environment in which political correctness silences faculty and students, multiculturalism and Marxism pervade classrooms, and American tradition and heritage are less and less frequently taught, if not outright undermined. On the heels of this assault, the volume pointed out, came less partisan critiques of universities—media reports that faculty were not teaching but seeking personal advancement through frivolous research, classes were overcrowded and taught by graduate students, undergraduates were graduating without basic skills and knowledge, and tuitions were skyrocketing—that further undermined the university's status in the public mind. Nelson and Bérubé (1995) described collective public perceptions of the academy as a "landscape so drastically flattened out by media depictions of the humanities, which render intellectual upheaval as nothing more than a succession of passing fads." (p. 17) Their text sought to diagnose the problem of the academy's popular delegitimation in order to suggest ways for progressive faculty to use the media to talk back and counter such critiques. Though theirs was a necessary intervention, the volume's analyses recognized but did not fully account for the shift to consumerism in the United States that increasingly frames the academy in the popular imagination and in practice (see Bok, 2003; Giroux, 2002; Kirp, 2003).

In this essay, we explore the effects of consumerist and technocratic ideologies and practices on the work of faculty and on the ways academics' responses do and do not challenge the privatization of the university's purposes. We are interested in academic practices that hold promise in altering the means through which faculty are being consumed by the demands of the "posthistorical" university. We begin with a brief discussion of the rise of the excellent university as it frames the personal professor. In the epoch of the culture wars, faculty's assertion of the personal often functioned as a gesture to embody the self and to make explicit differences that would assert the significance of subject positions in relation to subjects of study. The academic turn to the personal in scholarship and pedagogy has had an impact by questioning previously taken-for-granted academic practices in traditional disciplinary work, as well as raising new questions pertaining to the too-easy split between objectivity and subjectivity, the ethical implications of speaking for or as an other, and the often problematic relation of the personal to identity politics (see Bleich, 1998; Salvio, 1999; Taubman, 1990; Talburt, 1999; Tobin, 1993). However, as the nature of universities and the nature of academic work have changed, so have the uses and effects of the personal.

At a moment in which the academy's meanings and relevance are continually trivialized, it becomes increasingly difficult for academics to make a difference as persons whose intellectual labor carries weight in the public sphere. Indeed, within what we will describe as the university's emptying of content, academics experience a need to matter and thus seek recognition and confirmation as material, embodied beings. But does faculty's turn to personal accounts of their professional lives and the personal in teaching constitute a challenge to prevailing technocratic discourses, or does it inadvertently play a part in maintaining them? Our concern is that personal contestations of the corporate ethos of university life may, due to their individualizing nature, parallel the privatization of university knowledge that increasingly frames the public's understanding of education as an investment (see Duderstadt & Womack, 2003). Or to put this another way, the assertion of humanity may create critiques that are contained and isolated, much as the private knowledge and goods that universities allegedly purvey are cloistered from the public sphere. The very act of making public the seemingly private may not create sustained critique of the relations of institutional life and self but may encourage and end in personal consumption. We begin by laying out the features of the posthistorical university and its attachment to a rhetoric of loss that persistently, at times compulsively, seeks to conjure up human meanings in a consumerist system defined by a logic of accounting and accountability. We then elaborate on the proposition that the personal functions to redress a profound sense of displacement in the academy, a kind of academic homelessness that is felt more and more acutely as faculty are required to fashion personae and courses that have distinct market value. This combination of elements—an increasingly consumer-oriented, posthistorical academy and a modernist response of creating whole, meaningful academic selves—reveals a need for new approaches by faculty to creating and sustaining spaces that allow for the collective articulation of intellectual life.

Living and Working in the Ruins of Excellence

In *The University in Ruins*, Bill Readings (1996) takes up the topic of what he calls the "posthistorical university." He describes the development of the modern university, which has a unifying purpose or idea, and thus a role in history, by tracing the emergence of a Kantian university guided by reason and a Humboldtian university dedicated to culture-building through research and teaching, two ideas that defined the university and continue to play a part in fragments of university life. With the decline of the nation-state as the primary economic unit of production, culture-building and the development of reasoning subjects and rational communities are no longer the legitimating ideas unifying the university. Thus, as Readings describes it, culture and reason have been joined and transformed by a third term: academia's recent emphasis on the techno-bureaucratic notion of excellence, an undefinable abstraction that masquerades as an idea. As excellence, which is defined by the logics of production and consumerism, displaces culture and reason as fixed referents, students and faculty are left with a posthistorical university, or a "university without an idea." (p. 118) As Readings says, the posthistorical university is an "institution [that] has outlived itself, is now a survivor of the era in which it defined itself in terms of the project of the historical development, affirmation, and inculcation of national culture." (p. 6) It is a university whose meanings are neither given nor coherent but are continually up for grabs by university administrators, politicians, and corporations (Marginson & Considine, 2000).

That Readings' analysis resonates with Jean-François Lyotard's (1979) *The Postmodern Condition* should come as no surprise, as he translated a number of Lyotard's books and essays. Indeed, the core of his argument follows Lyotard's contention that in modernity, the university's alignment with metanarratives of emancipatory humanism, which values education "for its own sake" or its potential to "enlighten," has shifted to postmodernity's concept of performativity, which prizes efficiency and the production of functional skills for the sake of competition and economic growth. In the performative academy, Readings points out, "[a]ll that the system requires is for activity to take place, and the empty notion of excellence refers to nothing other than the optimal input/output ratio in matters of information." (p. 39) Thus the driving force of the posthistorical university is to become an "excellent," corporate-like institution that efficiently produces skills and information and effectively assesses student outcomes and faculty performance. Pedagogy and research are figured, not as Freud would argue, as incapable of closure, but rather as accountable to criteria of excellence and efficiency, answering to such phrases as "time to completion" (p. 128) or "usefulness to business or industry," thereby setting pedagogic relations and intellectual inquiry under the sign of the logos, shifting them further from the erotic. This shift requires faculty and individual departments to construct and represent themselves as aligned with the university's economic mission, which structures criteria used to determine tenure and promotion, course offerings, funding, and departmental organization.

Richard Miller (1998) has written of "the hybrid persona of the intellectual bureaucrat" (p. ix) as something of a betrayal of many academics' reasons for entering the university. Raising issues suggesting that faculty may simultaneously be living out two contradictory discourses of emancipatory humanism and excellence, Miller argues that faculty view "the academic and the bureaucratic spheres as both fully enmeshed and fully incommensurate." (p. 37) Academics may wish to imagine the academy as a space for "autonomy and freedom" of intellectual movement and thought, but have entered an intensifying culture of excellence that situates them as accountant-clerks:

> Given the shared bureaucratic and administrative structure of nearly every educational organization in this country, this is what all teachers do, regardless of discipline or position in the academic hierarchy: they produce and put into circulation evaluations; they solicit, assess, and respond to student work; they perform the bureaucratic function of sifting and sorting individuals (Miller, 1998, p. 36).

Though faculty would disavow their bureaucratic roles and idealize classrooms as at least one potential site of authenticity, students know better: "where teachers see a liberatory practice and rising opportunities, most students see a set of requirements, an arbitrary system of assessment, an impediment to advancement—a bureaucracy, in short." (p. 19) Indeed, Paul Lauteur (1995) has said of the loss of what he calls universities' "cultural authority," that "[t]o an increasing number of Americans, including our students, universities mean little more than a stamp on one's life passport—important but not all that serious." (p. 85)

The university's posthistoricism lends itself to the privatization of its functions, which are increasingly framed in the context of individual advancement, private consumption, and corporate interests rather than as a public resource. In the excellent university, Readings argues, students "are not *like* customers; they *are* customers." (p. 22) Following Readings' analysis, Masao Miyoshi (1998) contends that the decline of the university's role as builder and maintainer of national identity and culture is part of a larger process in which "[g]lobal corporate operations now subordinate state functions, and in the name of competition, productivity, and freedom, public space is being markedly reduced." (p. 263) Illustrative of the ways that corporate accounting procedures define the university's understanding of itself, Miyoshi (1998) describes a letter from his dean of humanities that reflected a quantitative anxiety with course enrollment, faculty–student ratio, the number of majors in the department, and the department's ranking by the National Research Council, and made "no reference whatever to substantial intellectual or pedagogic matters." (p. 261) In the university without a referent, the content of what goes on in the institution becomes less and less important:

> Courses are being canceled whether they teach basic mathematical theories, or the Achebe-Ngugi controversy about the use of language, or the South American testimonials, or Derrida's dependence on the ghost, or the power of hybridity, or fifteenth-century English poetry unless enough students enroll. Conversely, if a good many students are interested, any vacuous course can be taught" (Miyoshi, 1998, p. 266).

What Miyoshi points to in connecting globalization, bureaucratization, and declining concern with intellectual substance is a system of individual certification and advancement for students and faculty that increasingly disregards the university's role as a public social good:

> In fact, the university as a talk show that promises to entertain rather than discuss seems to be more and more the typical under-graduate expectation. Students also want to have been, but not to be, in the classroom. It is a sadly vacuous place that has little to offer except for licensing and professionalism—Readings' "excellence" plus diversion—without the substance of profession. Once professors

presumably professed; they are now merely professionals, entrepreneurs, careerists, and opportunists, as in the corporate world. (Miyoshi, 1998, p. 267)

In a productive academy, "work identity" is measured by departmental, institutional, national, and international recognition, which have become markers of who and what faculty are and may understand themselves to be in a system that demands endless activity to represent its excellence. As faculty are encouraged and enticed to move to national and international levels of scholarly involvement, they become less involved with activities that demand attention in their own workplace. The result is a quiet, insidious sense of homelessness. The nomadic "global academic" is alternatively described by Dominick LaCapra (1997) as a "resident alien": "a member of a university or college who spends minimal time on its specific problems and possibilities—including work with its students—in order to globetrot and expatiate on the great issues of the day. The result would be a particularly questionable, updated version of the old free-floating universal intellectual." (pp. 59–60) The traditional free-floating intellectual was "objective" and outside the confines of daily problems, rather than "subjectively" engaged and corporeally located in his or her surroundings. This free-floating status is even more compounded by the role of electronic communications. In a world of computerized data management, on-line course work, and instantaneous information, a person's sense of location is profoundly altered. Rather than experiencing life in actual time and space, the subject of the electronic society is, as Mark Poster (1990) writes, "multiplied by data bases, dispersed by computer messaging and conferencing, decontextualized and reidentified by TV ads, dissolved and materialized continuously in the electronic transmission of symbols." (p. 74) Una Chaudhuri (1995) describes this dispersal of subjective experience as a return to nomadic forms of existence, as faculty and students wander over vast global distances daily, changing channels, faxing letters, leaving messages on answering machines, and having the facts of our lives "gathered, stored and analyzed by myriad marketing concerns." (p. 4)

Aware that meaning ceases to inhere in academic work and life in the university and that faculty must actively seek and construct connections and engagement, Lauren Berlant (1997) urges academics to remain cautious about turning to a corporate discourse of flexibility and improvisation that, on the surface, appears to offer possibilities for intellectual agency and imagination. Berlant cautions educators to recognize in these terms the mobility that characterizes the institutions of labor, capital, and culture in the United States. She points out that flexibility and experimentation appear to offer the promise of a better world that is open to imagining new academic structures and relationships, particularly when they are set against the ideological apparatuses of the official public sphere that, as Harvey (1989) describes, emphasize "traditional ethics, family values, the solidity of domestic space as opposed to the contingencies of time." (p. 171) "Flexibility," Berlant says, "appears as a theoretical virtue; as a radical necessity of feminist and counterhegemonic world building; and as an administrative demand by panicking administrators." (1997, p. 156) However, as much as the forces of flexibility and creative specialization are becoming part of professional academic practice and despite the analysis of contemporary subjectivity as "flexible," the structural forces, pressures, and effects reappear, as Berlant insightfully explains, as expressions of individual identity and desire (also see Rouse, 1994, pp. 389–392).

In response to the sense of displacement academics experience in the posthistorical university, scholars such as Readings, LaCapra, and Berlant have worked toward rendering alternative accounts of how academic life and the place of the academy can be reshaped and reimagined. Implicit in their proposals is a speculation worthy of attention: The rhetoric of excellence associated with the posthistorical university provokes a range of responses that are tied to the problem of place within institutional life. The meaning, not simply the ownership, of place has given the past century much of its politics; thus, it is not surprising that it has also shaped the culture of becoming educated, and that a complex engagement with the significance, determinations, and potentialities of place courses through the body of the posthistorical university. Who one is and who one can be is a function of where one is and how one experiences the place of the academy. By threading the questions raised by the concept of place through projects pertaining to the self, the classic call to "know thyself" splays open. One does not address this question as a solitary individual or ahistorical being. Rather, the contingencies and complex politics contained in the places we live and the histories that linger there affect our modes of address, what we say, and what remains unarticulated. Scholars' efforts to explore the relations of place and history to pedagogy and scholarship through personal writing constitute one response to a sense of displacement.

Academics must be cautious about routes that appear to make it possible to redress a sense of homelessness, particularly pedagogical or scholarly routes that invoke the feel of intimacy ordinarily reserved for private relationships. Feminist pedagogy offers us, suggests Berlant (1997), a case in point. Although feminist educators have historically been committed to reimagining the practice of authority in the classroom so as to create an American feminist public sphere, early feminists did not anticipate the complex, invisible, and incoherent demands that occupy the professional time and labor of educators committed to counter-hegemonic teaching and research in the contemporary academy. In fact, she hints at dual sources of stress that become amplified in a culture of excellence. One is "the current downsizing of universities, which obligates faculty members to meet ever greater demands for pedagogical, administrative, financial, and intellectual productivity. Another source is quite different: what I will call the intimacy expectation that accompanies much politically engaged work in the academy, both among colleagues and in pedagogical contexts." (p. 143) The "intimacy expectation" is acute for politically engaged faculty who wish to make a difference:

> Deep in the ambitions and socialization of the feminist teacher . . . is the promise of women's studies to make learning personal, socially transformative, and generally supportive. This desire still inspires workers in the university system to make themselves vulnerable to the impossible higher expectations about institutionally and intellectually mediated personal relations that are hardwired into the feminist pedagogical project. It motivates taking on the kinds of therapeutic and mentoring functions that are way beyond our expertise; it motivates us to over identify with students' happiness or unhappiness as the source of our value; it motivates the ways we shield students from experiencing the various kinds of ambivalence we have toward being called to personhood in this way (Berlat, 1997, p. 154).

In universities centered on projects of culture and reason, intimacy, or the personal, in research or teaching, functioned to counter traditional disciplinary practices and pedagogical relations: "It proposed that new relations between knowledge, authority, and desire would not only affirm but create new general possibilities for identity and society. Central to this social transformation would be a revolution in the scene of teaching, turning it into a public, collective, and politically accountable practice." (Berlant, 1997, p. 147) However, the iconization of the feminist teacher's power to merge everyday life with political desire continually leads teachers and students into feelings of frustration, confusion, exhaustion, domination, and isolation. In excellent universities, the personal has not lived up to its promise but has framed individual faculty as delivering up yet another product.

The crucial concern is, as Berlant argues, that faculty are often unaware of the ways universities generate expectations for meaningful academic and personal identities that incite us to invest in our academic labor the need for mutual recognition that persons ordinarily seek within contexts of privacy and domestic intimacy. The project educators face is to become more eloquent about the "intimacy expectations" that shape our work with colleagues and students. In seeking meaning and connection in productive institutions, we fail to articulate to one another the degrees of intimacy and separation that we want in our lives, thereby losing track of unrealistic expectations for the kinds of sustenance, affection, and support that institutions and people in institutions can provide. It is this issue of how faculty try to create and sustain meaningful selves in institutions that are not inherently meaningful that concerns us. How do academics live out their professional placements? "[W]hat," as Berlant asks, "happens when people see their relations to an institution as vital to their self-understanding, their selfhood, their identities, and their hold on narratives of history and possibilities of the future" (p. 148)? Berlant urges educators to more fully articulate the ambivalence we feel about being personal in institutional settings, not because she is critical of modes of inquiry associated with the personal, such as memoir or autobiography, but rather because the closeness and intimacy feminist pedagogies call for is inclined to exact a price, depleting students and teachers in profoundly serious ways, leaving them confused about who they are to one another (p. 147).

Excelling at the Personal

As we have suggested, the academic turn to the personal belies a desire to endow oneself with a body and to compose a history as well as to connect with other subjects, past and present. The danger, however, is that the self that is composed inadvertently converts into a commodity, thus slipping into a lonely individualism that perpetuates the commodification of identities that Berlant encourages us to be suspicious of. In this regard, Jane Tompkins' (1996) *A Life in School* presents itself as a limit case. This memoir spills over with symptoms of feeling homeless in an excellent academy.

In her teacherly *bildungsroman*, Tompkins tells readers that education needs to address our private lives and to offer wholeness in the curriculum. Her first chapter begins with a string of typical dream sequences that teachers and students have before the first day of class or big exams, dreams that dramatize the fear of losing all sense of authority and mastery. Tompkins ties these dreams to her desire for recognition, and in the case of teaching, for the love and respect of her students. The narrative then flashes back to her early years in school. Readers meet dull teachers and the "teacher who made a difference" while learning of Tompkins' desires to be popular among her peers and her growing realization of the vacuousness of these desires. Tompkins uses her memories to build an argument for infusing the personal into scholarship and teaching in order to redress oppressive academic practices and a misdirected pedagogy that she traces, through Alice Miller's work, to child-rearing practices that instill fear in order to discipline and "properly educate" the body while satisfying the parent's need for power and revenge (p. 6).

In the early chapters of Tompkins' memoir, she renders a series of tableaux of frightened children standing in the presence of teachers who subject their students to such a pedagogy, taking their breath away and making them feel helpless, a helplessness registered in images of bodies falling into frozen positions, bodies so fearful that they ceased to "so much as breathe naturally." Tompkins creates causal links between the fear of authority she experienced in her childhood to the way she exercised and failed to exercise authority as an adult. In many ways, authority and authorship are the driving forces behind this narrative, for Tompkins' fear becomes an object of analysis, a long study that she cannot escape. Folded into this long study is Tompkins' evolution as an academic star and her increasing awareness of the vacuousness of stardom—a repetition, with variations, of her childhood longing for peers' approval. She describes her leap to the status of authority:

> Going to Duke with Stanley [Fish, her husband] brought to an end my struggles to gain professional recognition. My book appeared and made an impression; being at Duke helped. I was invited to lecture, to speak at conferences, to be on panels, to contribute chapters to scholarly volumes, to review candidates for tenure, to read manuscripts for presses, to serve on the editorial boards of journals. It was everything I had longed for in the days when I had commuted from Baltimore to Philadelphia to teach remedial writing and had envied the people I knew at Johns Hopkins with their light course loads and insider status. I enjoyed my success. Having a secure position at a prestigious university that supported me professionally gave me internal freedom. It was a few years before I realized that I no longer needed to worry so much about what other people thought of me. The habit was so ingrained in me that I'm still learning to let go of it. But gradually the truth dawned: I could do what I wanted (Tomkins, 1996, p. 113).

As she learns "to do what she wanted," Tompkins finds that recognition takes on a disembodied form within an individualistic, entrepreneurial university. Positioned excellently, she experiences anomie, a homelessness:

> The sense of always having too much to do is closely bound up with the lack of companionship, the failure of interchange, and with the higher productivity made possible by technological improvements that have recently entered our lives. Tenured faculty at research institutions come to exist in an elsewhere of print, phone, fax, and e-mail, their true communities embodied only in books

or on a disk, or at conferences they fly into and out of several times a year. Globe-trotting relationships with colleagues in one's field make for communities that are exciting, but they emphasize, possibly even contribute to the lack of just this feeling in the home institution, whose humdrum realities can't compete with conference glamour (Tomkins, 1996, p. 187).

It is no accident that a memoir that both calls for personalized teaching and enacts a personalization comes from an academic star. David Shumway (1997) has identified the star system as "a new form of intellectual authority and professional status." (p. 86) Autobiography, he argues, enables academics—and he explicitly names Tompkins as an example—to establish authority in a system in which "the construction of personality [has become] a means of acquiring cultural and academic capital." (p. 97) Faculty's construction of marketable identities that appeal to the imagination and desires of students and colleagues is neither strictly an affair of economics nor strictly a humanist striving for meaning. The personal and star status are not only commodities to be marketed, evaluated, and purchased in an academic economy but are bound up with our egos, desires, and longings, which come into play in the production and consumption of academic personae. Cary Nelson and Stephen Watt (1999) have commented that the star system is both institutional and psychic:

> Undergraduates are as likely to admire and try to emulate their teachers; graduate students and young faculty will look as [sic] least as often toward publications by distinguished scholars. Suddenly superstars had an audience to admire them. Fandom arrived in academia. Gradually, as Shumway argues, emotions of envy, ambition, and adulation entered the new structural place available to them. Of course students and young faculty could admire a discourse; they could entertain ambitions to enter a conversation. But wannabe followers in America sometimes find it easier to dream through the image of a person. And so it went. Academic superstars were born. (pp. 261–262)

At play, then, is the extent to which academics participate in creating a system of prestige in which certain academics take on the status of objects that perform fantasies of success that stand as ideals. These ideals have come to include the lone academic forging meaning and connection in an entrepreneurial culture and university.

In Toril Moi's (1999) analysis of the place of the personal in academic writing, she aptly points out that in her often-cited essay, "Me and My Shadow," Tompkins (1987) gets the diagnosis right: The oppressive discourses of the academy are indeed seductive, breathtaking, and all-consuming. They can create a sense of what psychoanalyst Michael Eigen (1993) attributes to the lost-I feeling. This I feels so lost to the desires and demands of others, so intruded upon and unable to breath, that it hardens and contracts almost to the point of insensibility. Tompkins' cure, however, misses a subtle but crucial point, for what brings on the lost-I feeling is an overwhelming sense of fusion with others and with institutional demands, thereby bringing about an impoverished sense of being precisely because, argues Eigen, one is driven by appetites that are dominated by an urge to do, an urge tied to a felt lack. The threat of implenitude runs deep in the ambitions and socialization of the feminist teacher, who focuses on fears that she lacks time, resources, or interest or is intellectually inadequate as she is compelled to satisfy the appetites of the institution for the ever-increasing labor of "service."

Tompkins' call to cultivate closeness between students and teachers in the academy, which she ties to the forms of intimacy associated with domestic scenes, unwittingly makes teachers vulnerable to being taken over, not only by the fear that there is not enough time or resources but that one will be suffocated by the demands of others, in turn breaking down completely. Tompkins' account of her evolution to a teaching style she deems "holistic," "experiential," and "experimental" is fraught with feelings of "precariousness, the constant sense of teetering on the brink." (p. 140) In teaching a course she titled "American Literature Unbound," Tompkins negotiated assignments and grades with students, both to redistribute authority and to encourage discussion about teaching and learning (pp. 169–70). As she describes the class, which included an excursion to the island of Ocracoke, she romanticizes the authenticity among students and professor, saying, for example, "So I loved our rebellion against grades and rules and conventional procedures, and I loved the group ethos. For both novels [*Moby-Dick* and *Beloved*] are also celebrations of communion and spoke to my longing to be rid of loneliness." (p. 175) Yet the loneliness returned when it was time for students to read their class evaluations, for they criticized the lack of structure and focus in the class. Recounting this moment, Tompkins tells her readers, "I would like to stop writing right here. For now my throat clenches." (p. 176) The logic of excellence appears to literally take Tompkins' breath away, undermining the collective spirit she believed she had cultivated with her students, a spirit that, for a time, rendered conventional procedures and forms of control invisible. Tompkins fails to recognize however, that the most potent forms of power are indeed invisible. The paradox inherent in her move to be personal with her students is that such a move can erode the personal lives of teachers, laying claims upon them that leave them feeling breathless, unable to connect with communal social and institutional life.

Tompkins' memoir refers repeatedly to the threat of lack that slowly chokes and binds her affective life, encrypting what she describes as an "inward drama." (p. 128)

What I see in [T.S.] Eliot now is what I saw in him then but couldn't acknowledge, the suffering. It was personal; it was long, drawn-out; it was unappetizing. There is a lot of sickness in Eliot, old unresolved fears and longings, half-formulated desires, unacknowledged hatred, and paralyzing despair. His innards are half rotted; they send up a kind of stink that curls between the lines but is denied. You can talk about the sources in *Purgatorio* while secretly identifying with his crucifixion. Reading his poetry was a way of experiencing something without letting yourself know you were experiencing it. The morbid fantasizing of unhappy intellectuals under the guise of doing literary criticism.

"Weave, weave the sunlight into your hair."

My relation to Eliot's fear and sickness is different now, mainly because I know how I feel when I read the poetry, whereas before I couldn't let myself know. He says in "The Waste Land," commanding us:

> Come in under the shadow of this red rock. . . ./[And] I will show you fear in a handful of dust." I obeyed. For years in an attempt to brighten grim surroundings, I had a cheap red rug in my university office, and I would say to myself upon entering, like an automatic reflex, "Come in under the shadow of this red rug," but never the second line, about fear, which I'd forgotten, since I lived it every day. Afraid that my classes wouldn't go well, afraid that my students wouldn't like me, afraid that my senior colleagues wouldn't think well of me. Living under the shadow of this red rug was hard to do! (Tompkins, 1987, pp. 129–130)

Possessed by the desires of others and utterly paralyzed in her search for students' and colleagues' approval and recognition, Tompkins suffers a lost-I feeling that undermines her capacity to feel the weight of meaning embodied in Eliot's poetry, to feel virtually anything at all, except fear and anxiety.

However liberating Tompkin's personal expression of fears and anxieties may appear, her *bildungsroman* spirals down into a commodity composed of the very individualism that she so despises. In her teaching and her relations with colleagues, Tompkins complains that she was "hungry for some emotional or spiritual fulfillment that university life didn't seem to afford. I craved the feeling that I was part of an enterprise larger than myself, part of a group that shared some common purpose." (p. 182) In this struggle against entrepreneurialism, Tompkins casts herself as a leading figure who falls to pieces only to be made whole through a "therapeutic" self-expression that is devoid of theoretical, pedagogical, or historical analysis. Why, for example, does Tompkins isolate herself from the scholarship in pedagogy and curriculum theory written by educators who have spent years working on questions she struggles with? In her preface, she notes that it does indeed seem strange that there would be so few references to books on educational theory in a memoir on teaching, "so little attempt to set my experience against the background of classroom practice as it's described in the literature. For a long time I was at a loss to explain this to myself. All I knew was, I had no desire to pick up a book on teaching—in fact, I had a positive aversion to doing so—and I couldn't even muster the energy to feel guilty about it." (p. xii) Tompkins attributes her aversion to a need finally to rely on herself for enlightenment, suggesting that a turn to such scholarly work as Deborah Britzman's (1998) *Lost Subjects, Contested Objects*, Jo Anne Pagano's (1990) *Exiles and Communities: Teaching in the Patriarchal Wilderness*, Valerie Walkerdine's (1990) *Schoolgirl Fictions*, or Carmen Luke and Jennifer Gore's (1992) edited volume, *Feminisms and Critical Pedagogy*—and here we name only a few—would undermine her individual path toward enlightenment. Given the ways these scholars conjugate literature, theory, history and autobiography, a turn to their work would indeed shatter the alluring ideologeme associated with the ideal of Enlightenment pedagogy. This ideal conjures images of tutors and teachers imparting true knowledge to their students, and in so doing, making a world possible for them in which their sensibility and ambition might merge in a lifelong sentimental education (Berlant, 1997, p. 151). Tompkins' attachment to this ideologeme is evident in her desire to seek out and sustain the position of the charismatic authority or virtuoso teacher who will help her students locate a true, secure self. This romantic pedagogical strain resonates with the pedagogy in *Emile*, or that of Jean Brodie, or Mr. Chips, or to be more up-to-date, to Jane Tompkins' leveling of the personal with the emotionally warm and giving teacher.

Critics of Tompkins have pointed out that the individualism in her earlier memoir resonates with the plot structure of the classic masculine autobiography as she goes it alone and emerges as the heroine of her own life story. One way to place this discourse of individualism in relief is to consider the modernist strain in Tompkins' pedagogy. This strain treats language as a transparent medium that has the capacity to reflect or disclose the true, interior life of the writer/teacher; language works somewhat like a glass house of the soul that harbors no secrets. Implicit in her memoir lies a belief that the language of the personal is a medium through which to render a faithful representation of her life that would lay bare the hidden contents that wreak havoc on her home and psyche.

What is also instructive about this memoir, however, is that Tompkins performs what LaCapra (1997) describes as a transferential repetition in which she unwittingly pursues specific problems in her teaching and scholarship without a thorough "working through." What didn't work in her classroom will work in her memoir: Her writing will forge connections among whole individuals. However, as Linda Kauffman (1993) points out, "[w]riting about yourself does not liberate you, it just shows how ingrained the ideology of freedom through self-expression is in our thinking." (p. 139) She warns "that there is something fatally alluring about personal testimony." (p. 132) Her choice of the word *fatally* is suggestive of the possibility that our very desires to tell or to know more about a person cannot, by definition, be satiated, for desire is always compelled by the lack of knowledge, the absence of insight, and by feelings of emptiness and unfulfilled appetites. To what extent is the reader's desire to tell or to know the autobiographical subject driven by a pull, a "fatal attraction," if you can bear the slip, to devour its subject by knowing and owning its meanings? (See Kristeva, 1980.) The question is not how to satiate a desire that is always ravenous, but rather how to render the personal in such a way that it does not get frozen in registers that are isolating, detached from the communal sphere, or utterly disembodied (Taubman, 1990). Bauer (1995) argues:

> The yearning for a truly public audience beyond the classroom or departmental experience might happen through a change in our discourse and the way we cast issues, not merely through personal disclosures . . . Although this seems the logical first step, for too many it becomes the only step. In the personal confession lies the logic of privatization, for the confession only veils the bourgeois academic personality's desire for public acceptance. Such recognition is indeed the goal of feminist discourse, but for the recognition of political commitment, not the confessor. In this sense, the confession of personal experience yokes together the rhetoric of individualism with the desire for a public audience. (Bauer, 1995, p. 64)

We believe Lauren Berlant (1997) begins to develop a more generative response to the problems articulated by Tompkins, provoking educators to take seriously what precisely happens when students and teachers feel displaced in performative, productive institutional settings, while at the same time relying on public life in institutions "for sustaining their identities, their opinions, and their relations to power, as well as their fantasies, rages and desires." (p. 150) Berlant's essay begins with the story of the suicide of the first feminist teacher she knew when she was an undergraduate at Oberlin College. Berlant remembers learning about pedagogy from her— learning, for example, that the classroom is not the place for professors to dramatize the brilliance of their own minds, but a space in which hard thinking could be generated collectively (p. 144). She recalls a conversation during her senior year in which her teacher disclosed profound feelings of inadequacy, desperation, difficulties in thinking clearly, finishing a sentence, wanting to write theory and teach with integrity but losing all capacity to remain present to her students and family. Berlant could not fully apprehend the pain or dire implications of such feelings, could not anticipate at the time, that she too could feel so vulnerable—until she attended graduate school. Late the next year, when Berlant was a graduate student in Ithaca, New York, her teacher called and asked how she was. Berlant recalls disclosing how inadequate she felt. "I told her, at great length," Berlant recounts,

> I was struggling terribly, partly because I felt stupid all the time, as usual, and partly because at that time there was very little feminism for graduate students in the English department, and I felt constantly inadequate and exposed as unserious for my lack of disinterestedness. We talked about this for awhile, and then she reported that she had stopped teaching and in fact had had a nervous breakdown. She said she couldn't face the classroom any longer. Shortly thereafter, she killed herself. (Berlant, 1997, p. 145)

Could it be that the emotional, intellectual, and administrative demands this teacher felt obligated to fulfill left her feeling breathless, lost to the sort of overwhelming fusion with her students and the institution that Eigen attributes to aspects of a "lost-I feeling?" The tragic paradox structuring Berlant's memory of her teacher is that the labor of making learning personal for her students eroded her personal life, leaving her in an abyss that appears to have laid claims upon her to the extent that her loss of breath stole her interest in writing, teaching, and participating in the life she had known.

Berlant does not create an easy equation between the insidious pressures of academic life and her professor's suicide. But her memories lead her to question the political and erotic demands that institutions make on teachers and that students and teachers make on one another. Although these demands spill over, as she points out, into the worlds they seek to change, challenging hierarchies of authority and entitlement, they also exact a serious price on our emotional lives. They induce, Berlant argues, "precarious lives," lives built on the conditions of ever-expanding volunteer obligation, conditions that politically engaged academics inhabit daily. In this sense, Berlant calls into question the institutional context in which the personal is composed and urges us to engage in sustained conversations about the ways in which the personal can be used to address how academics and students are complicit in sustaining a logic of excellence that fosters a profound sense of displacement and isolation.

Depersonalizing Academics

Rather than merely recognizing that the subjective and the objective, the personal and the social are always tangled up, personal writing best apprehends the tangles of the subject by proceeding along indirect routes that take the reader through theory, literature, history, and autobiography in order to decenter the subject. A decentered subject cannot easily be consumed, for it is not whole but implicated in fragments of what surrounds it in time and space. As she seeks a form in which to compose a self, Tompkins takes a direct route of disclosure, one that treats language as a transparent medium and thus fails to attend to the tangle of subjectivity and the social, history and the personal. The ambivalent place of the personal in teaching and writing theory coheres around the erotic, often tacit demands that confound what it means to be personal in our scholarship and in our teaching. The play of desire in the classroom, the envy, jealousy, and rivalry among colleagues, are continually created and recreated in the classrooms, departmental spaces, and institutional structures, at times stirring up a confusion that is associated with unease as shadows take occupancy in the places in which we meet, conjuring an imperceptible sliding of coziness into dread.

Dominick LaCapra (1997) suggests that academics' elusive sense of displacement might be confronted by thinking about one's subject position through inquiry that is informed by social and psychoanalytic concerns and "critically mediates between an essentializing idea of identity and an ill-defined, ideologically individualistic, and often aestheticized notion of subjectivity." (p. 65) This is a move from individual to collective resistance. Collective thinking about our subject positions has the potential to dilute the forces of commodification, individualism, and capitalism pervading academic institutions. How are we, as scholars and teachers, implicated in a transferential relation in which we repeat, at least discursively, the processes that we study and live? How might this relation be negotiated in ways that may variously reinforce or place in question one's existing subject positions? In what contexts can academics counteract the inevitable (and at times thought-provoking and heuristically valuable) processes of projection and work through the problems that one investigates?

LaCapra proposes that the process of composing a subject position entails the difficult labor of recognizing the transferential repetitions that we enact in our teaching and in our scholarship. Such a focus works against the impulse to shift immediately to national and international levels of analysis and bypass one's most specific ties, obligations, and desires. This is not to suggest that one's particular concerns and questions are not tied to larger political and social problems; rather, to bypass questions pertaining to one's specific location is "premature or even diversionary insofar as one's contribution is based on extremely indirect, truncated knowledge that one acquires primarily through the media." (p. 59) But to begin with the local and specific is not to offer consumable narratives of self, but to implicate self in surroundings, and to implicate readers and interlocutors in ways that avoid easy answers and instead encourage new questions.

A second rationale LaCapra develops to substantiate the value of beginning with one's subject position is to bring into focus the need to cultivate intellectual work that includes critical involvement with the academy and an informed desire to relate work in it to significant issues. In addition to the well-established categories of teaching, scholarship, and service, LaCapra adds a fourth category, that of "critical intellectual citizenship," which would alter how we assess the contributions faculty make to university and public life. This category includes participation in lectures, colloquia, and writing and speaking in the media in the insistent attempt to make them vital forums for inquiry that foster a role for the university in the public sphere by encouraging a rethinking of the problems of politics in the basic sense of what it means to live a life in common. (See LaCapra, 1997, p. 60.)

In her collection of essays, *What Does A Woman Want?*, Shoshana Felman (1993) argues that a generative approach to life writing requires that we decenter our subject by taking indirect routes through our autobiographies, literature, theory, and histories that link personae to larger historical fields, thus bringing the autobiographical "I" to form in ways that call upon students and faculty to be personal, but not about themselves. Such a move may make the self in autobiographical analysis less available for consumption and thus less vulnerable to the insatiable appetite of the consumer economy structuring the posthistorical university. This move finds historical precedent in the writing of Walter Benjamin (1978) and Virginia Woolf (1976) and has been extended by curriculum and composition theorists such as William Pinar (1991), Madeleine Grumet (1988), Jonathan Silin (1995), Peter Taubman (1993), Lad Tobin (1993), David Bleich (1998), and Susan Edgerton (1991). Their work resonates with Berlant's concerns about "public intimacies," for each urges us to test the limits of how much students and teachers need to know about one another. Fused through these scholars' life writing projects is an intentional challenge to the anti-historiographic intimations of the personal as a source of individual authority. To begin with the personal need not imply, argues Taubman (1993), a move that freezes identity, thus culminating in an aesthetic of individualism or a search for an authentic self. For example, Silin's (1995) *Sex, Death, and the Education of Children: Our Passion for Ignorance in the Age of AIDS* portrays possibilities for the life writer to create a discursive occasion that is open-ended and fluid, unfolding in such a way that subjectivity—located in the situation of the body—is restored to history. This scholarship stands apart from the work of scholars who individualize self and situation, for their analysis begins in a language that recognizes the possibilities for representing encrypted memories and their historical import. As a narrative mode, personal writing that decenters the subject is dependent upon a dialectical resistance that poses differences and strains between private life and the public sphere as the initiation of analysis. (See Brownstein, 1996.)

To resist being consumed by the demands made in the posthistorical university might require that faculty sustain an ambivalence toward the personal and recognize that there are no easy separations between the public and the private, the conscious and the unconscious, the past and the present, the real and the fictive. The detours and shuffling between theory, literature, history, and autobiography create a capacious narrative that can more fully engage the histories, theories, and biographies of those before us and around us. Such inquiry may enable academics to rethink the politics and implications of living together in posthistorical universities, in which it is incumbent on actors to create individual, institutional, and collective meanings.

Note

1. We wish to note that despite the seeming "ordering" of authors, this chapter is a fully collaborative project.

References

Bauer, D. M. "Personal Criticism and the Academic Personality." In *Who Can Speak? Authority and Critical Identity*, edited by J. Roof and R. Wiegman. Urbana, IL: University of Illinois Press, 1995: 56–69.

Benjamin, W. *Reflections: Essays, Aphorisms, Autobiographical Writings*. Edited by P. Demetz. New York: Schocken Books, 1978.

Berlant, L. "Feminism and the Institutions of Intimacy." In *The Politics of Research*, edited by E. A. Kaplan and G. Levine. New Brunswick, NJ: Rutgers University Press, 1997: 143–161.

Bérubé, M. and C. Nelson. "Money, Merit, and Democracy at the University: An Exchange." In *Higher Education Under Fire: Politics, Economics, and the Crisis of the Humanities*, edited by M. Bérubé and C. Nelson. New York: Routledge, 1995: 163–198.

Bleich, D. *Know and Tell: A Writing Pedagogy of Discourse, Genre, and Membership*. Portsmouth, NH: Heinemann Press, 1998.

Bok, D. *Universities in the Marketplace: The Commercialization of Higher Education*. Princeton, NJ: Princeton University Press, 2003.

Britzman, D. P. *Lost Subjects, Contested Objects: Toward a Psychoanalytic Inquiry of Learning*. Albany, NY: SUNY Press, 1998.

Brownstein, M. "Catastrophic Encounters: Postmodern Biography as Witness to History." In *The Seductions of Biography*, edited by M. Rhiel and D. Suchoff. New York: Routledge, 1996: 185–199.

Chaudhuri, U. *Staging Place: The Geography of Modern Drama*. Ann Arbor, MI: The University of Michigan Press, 1995.

Duderstadt, J. J., and Womack, F. W. *The Future of the Public Research University in America: Beyond the Crossroads*. Baltimore, MD: The Johns Hopkins University Press, 2003.

Edgerton, S. "Particularities of 'Otherness:' Autobiography, Maya Angelou, and Me." In *Curriculum as Social Psychoanalysis: The Significance of Place*, edited by J. Kincheloe and W. Pinar. Albany, NY: SUNY Press, 1991: 77–97.

Eigen, M. "Breathing and Identity." In *The Electrified Tightrope*, edited by A. Phillips. Northvale, NJ: Jason Aronson, 1993: 43–47.

Felman, S. *What Does a Woman Want? Reading and Sexual Difference*. Baltimore, MD: The Johns Hopkins University Press, 1993.

Giroux, H. A. "Neoliberalism, Corporate Culture, and the Promise of Higher Education: The University as a Democratic Public Sphere." *Harvard Educational Review* 72(4), 2002: 425–463.

Grumet, M. *Bitter Milk: Women and Teaching*. Amherst, MA: University of Massachusetts Press, 1998.

Harvey, D. *The Condition of Postmodernity*. London: Basil Blackwell, 1989.

Kauffman, L. S. "The Long Goodbye: Against Personal Testimony or, An Infant Grifter Grows Up." In *Changing Subjects: The Making of Feminist Literary Criticism*, edited by G. Greene and C. Kahn. New York: Routledge, 1993: 128–146.

Kirp, D. L. *Shakespeare, Einstein, and the Bottom Line: The Marketing of Higher Education*. Cambridge, MA: Harvard University Press, 2003.

Kristeva, J. *Desire in Language: A Semiotic Approach to Literature and Art*. New York: Columbia University Press, 1980.

LaCapra, D. "From What Subject-Position(s) Should One Address the Politics of Research?" In *The Politics of Research*, edited by E. A. Kaplan and G. Levine. New Brunswick, NJ: Rutgers University Press, 1997: 59–68.

Lauteur, P. "'Political Correctness' and the Attack on American Colleges." In *Higher Education Under Fire: Politics, Economics, and the Crisis of the Humanities*, edited by M. Bérubé and C. Nelson. New York: Routledge, 1995: 73–90.

Luke, C., and Gore, J., eds. *Feminisms and Critical Pedagogy*. New York: Routledge, 1992.

Lyotard, J-F. *The Postmodern Condition: A Report on Knowledge*. Minneapolis: University of Minnesota Press, 1979.

Marginson, S., and Considine, M. *The Enterprise University: Power, Governance, and Reinvention in Australia*. New York: Cambridge University Press, 2000.

Miller, R. E. *As if Learning Mattered: Reforming Higher Education*. Ithaca, NY: Cornell University Press, 1998.

Miyoshi, M. "'Globalization,' Culture, and the University." In *The Cultures of Globalization*, edited by F. Jameson and M. Miyoshi. London: Duke University Press, 1998: 247–270.

Moi, T. *What Is a Woman?* Oxford University Press, New York, 1999.

Nelson, C., and Bérubé, M. "Introduction: A Report from the Front." In *Higher Education Under Fire: Politics, Economics, and the Crisis of the Humanities*, edited by M. Bérubé and C. Nelson. New York: Routledge, 1995: 1–32.

Nelson, C., and Watt, S. "Superstars." In *Academic Keywords: A Devil's Dictionary for Higher Education*. New York: Routledge, 1999: 260–280.

Pagano, J. *Exiles and Communities: Teaching in the Patriarchal Wilderness*. Albany: SUNY Press, 1990.

Pinar, W. "Curriculum as Social Psychoanalysis: On the Significance of Place." In *Curriculum as Social Psychoanalysis: Essays on the Significance of Place*, edited by J. Kincheloe and W. Pinar. Albany: SUNY Press, 1991: 167–186.

Poster, M. "Words Without Things: The Mode of Information." *October* 53 (1990): 63–77.

Readings, B. *The University in Ruins*. Cambridge, MA: Harvard University Press, 1996.

Rouse, R. "Thinking through Transnationalism: Notes on the Cultural Politics of Class Relations in the Contemporary United States." *Public Culture* 7(2), 1994: 353–402.

Salvio, P. M. "Teacher of Weird Abundance: Portraits of the Pedagogical Tactics of Anne Sexton." *Cultural Studies* 13(4), 1999: 639–660.

Shumway, D. R. "The Star System in Literary Studies." *PMLA* 112(1), 1997: 85–100.

Silin, J. *Sex, Death and the Education of Children: Our Passion for Ignorance in the Age of AIDS*." New York: Teachers College Press, 1995.

Talburt, S. "Identity as a Bother: Forms and Locations of Speaking." *Review of Education/Pedagogy/Cultural Studies* 21(1), 1999: 15–39.

Taubman, P. "Achieving the Right Distance." *Educational Theory* 40(1), 1990: 121–133.

——— . "Separate Identities, Separate Lives: Diversity in the Curriculum." In *Understanding Curriculum as Racial Text: Representations of Identity and Difference in Education*, edited by L. Castenell and W. Pinar. Albany: SUNY Press, 1993: 287–306.

Tobin, L. *Writing Relationships: What Really Happens in the Composition Classroom."* Portsmouth: Heinemann Press, 1993.

Tompkins, J. "Me and My Shadow." *New Literary History* 19(1), 1987: 197–200.

——— . *A Life in School: What the Teacher Learned*. Reading, MA: Perseus, 1996.

Walkerdine, V. *Schoolgirl Fictions*. London: Verso, 1990.

Woolf, V. *Moments of Being: Unpublished Autobiographical Writings*. Sussex, U.K.: Sussex University Press, 1976.

2
Picturing Institutions: Intellectual Work as Gift and Commodity in *Good Will Hunting*

JO KEROES

As we are about so many things, Americans are conflicted about higher education. Given the insistently tiered nature of institutions of higher learning, along with the influence of popular forms on cultural attitudes, it's not surprising that these conflicts surface in commercial films set on college campuses. To take a recent example, underpinning the 1997 film, *Good Will Hunting*, is a set of complex and often contradictory assumptions about intellectual work and the institutions that foster it. Intellectual talent is both a blessing and a product to be purchased, one that will eventually become currency in the market place. It is, in other words, both gift and commodity.

These metaphors of gift and commodity provide a lens through which to examine the ways this film, as others have done before, uses institutions of higher learning to play out unresolved, possibly irresolvable, conflicts about class, loyalty, and the nature and value of intellectual work. What's revealing is how intellectual capacities get defined—whose get bought and sold and whose are treated as gifts.

According to Lewis Hyde, whose book, *The Gift* (1979), builds on the work of cultural anthropologists to explore the way art functions in a market economy, a gift exchange between individuals or community members involves reciprocity and invokes permanent social bonds; it depends upon relationship rather than a formal contractual arrangement. The gift's benefit derives from its being freely offered, its value from its being "priceless." Thus talent, inspiration, and creativity are gifts, as can be an organ donated at the time of one's death, or a pair of gloves offered as a birthday present. A commodity, on the other hand, functions independent of social relations and personal obligations between those who exchange it. The commodity moves to turn a profit. Once it is sold, nothing ensures its return; it is "used up." We buy a car or the pair of gloves in a purely economic transaction, giving the dealer or shopkeeper a sum of money in exchange for the automobile or gloves, expecting nothing in return but the product itself in good working order. When a gift is given, however, it theoretically begins a process that implies its return. Something inherent in the giving itself assures that it will be replenished, for the very essence of the gift is that it not be converted into capital. Though the gift exchange may incur an obligation for the recipient eventually to return the favor, in that favor's return rests the potential for restoring balance to the relationship. In other words, there's an ethical component to the gift exchange that differs from the rules guiding the market transactions of buying and selling.

Not surprisingly, the values inherent in gift exchange operate in continuous tension within a capitalist market economy. Occupations such as banking, law, manufacturing, and sales operate clearly in the market on a cost–benefit basis. Gift labor is closely allied with more spiritual and social concerns often perceived as feminine, such as schooling, childcare, culture, or religion. It doesn't lend itself as readily to market quantification, precisely because the products of such work aren't commodities. As Hyde notes, "gift labor requires the kind of emotional or spiritual commitment that precludes its own marketing." (1979, p. 107)

Although any object or any kind of commerce can become either gift or commodity, depending upon how we treat it, certain kinds of work more closely approximate gift rather than commodity exchange. Though few jobs are "pure" gift labors—as Hyde observes, nurses are committed to healing but they are also participants in the marketplace—the more gift labor an occupation contains, the less lucrative it is likely to be (1979, p. 106). These entwined concepts of *gift* and *commodity* tap roots that are deeply embedded in Western culture.

From the time of the ancient Greeks, culture in Western societies has been yoked with prestige, marking those with certain kinds of knowledge as members of a superior social group. In the early American university, this came to imply a curriculum focused on literary and historical studies, knowledge of classical texts, and mastery of certain foreign languages. Since the last part of the nineteenth century, however, when business standards came to dominate American culture, the main purpose of higher education in America has been to prepare students to take their place in and to serve society in tangible ways. The purpose of schooling is not so much to cultivate learned habits of mind but to make personal advancement possible; the kinds of knowledge schools and universities purvey ought to enable graduates to acquire and implement *useful* knowledge.

Though commercial films have long provided us with vivid and romantic pictures of how the privileged are supposed to live and how such worlds as business and medicine presumably work, very few movies have attempted to deal with the life of the mind. Popular films typically represent intellectual talent as either the spontaneous product of genius or as something suspect, silly, or simply obscure—as anything but "real work."

Consider *Good Will Hunting*. Early in the film the title character dashes the pretensions of a Harvard student who ridicules Will's best friend. "You dropped a hundred and fifty grand on a fuckin' education you coulda got for a dollar fifty in late charges at the library," Will taunts. The Harvard student retorts—"yeah, but I will have a degree and you'll be serving my kids French fries at a drive-thru on our way to a skiing trip"—which speaks to the utility of that Harvard diploma. But consider something else about this encounter: Will, a glib, working-class genius whom we never see studying, has assaulted the arrogant but nonetheless diligent history student who has, at least, worked at mastering his subject, whereas Will can rely on his extraordinary gifts. Yet the scene compels us to side with Will rather than with the Harvard student who has presumably done some serious intellectual work. The screenwriters understand that their audience is of two minds about superior intelligence and higher education: It's okay to be smart and to be educated, but only if one doesn't take it all too seriously and work too hard at it. Will's rough arrogance and spontaneous brilliance are more tolerable than the student's intellectual effort simply because the student trades on the commercial value of his Harvard credential.

It is because Will Hunting's intellectual prowess is so insistently defined as "genius," as "easy," as a gift he doesn't "work for," that this film makes a particularly apt text for exploration. *Good Will Hunting* articulates a fundamental American ambivalence about the power and purpose of higher education, the fears it inspires, and the promise it implies. By casting Will Hunting as a genius, rather than just a smart kid who studies, the movie illuminates tensions that shape our vexed public policies about higher education. Will's genius is discovered within an institution allied with the cold, striving, competitive intellect, but it's nurtured and taught to flourish by a teacher who has chosen another path. Using MIT and the community college and the teachers who represent them as emblems of conflicting life choices, the film promises that the young genius will use his gift to ascend from the "working" class and discover a niche that will neither commodify his talent, corrupt his innocence, nor compromise his loyalty to his friends.

Good Will Hunting enacts a tug-of-war between allegiance to class roots and the equally powerful pull of individualism—the belief that to fulfill one's potential means to confirm or to rise above one's native status. The battle sites are MIT, a quintessentially elite university, province of the "haves," and Bunker Hill Community College, the sort of institution considered a refuge for underprivileged students, those too poor or academically undernourished to gain admission to a more prestigious institution. The faculty here are those professional academics presumed to be insufficiently ambitious or talented or without degrees from those elite institutions that would allow them to market their talents elsewhere. To a significant extent, because it is poorly compensated, their teaching constitutes gift labor. The film enacts these tensions paradoxically by seeing the community college as a source of "real" values, a place where somehow the whole person is educated, rather than the site of cut-throat ambition and selling out whose only concern with Will is his intellect, detached as it may be from his self.

For those unfamiliar with the film, *Good Will Hunting* is the story of a troubled young South Boston man who works as a janitor at MIT. A working class genius with a photographic memory who has mastered art, literature, history, and philosophy but whose special gift is mathematics, Will comes upon a problem a professor has left for his students to puzzle over and quickly but anonymously solves it. The professor, Gerald Lambeau, once a prodigy himself, discovers Will's identity and takes him under his wing, rescues him from being sentenced to jail for barroom brawling, and makes him a member of his mathematical team. To deal with his antisocial behavior, the professor enlists as Will's therapist a community college psychology instructor Sean McGuire (played by Robin Williams), who is also the MIT professor's former Harvard roommate. The two vie for Will.

Intellectual work of the sort presumably done at places like MIT and Harvard is customarily the province of the privileged; those not so fortunate are consigned to second- and third-tier institutions, state universities, and community colleges in this country—in England almost any place other than Oxford or Cambridge. American films about higher education typically align elite institutions and the students and faculty who inhabit them with a commodity culture, whereas working class institutions embody a gift economy. *Good Will Hunting* is no exception. Professor Lambeau, winner of the Fields Medal, mathematics' most prestigious prize, is elegantly dressed and surrounded by obsequious though brilliant graduate assistants who help advance his work. He will expect Will to put his talents to use. McGuire, the community college teacher, sitting rumpled in his basement office at a third-tier institution, physically embodies the notion of teaching as gift. Yes, he has a job, but not the title of "professor." Yes, he must be paid, but not very much. The spirit of what he does is the spirit of the gift exchange. We want, even expect this character to offer the gift of transforming Will's life, opening him up to love and possibility. Their encounter is supposed to be a therapeutic one; the MIT professor brings Will to Sean McGuire for therapy, not to take a class. Yet by setting their meetings in his community college office, the film insists upon McGuire's identity as a teacher, suggesting a yearning for the teaching encounter to be as private a recognition of the individual and as curative as the therapeutic one. It's worth noting that though therapists are usually compensated, since Will himself doesn't pay for his meetings with McGuire, their encounters constitute a pure gift exchange. The problem is that in a modern capitalist society, only by exploiting one's gifts can a person travel the path to material success. This means, quite literally, putting those gifts to work.

But it's a curious feature of films about higher education that they rarely show people *engaged* in intellectual work—students studying and teachers preparing lectures, writing academic papers, and so forth. Even more telling is what they show when they do devote screen time to intellectual activities. Will Hunting has a prodigious store of general knowledge but is shown reading, acquiring that knowledge, in only one brief scene. Lambeau, the MIT math professor who discovers Will's talent, works hard at mathematical problems, compelled to justify and sustain his reputation as the winner of mathematics' equivalent of the Nobel Prize, but for Will himself it's no effort at all. As Will becomes bored watching Lambeau struggle to do a proof, he explodes, "Do you know how easy this is for me? Do you have any fuckin' idea how easy this is?" Skylar, Will's romantic interest, a Harvard student bound for Stanford Medical School, figures that "at the end, my brain's going to be worth $250,000." A valuable commodity, her degree promises financial security and social prestige. Still, she has plenty of time to hang out in bars, and on the one occasion we see her studying, Will pulls her away "to have fun."

Those less blessed must often work toward material success at places where it's less likely that they'll achieve it; some sacrifice it entirely. Sean McGuire, Will Hunting's mentor and a man of formidable intellectual gifts, has opted not to compete for medals or prestige or a high salary but simply to teach, to pass his gifts along. When such figures do "succeed," their achievement is portrayed as something that will promote personal happiness and satisfaction rather than economic gain. (In *Educating Rita*, an earlier film that similarly treats the issue of class head-on, Rita, a cockney hairdresser, studies great works of literature in order to "find herself," to become educated and so to make better choices about her life.)

The community college office of Will's mentor provides the place from which Will Hunting gains the strength to emerge and seek his "true self," to use his own extraordinary gift in a productive and generous way. In either case, though knowledge ensures a rise in class status, its connection to personal happiness appears to lie elsewhere, in self-respect or service to others.

Still, this view of higher education as a commodity doesn't completely obliterate the film's respect for learning and culture for their own sakes and for the confidence, intellect, and taste they foster. The ancient idea that practical knowledge requires less intelligence than more abstract forms, let's say philosophy or higher mathematics, and that earning one's living and engaging in commerce ought not to be activities engaged in by the intellectual elite linger even in the industrialized Western mentality. But this opposition is too simple, of course; it is one that begs to be deconstructed. Few engaged with higher education would quarrel with Martha C. Nussbaum's assertion that a university education should "cultivate humanity." Few would dispute the idea that liberal education "should be Socratic, committed to the activation of each student's independent mind and to the production of a community that can genuinely reason together. . . ."(Nussbaum, 1997, p. 19) Such a humanistic education is dedicated to the cultivation of mental discipline and a critical intelligence through the mastery of academic subjects. Though a truly liberal education includes science and economics as well as literature and philosophy, education for tangible, practical ends remains aligned in society's mind with business, science, and technology, whereas the more abstract forms of knowing are assigned to the humanities, which have no obvious practical application and whose benefit, like religious belief, must be taken on faith. Our persistent confusion shows up in the way *Good Will Hunting* turns the abstract mathematics of MIT toward the ultimate antihumanism of espionage.

As it did in Europe, religion in America provided the first arena for intellectual life. The Puritans were learned intellectuals who expected their clergy to be scholars, and in fact, most clergy had college degrees. But our progenitors also held to the Calvinist conception of usefulness and believed that those who achieved material success were assured entry to heaven, the rich person's wealth a sign of not just business acumen but God's favor—a *gift* from God. Those less fortunate were, by implication if not definition, simply less good, a notion that unfortunately persists, most visibly in current efforts to eliminate welfare, affirmative action, and college remedial programs. By the end of the nineteenth century, a person's success in the marketplace or in public life was taken as a sign of his own accomplishments. He (it was virtually always and only a "he") was a "self-made man," one to be admired, even envied, whereas the scholar opting for a life of the mind drew skepticism for his dubious worth in the marketplace. Yet a genuine longing for culture and what it represents persists alongside this ingrained distrust of the intellectual, a tension that surfaces in popular forms.

In the ancient world, it was believed that everyone had a personal spirit that could and ought to be cultivated. The Romans called this tutelar spirit the person's *genius*, and the task of setting free one's gifts was a recognized labor. The genius (or daemon[1] to the Greeks) comes at birth, carrying with it the fullness of undeveloped powers. In Rome, according to Apuleius, on his birthday a person not only received gifts but would also give something to his genius, for it was believed that those who do not reciprocate the gifts of their genius will leave it in bondage when they die. Thus, an abiding sense of gratitude moves a person to labor in the service of his gift, his *genius*. As Hyde explains, "a gift isn't realized fully until it is given away. Those who don't acknowledge gratitude or who refuse to labor in its service neither free their gifts nor really come to possess them." (1979, p. 50) What Hyde calls a "reciprocal labor" is essential to the cultivation of a talent, for the gift will continue to discharge its energy only as long as it is attended to in return. Whatever we have been given is supposed to be given away again, not kept; if it *is* kept, something of similar value should be given in its place.

This explains why everyone involved in his life either expects or wants this troubled boy-genius to *do* something with his talent. It's a gift, they understand, and as such, it must be put in circulation and remain there. Hyde emphasizes the communal nature of the gift economy; it flourishes among small groups and binds them together. Will's buddies want *him* to use his genius to become something better than they think they can be— not terribly difficult, as the film portrays them as crude, foul-mouthed sexists redeemed only by their loyal hearts of gold. "You need to do it for me," says Will's best friend, Chuckie. "You're sitting on a lottery ticket and you're too scared to cash it in. You owe it to me and the other guys cause you have something the rest of us don't have."

Respect for the intellectual life is leavened with suspicion, though. In the case of the MIT professor hard at work attempting to solve his mathematical equations, we're meant to admire the scope of his talent, which has garnered him the equivalent of a Nobel Prize. Though it's beyond our comprehension, or perhaps *because* it is, this is intellectual work we can respect. It's abstract intellectual work, but of a sort that can be put to tangible use, as Lambeau's connection to the NSA, a secret government agency, attests. He's won a prize *and* can sell the product of his work in the marketplace. The film is too clever to set the professor up as unambiguously evil; he does rescue Will, recognize his talent, and want to help him be gainfully employed, after all. But in the hint of a homosexual attachment to his teaching assistant, in his excessively elegant dress, in his slightly effete manner, and mainly in the contrast between him and Sean McGuire, we're meant to look at him slightly askance. Hyde maintains that when gifts are sold, they change their nature "as much as water changes when it freezes." (1979, p. 21) When Lambeau wants Will to exchange his genius for the reward of a job in espionage, the mathematics he pursues is no longer quite so pure. Richard Hofstadter has observed that our attitude toward intellectual work has changed in this century from a "benign ridicule and neglect" of intellect born of skepticism about its practicality, to a "malign resentment of the intellectual as expert." (1963, p. 34) Sufficiently cynical to understand that his talent can be exploited, Will rejects an offer to do code breaking for the government intelligence agency because he believes his efforts will be put to sinister use.

McGuire, pointedly a former Southie kid like Will, takes pains to tell his rival that he has *chosen* his life as teacher in an obscure community college; he has deliberately opted not to use his gift as a tool. He represents the capacity of Will's gift to bring a different sort of satisfaction—the pleasure of choosing how and what to give, a pleasure that first requires being willing to accept and acknowledge his gift and the responsibilities that accompany it and then to give of himself. McGuire isn't really interested in Will's genius or what he does with it. He wants Will to "do what's in your heart." It's part of the anti-intellectualism of this film about intellectual life that their discussions never do center or even touch upon Will's talent. Rather, they focus on getting Will ready to open up sufficiently to follow the girl he loves. Certainly there's nothing wrong with this, but it's typical of *Good Will Hunting* that it raises but then skirts the question of just what one does with one's gifts, what obligation its owner has to his talent and to the larger communities of which he is a part. But the film does raise the question, even though, like the society it reflects, it can't resolve the conflict between teaching and learning as both gift and commodity.

When Will finally decides to leave South Boston to follow his heart, his friends give him the car that will take him across the country, a car they've restored with their own hands. The film's sentimentality obliges that it be the buddies whom he would desert who push him on. This way, we can ignore the reality that education is always about class, and that leaving home often means that one can't go back. Though it's questionable whether in real life his buddies would in fact be as encouraging as they are in the film, they *could* do more with their lives than go from low paying jobs to barroom brawls and back again, which is the reductive picture of uneducated working people the film perpetuates. It's precisely people like Will's friends for whom community colleges have been such a boon. But by sustaining this myth that brands working class youth with being "stuck," the film serves to keep them in their place. Despite the boys' encouragement, the film reinforces the fear that emerging from such places will mean being transformed, reconfigured with new manners, new modes of dress, and most important, disdain for and alienation from the people they once were.

This is why the character of Sean McGuire is so immediately lovable and comforting, something Robin Williams intelligently capitalizes on in his portrayal. McGuire is the brilliant, critical non-conformist, but he has renounced the world of the elite intellectual class for the world of workers, given up being a man of the intellect to become a man of heart. In the tried and true manner of dissenters, he has alienated himself from the alliance with power and prestige and money his talent might earn him, forsaking the intellectual life of the sort his MIT colleague lives for the world of more mundane educational work. This work, we understand, is offered as a gift. This is what we secretly still believe of schooling: that, like religion, knowledge instills true values, right thinking, and a purified heart. And that educators, eschewing adequate compensation for the rewards of altruism, ought in part, at least, to be spiritual leaders. The film sustains the stereotype of the man of heart, beloved but powerless, and offers the conviction that the emotional life is best for those aligned with the working class. It also sustains the idea that teaching in such a setting is a labor of love.

Like most popular films, this one smoothes out reality's bumps. Society is dominated by commodity exchange. Students, privileged and not, do go to college in order to take their places in the market economy, and they have good reason to expect that their education will enable them to get decent jobs. The community college in reality functions as a site for the most fundamental of economic transactions: people go to community colleges to acquire skills, trades, and certificates in fields such as hospitality management, landscape design, and computer technology that will enable them to participate in the commodity culture. They go to get trained for jobs or to prepare for further study. Substantial numbers of them continue on to prestigious public and private universities. But their instructors are among the most exploited in the profession, teaching the greatest numbers of classes and students and receiving the lowest measure of prestige. The film elevates McGuire's message, romanticizing him and his institution as the place where the gift exchange flourishes, as it insists upon his low status in both the intellectual and market economy but says his work is worth it. In doing so, the film perpetuates rather than challenges these values.

We can see in *Good Will Hunting* an attempt to work out the relationship between utility and knowledge, to comprehend and perhaps reconcile society's need to see higher education as serving both the pragmatic, practical needs of a capitalist society, including the need for scientific research, and those more abstract but equally important concerns for knowledge and the critical habits of mind that we understand to be products of a university education. One message of the film is that knowledge ought not to be "pure." As commodity, it needs to be put to use, though precisely to what use, with what consequences, we cannot guarantee. As gift, it needs to be passed on.

American society values intellect, of course, but it understands or approves of it wholeheartedly only when it works toward tangible results. We shouldn't condemn this attitude out of hand. It's not unreasonable for a society to want its members to function purposefully and productively in it. What's distressing is its inability to fashion a vision that goes beyond the practical to include the aesthetic and the metaphysical as forms of knowledge useful because they involve reflection, analysis, reasoned debate, and the cultivation of ethical principles. As those who are likely to be reading this know, the intellectual life involves engaging in reasoned dispute and critical speculation about the nature of knowledge, the art of interpretation, and the meaning of the human condition, activities essential for the development of critical intelligence and even wisdom. In the world of the university, we tend to cluster these goals under the rubric of "the humanities"—literature, philosophy, language, and history—too often paying weak homage to their honorable past while allowing their resources to shrivel and their departments to shrink as power and prestige are granted elsewhere, typically to departments of business and technology.

In general, popular films exhibit little understanding of what an intellectual is. We know what scientists do—or we think we do. We sort of know what teachers, writers, and even poets do—or we think we do. Popular films tend to portray these activities in very concrete and practical terms: Scientists test and experiment and observe and make discoveries; writers produce novels or plays; teachers transmit information; math geniuses go to work for the government. But unless we're engaged ourselves in those activities, we don't really seem to spend much time considering the *work* involved. So intellectual work gets misrepresented in popular forms as either airy-fairy, pencil-pushing stuff separate from the real world, or as genuine effort, but of the sort too abstract or mysterious for ordinary folks with common sense to understand. Because we can't understand it, we harbor the suspicion that it's the province of the arrogant, weird, or even dangerous. Though math and science are seen as more concrete and more "useful," with practical applications to everyday life, the higher math shown in *Good Will Hunting* is intellectual work both abstract and incomprehensible. Moreover, the popular conception of intellectuals is that they talk only to one another in arcane language about topics they take little trouble to make intelligible to the lay public, a conception not always far from the truth. All of which is to say that intellectual work can intimidate or shame us. Richard Hofstadter has pointed out that intellect is resented as a form of power or privilege, a claim to distinction and thus at odds with the egalitarianism fundamental to American consciousness (1963). Intellectualism tends also to be allied with slightly left-of-center political positions, so along with resentment of its elitism goes the suspicion that intellect is a subversive force, a skepticism that stems from not understanding what intellectual work is and a fear of the mind left relatively unfettered.

It's tempting to call *Good Will Hunting* and other works like it profoundly anti-intellectual, privileging as they do the heart over the head. But it's more accurate, I think, to point to their ambivalence. Will may be a genius and may not have to do much actual "work," but it's clear that we're supposed to admire his gift and expect him to use it well. Still, it's his "heart" that's most urgently at stake. If the work of the heart brings few financial rewards, then encouraging the less privileged to pursue it may enrich their souls but will keep them powerless in a world in which power and money are synonymous, and perhaps this is one purpose a film such as *Good Will Hunting* serves. Its romantic appeal rests on the fact that, like all fairy tales, and like most commercial films, it plays with our anxieties and then assuages them. Another way to look at it, though, is that these films yearn for an altruism we've lost and see those who haven't yet been co-opted as a last hope for humanism. They take as an act of faith that knowledge can disclose the meaning of life and that the purpose of higher education is to search for that meaning. Still, the teachers in these films either get their rewards elsewhere, winning a medal, receiving support for their research, conducting their private law practice, writing their own poetry, or they are altruistic "failures," altruism and fair compensation continuing to be a contradiction in terms. Though that may not be their stated purpose, the films allow us to continue to consign teaching to a gift economy and thereby justify its not yielding adequate financial return.

The traditional low salaries of teachers have their roots in the notion that teachers were public officers who, in the American egalitarian spirit, ought not to be too highly paid. (They were, of course, also often women, who from the beginning of the common school movement were, as a matter of course, paid less than their male counterparts.) We want teaching to be a transformative gift, freely given. But we're ambivalent about this, too. We want the teacher to remain generous, tied to the gift economy, but as recipients we want to be able to exchange the fruits of his or her labor, as well as our own, in the marketplace. Rather than compete for prestigious academic prizes, McGuire has chosen to hide his light under a banged-up, community college, public-issue desk, and we're given to understand that though this was his noble choice, there's something slightly wrong with him.

Ignoring the fact that in real life many supremely capable academics choose positions in state universities and community colleges because they're philosophically committed to the idea of public education, the film emphasizes that McGuire has been hiding from life since his wife's death. This is why the twin departures of both McGuire and Will Hunting at the end of the film seem so satisfying. In timeworn tradition, the teacher has been taught. Our uplift at the film's ending comes from our belief that by going off to follow his heart, Will Hunting will find the right path and discover a way to pass on his prodigious gifts and that McGuire's generous encounters with Will have likewise freed him to open up his own. But McGuire leaves the community college where, we had been led to believe, he was engaged in honorable work, for a presumably more satisfactory existence, though we're given no more idea of what that might be than we are of what will happen to Will when he gets to California. Though McGuire's departure from the gift-giving teacher stereotype suggests the need for a new plot about intellectual life, the film can't imagine either his or Will's future, perhaps because our society has yet to invent one.

Note

1. No doubt it's coincidence, but it's worth observing nonetheless that one of the authors of the script for *Good Will Hunting* is Matt Damon and that he was a Harvard student who quickly commodified his education, entering the lucrative Hollywood marketplace by valorizing the meagerly compensated life of the spirit.

References

Gilbert, L. (Director). *Educating Rita* [Motion picture]. UK: Acorn Pictures, 1983.
Hofstadter, R. *Anti-Intellectualism in American Life*. New York: Vintage, 1963.
Hyde, L. *The Gift: Imagination and the Erotic Life of Property*. New York: Vintage, 1979.
Nussbaum, M. C. *Cultivating Humanity*. Cambridge, MA: Harvard University Press, 1997.
Van Sant, G., Jr. (Director). *Good Will Hunting* [Motion picture]. United States: Miramax, 1997.

3
Education for Fun and Profit: Traditions of Popular College Fiction in the United States, 1875–1945

SUSAN IKENBERRY

The college novel has a long tradition in American popular literature. The vitality of the tradition is evident in diverse works capturing the popular imagination in recent years. These range from nostalgia stories romanticizing student radicalism, such as the film *The Big Chill*, or fast times sorts of stories such as *Animal House*, which has achieved cinematic cult status, to an array of novels treating the experience of college life. This chapter explores the pulp fiction roots of this rich tradition. In particular, core thematic elements of popular college fiction will be described and placed in sociohistorical context.

By the beginning of the Civil War, an explosion of novels and magazines was well underway. Printing technology, cheap paper, the transportation revolution, urbanization, and literacy widespread enough to create a substantial popular market were the major causes. As the illustrated weeklies, best-selling novels, and the much-maligned dime and half-dime novels emerged, their fare quickly became formulaic. It's not surprising, for not only did stories need to be turned out quickly, but editors also needed a predictable product that matched readers' expectations. Along with the Detective story and the Western, the College novel was one genre of many to emerge during this period in which so much of our popular culture was born.

Stories about school and college reflected an idealized, dramatized formula version of the reality of the role that school and college had begun to play in the lives of the readers to whom they were directed. These stories were not chronicles of college life, but they may give an even more vivid picture of popular attitudes, for they illustrate the stereotypes, class resentments, and aspirations that came to be involved America's unique involvement with higher education.

Along with the better-known tales of "Wild West" heroes, frontiersmen, and plucky boys who made their way to respectability if not riches, all of which emerged around the time of the Civil War, stories about school and college students became a small but recognizable part of juvenile and adult fare. Stories typically make little distinction between school life at an academy and the college experience, reflecting the reality that boys (for women were only just becoming part of the American higher education movement at this point) in either situation were part of the social class who would be prepared for college. The public high school had not emerged on a large enough scale to democratize schooling above the elementary level, so often writers made little distinction. If the hero's antics and adventures at the Lawrenceville School were popular, the writer could simply follow him and his friends to Princeton.

In the earliest dime and half-dime weeklies, such as *Wide Awake* or *Tiptop Weekly,* there were stories of resourceful, practical-joke-playing school/college boys as part of the standard fare. Schoolboys must have relished these prankster heroes, whose tricks resulted in the humiliation of stuffy professors or in the embarrassment of members of various immigrant groups according to expected crude stereotypes: The dimwitted Irishman was easily tricked into making a fool of himself, the German immigrant was easily duped, and the "Chinaman" was tripped up in ways that caused him to lose his temper, remonstrate in his native language, and then lose a package or dirty a bundle of clean laundry while chasing his tormentors.

By the last two decades of the nineteenth century, the crude prankster had been refined, and the school story and college novel had become a staple of the publishing industry. Two separate traditions developed: From lowly dime novel origins came a slightly more elevated hero, such as Frank Merriwell, an athlete, detective, ventriloquist, and still a prankster. But a new genteel tradition involved a more realistic depiction of school, and increasingly college, life from the standpoint of the upper-middle class student with plenty of spending money and social connections. Such books sold widely enough to interest publishing houses, and though they were hardly intended for a mass audience, they were common enough to have their formula known.[1]

No series better illustrates the popular college novel than Gilbert Patten's series of stories, which included the famous Frank Merriwell books and many others less remembered, such as *Boltwood of Yale, The College Rebel, On College Battlefields, The Call of the Varsity, Clif Stirling: Sophomore at Stormbridge,* and many others, published just after the turn of the century and well into the 1920s. Patten's books were best sellers even by today's standards. It is estimated that at least 125 million copies of the Frank Merriwell series (which itself ran to at least 209 books) were sold. Estimates of readers are as high as three million.

Patten's heroes were athletes, sometimes reluctant but always accomplished and victorious when it really mattered. Actual schoolwork interfered little with Frank Merriwell's busy life. A champion of the democratic college environment, Frank and those like him fought snobbishness and illustrated, in their play and in their reaction to setbacks, a simple nobility of character. Merriwell and the other Patten heroes "stood for every boy's dream. For truth, faith, justice, the triumph of right," as George Zuckerman put it in his 1973 novel, *Farewell, Frank Merriwell* (p. 45).[2]

The reader—more often the parent than the child—who chose the more elevated book about student life at Harvard, Yale, or Princeton probably had certain expectations about its content because novels about life at the Ivy League colleges rapidly became a staple of the publishing houses. Often written by alumni who looked back nostalgically on their college experience, these books were read by the early generation of prospective college students, who may have received one as a gift. They were often the children of the new industrial middle class. For them, a college education was both a manifestation of their father's success and, increasingly, a necessary step even to stay on economic par with the family. After all, Father's good income was so often a matter of salary, not land or a business that could be passed on. There was a very good chance Father himself had not been to college or, if he had, the experience had borne little resemblance to those provided by the colleges as they were emerging by the century's end. (It was even a better bet that Mother had not been to college, though for her late nineteenth-century daughter, college was, indeed, an option if by no means a necessity.) These novels played a crucial role in defining the college experience, projecting idealized expectations of college life to a large audience and to some extent shaping the reality of college life. The stock campus images no doubt reassured parents as well as prospective students that the institution would build character and ensure their sons' or possibly daughters' meeting people whose help and influence would be important to them all their lives. They also allowed alumni to look back sentimentally on their own experience.

Tripp's (1876) *Student Life at Harvard*, a well-drawn example of the early elite college novel, lays out a surprising number of elements of college life that novels and stories continued to examine over the course of the next hundred years: A keen interest in athletics is already assumed in the story, though at that time the sport chosen was more likely to be rowing than football, the sport that was to dominate the literature within two decades. Tripp paid considerable attention to behavior involving "class spirit" and to hazing and pranks. But he was also at pains to illustrate that the "dig" (the hard-working student) often deserved respect—especially if his studying was for " the pure love of truth" and the student was not actually in league with the faculty (Tripp, 1876, p. 327).[3]

Tripp's Harvard was no exemplar of democracy. With no sense that it could or should be otherwise, Tripp seemed to say that it was dominated by the wealthy and socially prominent, who set the tone. The expenditures of a typical student for "gloves, flashy scarfs, and French boots" could amount to "an alarming sum-total," yet Tripp could laugh indulgently at the protagonist's spending too much of Papa's "allowance to him."[4] (p. 368)

Despite his preference for affluence, Tripp seemed to approve of the University's going to some lengths to attract less affluent students:

> Though the number of poor students is perhaps proportionally smaller at Harvard than at any other college in the land, there are many brave hearts (and this is especially true of the professional students) who toil on sometimes without the common creature-comforts, and struggle manfully along the rough path to golden knowledge, sacrificing enjoyment and leisure, and sometimes health, and even life itself. (Tripp, 1876, p. 313)

Young Sam, Tripp's hero, is shocked to learn of the small sum on which one of the law students lives: " 'Eighty cents a week!', exclaimed Sam, in astonishment. 'Why, our 'marm' charges eight dollars for meals; and . . . she grumbles at that.'"[5] (pp. 318–319) Taken as a whole, Tripp's compassion for the ethnic scholarship student was only slightly less shallow than other authors, who used the penniless first-generation immigrant on campus to provide comic relief and to reassure the upper-class reader that he was, by comparison, a specimen of the first rank. A popular example of this is a story published about two decades later, *Philosophy 4*, written as a short story in the *Saturday Evening Post* by Owen Wister (better known as the author of *The Virginian*). Wister's friend Theodore Roosevelt was fond of this story of two fun-loving Harvard students with "Colonial last names" who hire Oscar Maironi (his Jewish parents had come over in steerage, the reader is informed) to tutor them. Oscar is sneaky, stingy, and apparently capable of little originality in his work. As for the two well-off students, Bertie and

Billy, "Money filled [their] pockets" and thus with "their heads empty of money, they were burdened by less cramping thoughts." (Wister, 1903, p. 37) Bertie and Billy sought harmless diversions. The closest they came to going astray was to consume a bit of wine and speculate on possible artifice that might have enhanced the barmaid's red hair. Oscar's pleasures were less innocent: "There were sly times when he took what he had saved by his cheap meals and room and went to Boston with it, and [for] a few hours thoroughly ceased being ascetic." (p. 37) When the time comes for the philosophy exam, Bertie and Billy spend a day in the country rather than cramming. But not only do they get better philosophy grades than Oscar, they go on after college to manage important companies, while Oscar ends up writing book reviews for a minor paper.[6]

Wister, and many authors like him in the period from the late nineteenth century to World War II, spoke to members of the secure middle class who liked to think of Harvard and Yale as their special training grounds and who felt threatened by the sudden presence of so many children of new immigrants whose tenacity and ability were, if the truth be told, quite remarkable. Jewish and Catholic immigrants (Oscar Maironi might stand for both groups) had little to teach and much to learn from the more refined undergraduates at Harvard. The dime novelists such as Gilbert Patten, still penning Frank Merriwell books well into the twentieth century, made similar if cruder assumptions about social class: Roger, the hero of the *College Rebel*, for example, is a rich boy disowned by his father and forced to shift for himself. Fortunately he is a racecar driver as well as a good football and baseball player, pursuits that were enhanced when he stopped drinking and associating with his former "fast" companions. With all these talents, apparently bred into one of his class, being temporary disowned was no real setback (Patten, 1914).

But the democratic vein in college stories grew, and over time the idea of college as a means of social mobility became increasingly important. Illustrative are the novels of Francis Wallace, whose stories became popular during the second decade of the twentieth century. A Wallace hero might be, for example, a mill worker who had become a football star at "New Dominion." His preoccupation with his own social class, and his sense of leaving it behind is detailed with some directness.

> Ted was riding a day coach. His companions were of the class he was trying to escape; greasy foreigners eating oranges . . . Most of them never had a chance. Ted didn't want to grow old like that; he had his chance and he was going to give it a battle." (Wallace, 1930, p. 24)

These new college novels of upward mobility, a refined version of the old Gilbert Patten classics, remind us that for men a college education had become the most dependable means of upward mobility by the twentieth century. Ted Wynne, hero of Wallace's *Huddle*, surprises himself when he "suddenly realized that to ride an ocean liner was one of the really big things he wanted—when he first stepped on board a boat, first class, it would be more of a diploma than any sheepskin they might hand him." (Wallace, 1930, p. 102) Such novels begin to reflect the new reality of student life. As college gradually became the ticket of entry into the echelons of the new corporations and as professions such as medicine, dentistry, social work, and engineering became codified and organized so that they required college, bright children of immigrants began to demand admission. And as urban and small town high schools developed college preparatory programs, their students could not be denied. Getting in was not easy for these "outsiders," to use Helen Lefkowitz Horowitz's phrase, but despite quotas and a lack of privilege, they increasingly found their way to colleges. At first the genteel tradition of the college novel appeared to ignore them—or include them as part of the interesting fabric of the institution. But gradually even the more elite stories began to plot along these more democratic lines. This was evident by the beginning of the last century: "A college such as Princeton had its own distinct workings," said Day Edgar, author of *In Princeton Town*. The boy from the important prep school had an initial advantage, but often that could weigh him down over time. It was the more democratic process of seeking offices and honors in which the best generally rose to the top. "In Freshman year a man's position is given to him by his reputation," explained Williams, but by the senior year the young man "takes his proper place with his character. What a man seems to be cuts a lot of ice at the beginning; but what he really is wins out at the finish." The snobbish boy was turned "inside out and upside down, and rubbed him this way and that way" until he had become one of them (Edgar, 1929, p. 135).

As the elite tradition mellowed, poor students became standard characters. The Western student was slightly older than the average and was working his way through college. His function in the plot was as a character builder. Wealthy young men learned from the grit and rugged integrity of this poor but noble student. In the same democratic tradition, the affluent student also had his function: Rich people had manners, class, and power, while poor people had ambition and courage. The mix was important. The soft, wealthy boy learned democracy, pluck, and heart from the rough-edged boy from the West or an eastern mill town who had not gotten to college by accident of birth. The poor boy acquired some refinement. His college experience taught him how to mix with powerful people, helped him make the right sort of friends, and sometimes allowed him to meet a useful wife. In short, by the turn of the century, the difference in attitude on this subject between the two traditions was mainly a matter of perspective.

In one important area there was agreement between the writers of popular and elite college stories for boys: Nothing in the education itself was of any particular benefit, though occasionally exams taught basic lessons about the evils of procrastination or furnished an occasion for the plot to turn on a matter of cheating. Character was built in the peer group or on the playing fields, not in the classroom. Jesse Lynch Williams (1908) has a wonderfully illustrative story of a young man who gains prestige by explicating Robert Browning to his roommates and their friends. (Browning occupied a good deal of the literature curriculum in many of these stories . . . and in most others of the period.) Browning's content is not important here; what is significant is that a student has the ability to amusingly convey themes in "My Last Duchess" to fellow students. Stories of young men who did not study were common. Professors and deans are seen as kindly, long-suffering people who try their best to make subjects interesting. But students are simply too busy to give a great deal of attention to such matters when there are football, crew literary magazines, and secret societies to worry about.[7]

As women began entering college in large numbers, there appeared at the beginning of the century stories for girls and college novels in the genteel tradition. Parents of young women, as well as the young women themselves, were assured by books such as *Smith Stories*, *Vassar Stories*, and *A Book of Bryn Mawr Stories* that students at such colleges would graduate as well-balanced, poised, and resourceful young women ready to make their way in Society. If the graduate emerged with more than a nodding acquaintance with Latin, French, and Browning and had survived a roommate who collected insects and frogs as biology specimens, so much the better.[8]

In fact, unlike the stories about men's colleges, women's school stories devoted a good deal of space to describing the actual coursework of college. *Vassar Stories*, for example, contains typically precious academic jokes: about the Latin professor "who specialized on the first declension" and whose last words were: "Oh, if only I'd devoted my life to the dative case" or of the "pie girl" who "acquired her name by translating *deus pietate propitiant* as 'they appease the gods with a pie. . . .'" (Gallaher, 1907, pp. 37–38)

A picture is drawn of pretty, well-groomed young women in well-furnished rooms studying their Horace and receiving guests, or first attending an "Alpha Meeting" and then returning to the room or library to finish a writing assignment. Though Horowitz tells us that the backbone of the first classes at women's schools were usually middle-class girls with aspirations to be teachers or scholars, by the point at which these books became plentiful, the tone was set by the upper-middle class. At Vassar, Grace Margaret Gallaher tells us, "She who can stand high in her class and yet keep in with most of the fun can 'have' the other girls." p. 74 In the tradition of genteel men's college fiction, a poor academic record is of no concern unless it puts a student in badly with Father or gets him put out of school. But flunking a course is a source of shame to the women attending college. Though the most highly prized student was neither "Miss Grind"(probably a student trying to maintain a scholarship, although authors were generally oblivious to such handicaps) nor "Mademoiselle Fripon," the authors were well aware of the gender difference:

> "They act as if you had robbed a bank and eloped with your coach-man, and they make you feel so, too." [says a fictional Vassar student about flunking and cheating] "Why don't they look at it as the usual thing, and the getting through as the surprise. That's the way men feel. My brother flunks right and left, and he thinks it's grand." "I don't," replied a roommate. . . . "I'd be ashamed if I were so stupid or so careless I couldn't pass ordinary undergraduate work." (Gallaher, 1907, p. 70)

At the turn of the century, physical and emotional relations among young women were rather more intimate than what was to become customary a few decades later. One of the *Wellesley Stories*, for example, has young women holding dances with no young men around and with no one feeling any sense of deprivation about their absence, for these were described as formal dances with cards and the concomitant jealousies and misunderstandings. "I've saved my last dances for you and, and you ought not to promise dances when you know you're going to town." remonstrated a student described as "indignant" and whose "hot face shown with honest wrath." (Cook, 1901, p. 21) This was a self-sufficient female world in which the main role young men played was to remove young women from school. The young women hugged and hung on to each other. And had, in these novels, what might be described as "chaste crushes."[8]

In both the popular and genteel traditions of college fiction, from the 1890s through the Progressive era, the opposite sex was dealt with tangentially in stories for men and for women. In the stories of men's colleges, women might be seen as gold-diggers, distractions, or a source of splendid inspiration. But as the century progressed, women took on a larger role in these stories and novels about men's colleges. Even before the 1920s, women began to appear as mysterious, devious creatures who might use underclassmen to meet older, more powerful upperclassmen, or who might gravitate to a younger student as the present interest is about to graduate, thus extending her stay among the college parties and fun.

By the beginning of the twentieth century, the elite schools began to share literary space with stories about state schools. These stories examined, humorously or seriously, the athletic and fraternal traditions of such institutions. The *Siwash* books by George Fitch, originating in 1908 and running until the author's premature death from a burst appendix in 1915, are among the most enduring of these State U tales. The stories remained popular through the 1930s, when movie rights were negotiated with the author's widow. Like many college tales, Fitch's first story was first published in the *Saturday Evening Post*, which had early on recognized the broadening interest in undergraduate life. *The Big Strike at Siwash*, a coarse story of an unlettered Scandinavian immigrant recruited as a top football player, who suddenly refuses to play unless he is pledged by a fraternity, helped to establish many of the popular stock characters that became a staple of college stories and movies through the 1930s: the luggish football player who was nonetheless adored; the brainy girl who could be found in the library and might be willing to help a scatterbrained student cram for a test; fraternities and sororities such as the Eta Bita Pies, the Sigh Whoopsilons, and the Delta Flushes—whose snobbishness and brutality of hazing were as legendary as their loyalty to one another and to "good old Siwash." Most important, there was Petey Simmons himself, a type of "steam-heated little chap, who was one of the tall buildings in college life." (Fitch, 1909, p. 21) As "assistant treasurer of the athletic association, leader of the banjo club, member of the Clavicle and Sesamoid . . . and author of the famous 'Big, Big Bjla' song with which we made ninety yards and a touchdown against Kiowa in the fall of '99 . . ." Petey "knew about everything worth knowing long before it happened". pp. 21–22 Petey assumed that his reason for being part of campus life lay in the extracurricular aspect. As was common in the stories of this earlier period (about young men), it was only when failure threatened one's status as a member of the crew team or the lit magazine staff that some measures had to be taken.

As in the stories of the more elite institutions, it was the friendships made—never academics—that mattered. Petey and his friends illustrate this with their invention of "Grabbenheim," a fictitious student who helps amuse them in a very boring calculus class. The professor, being—as readers by now had come to expect—absent-minded and nearsighted, couldn't distinguish his male students from one another, and so students devised a scheme whereby whoever had actually prepared for the class would recite as "Grabbenheim" and take tests. Needless to say Grabbenheim became famous as the best math student at Siwash.

So many college stories appeared in so many periodicals and books that by the early 1920s the role of the college-novel formula was well established. Nothing speaks to this better than the great Harold Lloyd movie *The Freshman*. In this silent classic, the hero, "Speedy," has absorbed all that the popular culture has to show him on the subject of college—novels, stories, movies, and even "how-to" articles in the magazines. Some of these ideas and advice didn't correspond with reality, and so once he gets to college "Speedy" makes a fool of himself with silly handshakes, dances, and his pathetic attempts to play football to achieve popularity.[10] Of course, "Speedy" manages to win both a football game and the girl of his dreams in spite of the books he has read, not because of them. State universities were by definition rather more democratic institutions, though clearly students whose parents had money and influence tended to run the show.

Harold Lloyd poked fun at the college-story formula. The publication of *This Side of Paradise* and such imitators as Percy Marks' *The Plastic Age* shattered the old framework. These new stories of "flaming youth" described a college life that was morally dangerous and altogether not uplifting. To the modern reader, the issues raised—petting and a bit of cheating or unsportsmanlike behavior in athletics—seem minuscule. But these topics represented a radical departure from an accepted and comfortable formula that had reassured student and parent alike since the 1870s in books such as *Student Life at Harvard*. College-story formulas began slowly to die out. Though some authors continued to milk the old expectations through the 1930s, in general, the college novel became a far less predictable genre, one increasingly intended as serious belles letters.

Olive Dean Hormel's *CO-ED*, for example, examines a very different college life from the perspective of a woman student, Lucia, whose lifelong plans to attend Vassar are changed at the last moment when she catches a glimpse of the excitement of a midwestern university. Lucia, who is pretty, popular, and talented, becomes totally enmeshed in the social minutiae of her sorority and the complex rituals of dating (still a term demarcated by quotation marks at that time). The opposite sex is part of the everyday picture in classes, and everywhere else on campus, yet the world that Lucia inhabits is primarily a female one, with men entering at set points—on weekends or on the allowed weekday night "date." Lucia seems to feel much less pain at losing an occasional boyfriend than at losing a potential Gamma pledge to Alpha. As to the girls who cross the chastity line and in one case get married out of necessity, Lucia has contempt for their hedonism. By the time of her graduation, Lucia has developed a seriousness of purpose. She looks back wistfully at her sorority days, thinking that she perhaps should have devoted more time to her studies. Still, she acknowledges, she enjoyed her life at State. [11]

This sober note typifies the trend novels of the 1930s and early 1940s. Increasingly they tended to be written much less by formula. Julia Lake Skinner Kellersberger's *Betty: A Life of Wrought Gold*, published in 1943 by John Knox Press, was set in the early 1930s. A serious and inspirational book, Betty represented an ideal white, female student at a southern school, Agnes Scott College in Georgia. Like a nineteenth-century Christian heroine, Betty is too good to live a long life. She exemplifies Christian patience. Indeed, it would be hard to imagine Betty at Vassar or at Wellesley unless she were leading chapel, tending to freshmen problems or praying that God either help her find a way to acquire a new dress or help her to do without. p. 73 But like her northern counterparts, "Betty participated: She helped to win the 'Black Cat' trophy for her class in the annual freshman-sophomore contest. She helped . . . by sacrificing good disposition . . . and two nights of sleep in the fabrication of [a] daisy chain [for the investiture ceremony]." (Kellersberger, 1943, p. 71) She also sang in the glee club, "the first college musical organization to eliminate jazz bands" from its repertoire, and wrote for *The Aurora*, the Agnes Scott literary magazine. Betty was a hardworking student but not always oriented academically. "Betty majored in people."[12] p. 72

There were other novels from this post-1920s period that gave more attention to the intellectual life of the student. Occasionally a professor even proves to be a worthwhile influence, especially if the protagonist hopes to (and does) become a writer. James T. Farrell's *My Days of Anger*, the third in the "Danny O'Neill Trilogy," is illustrative: Unlike heroes of earlier college novels, Danny is a working day student at the University of Chicago. He's an "outsider," and one of the earliest of many to appear in the college novel who isn't preoccupied with athletics, though even he takes playing football seriously. He has little time for college fraternities or activities. Danny works in a gas station to pay tuition and buy books, trying to read on the job as much as is allowed. As in many of the novels written for and about the second-generation immigrant, Danny lives at home and commutes. He is first encountered on the elevated train poring over his copy of Charles A. Beard's *Readings in American Government and Politics*, "his mind . . . lost in American history":

> He sat down and carefully read the decision of Chief Justice Marshall in the case of Madison versus Marbury. How could there be a government of laws rather than of men? Men administered the laws. And they acted according to their economic interests . . . In this world was force . . . was force and money. Where did he fit in this scheme? (Farrell, 1943, p. 257)

Charles A. Beard's ideas preoccupy Danny, who also engages in conversations on such topics as whether the ideas of John Dewey have ruined the University of Chicago.

No single professor dominates *Mud on the Stars*, William Bradford Huie's novel of the University of Alabama, a place where in the 1940s fraternities and sororities abounded, dividing the student body socially and ethnically, serving not only as living quarters and occasional social headquarters, but even as a the location of the protagonist's sexual initiation (deliberately interracial). Huie clearly set out, as did Julia Lake Skinner Kellersberger, to write a distinctly southern college novel, and for all its racism, the novel has a distinct sense of place.

By the 1950's novels about college were increasingly the genre of choice for aspiring writers such as Huie, and often they began to look at the problems of ethnicity. Skirted over before, these issues are now laid bare. The protagonist is now typically an "outsider." College is tough stuff. The old conventions seem pointless to these postwar authors. In fact the old conventions are often seen as downright pernicious. A Harvard novel, *Remember Me to God*, by Myron S. Kaufmann, follows a Jewish student through anxious days of attempts to join exclusive clubs that make him ashamed of his Judaism. The protagonist becomes so obsessed with opening these clubs up to Jewish membership that he seems to lose his soul and certainly his girlfriend.[13]

Concluding Remarks

In sum, the college novel has a long tradition in American popular literature, with origins in early pulp fiction. Two sorts of novels had emerged by the twentieth century: a lengthy, formulaic novel of college athletics and upward mobility, and a more genteel novel or set of vignettes that sentimentalized the college experience for upper–middle-class readers. Though a far larger number of books were published in the more popular tradition, both types were recognizable as genres with a strong following that continued until the "exposé" novels came along that associated college life with drinking, petting, and other popularly regarded excesses of "flaming youth." Though the formula novels continued for a while, they now seemed dated and the tradition faded away. College novels didn't necessarily become any better, but by the mid 1930s, increasingly the intention of the authors was that these novels be regarded as serious literature, though the image of the carefree student lived on in movies throughout the 1930s and beyond. By the 1950's the college story had become common as the first novel of an aspiring writer.[14] And unlike F. Scott Fitzgerald, who had so wanted to be part of the movers and shakers of student activity, these writers, often reflecting the detachment of students on the G.I. Bill, had little sense that it was a reasonable aspiration for them and were inclined to think it was rather a waste of time.

The tradition of college novels and movies after this period is beyond the scope of this chapter. The tradition is a rich and complicated one that is more difficult to summarize. Recent novels about the college experience show considerable diversity. Donna Tartt's (1996) *The Secret History* is certainly one of the best and most interesting but is very difficult to classify. Certainly college life described there has an old-school flavor. Other recent novels, such as Tom Perrotta's (2000) *Joe College*, seem to enjoy describing the modern college experience as Bildungsroman. The content is different, but there is something reassuringly familiar in the idea that college is still an experience worth an individual's writing about. One interesting recent novel that takes up the common experience of college admissions is *Getting In*, by James Finney Boylan (1998). This wonderful picaresque story of a surrealistic college-visiting trip to Yale, Harvard, Bowdoin, Colby, Dartmouth, Middlebury, Williams, Amherst, and Wesleyan gives a wonderful new dimension to the tradition of the college novel, but one that no less than before reflects both the reality and the aspirations involved in the process of going to and attending college.

Notes

1. According to John Thelin and Barbara Townsend (1988), there were 986 consecutive weekly stories, 415 paperback novels, and a readership of close to 3 million. By 1906 the Harvard Lampoon gave free advice on how to write novels about Harvard. Advice included street names to provide local color and extravagant characters in robes before fire places, who were prone to drink and smoke, meet girls innocent and not so innocent, and sit in Morris chairs. Quoted in William Bentinck-Smith *The Harvard Book: Selections from Three Centuries* (Cambridge, Harvard University Press, 1953).

2. The Frank Merriwell novels originally published by the well-known series publisher. Street and Smith are available online from Standford University at http://www.sul.stanford.edu/depts/dp/pennies/texts/. Useful commentary about these books is found in Jowett (1982) and Umphlett (1975).

3. Even as this novel was being written, the author was aware of changes the more modern courses offered under the elective system were bringing about:

> What an endless amount it seemed, to look at it in the lump!—mathematics, chemical physics and chemistry, Greek and Latin, Anglo-Saxon, themes, elocution and lectures; there was enough to keep the most inveterate dig busy, and to create in the mind of a man of fair ability and average ambition a disgust for study that would endure long after the faint smattering he acquired had passed away. At least it used to be so under the 'old regime'" (Tripp, 1876, p. 291).

4. It's interesting to note that the awareness of dress is an enduring theme in the college novel. As late as the 1950s, when college novels began to take themselves much more seriously, one sees the attention to minute details of sweaters and ties. John Knowles, writing as

late as 1983 about a socially stratified Yale in the early 1950s, dwelt on subtleties of dress to convey gradation of distinctions in social status.

5. Thus explored were the social dynamics behind the tendency for undergraduates to "consider the professionals ... as so many scrubs, altogether unworthy of their notice; and the professional men [to] look down upon the college boys as a set of conceited young dogs, who ought to be taken in hand and have some of the nonsense rubbed out of them." (p. 321) Tripp also railed against the practice of a student's taking a scholarship "just because it happens to be with his reach when he is not really dependent on himself for his support," when "so many are needy ... who don't happen to rank high, for the most part because their advantages have been poor." (p. 325)

6. More exactly:

> Oscar never understood. But he graduated considerably higher than Bertie and Billy ... Today Bertie is treasure of the New Amsterdam Trust Company, in Wall street; Billy is superintendent of passenger traffic of the New York and Chicago Air Line. Oscar is successful, too. He has acquired a lot of information ... He has published a careful work entitled "The Minor Poets of Cinquencento," and he writes book reviews for the *Evening Post.*" (p. 95)

A more succinct argument for the "gentleman's C" would be hard to find.

7. The need for achievement on campus bring certain novels to mind: One is certainly Owen Johnson's *Stover at Yale*. Originally published in *McClure's* as a muckraking novel to expose the shallow secret society system at Yale, the novel seems to have quickly had the opposite effect, in part because Dink Stover embodied the qualities of athlete and popular student, and in part because in the end he was tapped for Skull and Bones.

8. Carroll Smith-Rosenberg (1986) has some discussion of this issue. See especially "The Female World of Love and Ritual." 53–76

9. Fitch Petey Even the famous "five-minute rule of waiting for Professors," a piece of academic folklore that still persists, is articulated clearly in the Fitch stories. See also Litvin (1991).

10. *The Freshman* is in the film collection of the Library of Congress. Harold Lloyd, Producer; Fied Newmeyer, Director; reissue of a 1925 silent film, Patne Exchange 1959.

11. Lucia shows lots of knowledge of the "debunking" college novels by Marks, Fitzgerald, and others. "Fiction isn't an imitation of life

any more—life's an imitation of fiction—in college, at least" says Lucia, "The girls get their live from *Flaming Flappers*—and the boys get theirs from *The Other Side of Purgatory*." p. 155

12. Since this research was completed, a new book, *The Past in the Present: Women's Higher Education in the Twentieth-Century American South*, by Amy Thompson McCandless (University of Alabama Press, Tuscaloosa, ALA, 1999) has useful insights not incorporated into this text.

13. The influence of the G.I. Bill on college novels is really the topic of another paper, but suffice it to say that the older, wiser, and more critical protagonists depicted in these postwar novels had neither the time nor the interest in college songs, pranks, or spirit, and fraternities were reduced to simply places where young men lived and ate together.

14. In *Oakey Hall, The Corpus of Joe Bailey* (Viteing Press, New York, 1953), the frat is described as a messy eating arrangement that means very little except to a few who seem dimly interested in recapturing some of the glory days of the past. Earlier authors had been critical of the excesses of the fraternity system, but by the early 1950's they are often depicted as unredeemably stupid hothouses of snobbishness and meanness. A few minutes after serenading a sorority with strains of "Here's to old Omega Alpha . . . We'll give our all for Old Omega Alpha," a member turns to a fellow member and calls him a "San Diego jerk." (p. 171) See an equally interesting exchange on p. 252.

References

Bacon, J. D. *Smith College Stories*. New York: Chas Scribner's Sons, 1910.
Boylan, J. F. *Getting In*. New York: Warner Books, 1998.
Cook, G. L. *Wellesley Stories*. Boston: E. H. Bacon & Co., 1904.
Edgar, D. *In Princeton Town*. New York: Chas Scribner's Sons, 1929.
Farrell, J. T. *My Days of Anger*. Cleveland, OH: World Publishing Comp., 1947.
Fitch, G. *The Big Strike at Siwash*. New York: Doubleday, Page & Co.,1909.
———. *Petey Simmons at Siwash*. Boston: Little Brown and Co., 1916.
Fitzgerald, F. S. *This Side of Paradise*. New York: A. L. Burt Company, 1920.
Gallaher, G. M. *Vassar Stories*. Boston: RG Badger & Company, 1900.
Hormel, O. D. *Co-Ed*. New York: Chas Scribner's Sons, 1926.
Horowitz, H. L. *Alma Mater: Design and Experience in the Women's Colleges from Their Nineteenth-Century Beginnings to the 1930s*, 2nd ed. Amherst: University of Mass Press, 1993.
———. *Campus Life: Undergraduate Cultures from the End of the Eighteenth Century to the Present*. AA Knopf, NY, 1987.
Huie, W. B. *Mud on the Stars*. New York: University of Alabama Press, Tuscaloosa, 1996.
Johnson, O. *Stover at Yale*. New York: Frederick & Stokes Company, 1912.
Jowett, G. S. "The Emergence of the Mass Society: The Standardization of American Culture, 1830–1920," *Prospects the Annual of American Cultural Studies Jack Salcman Ed. Vol. 7*. New York: Burt Franklin, 1982.
Kellersberger, J. L. S. *Betty: A Life of Wrought Gold*. Richmond, VA: John Knox Press, 1943.

Knowles, J. *The Paragon*. New York: Randon House, 1971.
———. *A Stolen Past*. New York: Holt Rinehart and Winston, 1983.
Kaufmann, M.S. *Remember Me to God*. Lippincott, Philadelphia, 1957.
Litvin, M. *I'm Going to be Somebody!: A Biography of George Fitch*. (*Originator of the Word "Siwash"*) Woodston, KS: Western Books, 1991.
Marchalonis, S. *College Girls: A Century in Fiction*. New Jersey: Rutgers University Press, 1995.
Marks, P. *The Plastic Age*. Cambridge: Southern Illinois Press, 1924.
Morris, M., and Congdon, L. B. *A Book of Bryn Mawr Stories*. Philadelphia: George Jacobs and Company, 1901.
Patten, G. *The College Rebel*. New York: Barse and Hopkins, 1914.
———. *Clif Stirling: Sophomore at Stormbridge*. Philadelphia: D McKay, 1916.
Perrotta, T. *Joe College*. New York: St. Martins Press, 2000.
Smith-Rosenberg, C. *Disorderly Conduct Visions of Gender in Victorian America*. New York: AA Knopf, 1985.
Solomon, B. M. *In the Company of Educated Women : A History of Women and Higher Education in America*. New Haven: Yale University Press, 1985.
Tartt, D. *The Secret History : A Novel*. Knopf, Randon House, 1992.
Thelin, J. R., and Townsend, B. K. "Fiction to Fact: College Novels and the Study of Higher Education." In *Higher Education Handbook of Theory and Research*, Vol. IV, edited by J. C. Smart. New York: Agathon Press, 1988, pp. 183–211.
Tripp, G. H. *Student Life at Harvard*. Boston: Lockwood, Brooks, and Company, 1876.
Umphlett, W. L. *The Movies Go to College: Hollywood and the World of the College-Life Film*. Rutgers: NJ, Fairleight Dickinson University Press, 1984.
———. *The Sporting Myth and the American Experience: Studies in Contemporary Fiction*. Lewisburg, PA: Bucknell University Press, 1975.
Wallace, F. *Huddle*. New York: Farrar & Rinehart, 1930.
Williams, J. L. *The Girl and the Game and Other College Stories*. NY: Chas Scribner's, 1908.
Wister, O. Philosophy 4: A Story of Harvard University. New York: The MacMillan Company, 1903.
Zuckerman, G. *Farewell, Frank Merriwell*. Dutton, NY, 1973.

4

Those Happy Golden Years: *Beverly Hills, 90210*, College Style

MICHELE BYERS

Introduction

I will begin this work by stating that I am a fan of *Beverly Hills, 90210*. I have been watching the show since it came on the air in 1990. Through the ups and downs of its ten seasons—even when it became a chore—I spent every Wednesday night on Fox. For a decade I watched "the zip" and thus the perspective that informs this chapter is inflected by the vision of a (critical) fan.[1] My intention is to examine the portrayal of education and educators in popular culture through a critical examination of the 1993 to 1997 seasons of *Beverly Hills, 90210*: the college years. Although *90210* continued to air for several seasons after its characters had graduated from college (the series ended after the 1999–2000 season), it is with the seasons during which the central characters were attending college that I am concerned. I will carry out this analysis by juxtaposing theories of education and performance with illustrations of how education and educators are performed on *90210*.

The concept of performance will be important to this work. Performance in television is related to the active quality of the text. The importance of performance is its spectacular quality, which defies traditional notions of reality and disrupts long-held beliefs about the construction of identity.

Television images evoke a thousand others, every image offering another version of "reality," another thousand possible moments of identification. Our possible whos, whats, wheres, and whens are increasingly on display on television, and it is often through our perusal of these media pageants that we learn who, what, where, and when we want to be.

Identity refers to how we understand ourselves, the "I" of who we are. At one time it was thought that this "I" was unified and monolithic, but we have come increasingly to view it as complex and multifaceted. Today identity is often thought of as fragmented, something brought about, at least in part, by the expansion of processes of identification made possible by the global media and consumer markets. The complexity of our personal identities has to do with how identity is shaped by processes of identification by which each of us searches for some connection, some sign of commonality (real, imagined, or desired) with another. Television offers the viewer a lot of perusable, consumable identities and opportunities for identification. The images we see every day on screens, glossies, and billboards offer moments that we may try to paste together into potential identities, as reality becomes synonymous with the more elaborate realities and identities of the mediascape.

The term (mis)education, as I am using it here, refers to the process by which media images concretize themselves into everyday life. It is the distance (or lack thereof) between the screen and the self, and how gender, race, class, and other axes of difference are performed through hegemonic (serving in the maintenance of the status quo) and sometimes transgressive (upsetting the status quo) televisual discourses: the ideological underpinnings that lie beneath every story and how they are put together in language. (Mis)education refers to the way stories become invested with political undercurrents that can be interpreted by audiences in multiple ways. I use the term (mis)education to try to show how *Beverly Hills, 90210* plays into myths about higher education in North America today.

In 1990 we were introduced to high schoolers Brandon (Jason Priestly), Brenda (Shannen Doherty), Kelly (Jennie Garth), Donna (Tori Spelling), Dylan (Luke Perry), Steve (Ian Ziering), David (Brian Austin Green), and Andrea (Gabrielle Carteris). For the next ten years, we followed them from West Beverly High to California University (hereafter C.U.), and finally to the Los Angeles job market, marriage, and family life. The college years on *90210* offer a paradigmatic display of the social and intellectual turmoil surrounding postsecondary education in the popular imagination today. I am not suggesting that *90210* depicts the way things are in college life in any "true" sense. But it provides space for an interrogation of television's depiction of hegemonic collegiate experience, as well as moments of transgression.

Performances of (Mis)education

Educators and educational theorists from many disciplines have begun to look long and hard at popular culture. Holland and Eisenhart (1990) write that "students bring values and understandings from other realms of their lives and, together with fellow students, generate a system of meaning and practice in response to the social barriers they face." (p. 7) One of the most important of the other realms students bring to their experience and understanding of education is the mass media. Henry Giroux (1994) insists that

> Electronically mediated images, especially television and film, will represent one of the most potent arms of cultural hegemony in the twenty-first century. Constituted as a public sphere with an enormous global reach, the electronic media have a power that reinforces Stuart Hall's claim that there is no politics outside of representation (p. 44).

And Morgan (1995) writes that "[T]he fluctuating spatial horizons fostered by living in a televisual culture have important consequences for the way in which we conceive of the place of schooling and the forms of cultural identity it has privileged." (p. 40) And so whether the media slides off us, infects us, or allows us space for reinvention—or all three—it is always present in our lives and is central to the contemporary study of pedagogy and the cultural production of education and educators.

In keeping with the educational focus of this work, imagine the following examples of (mis)education as a Venn diagram with many overlapping spaces: First, we learn about the world, including the academy, through the mediated images of the small and large screens. This helps to create a space of post-high school fantasy in which audiences may vicariously live out their hopes, dreams, and fears about higher education and what their futures might be like.[2] Second, (mis)education refers to the falsehood of media performances in relation to the realities of education and its practitioners. This includes film and television portrayals of campus life as devoid of academics, political turmoil, and discrimination on the basis of difference. Third, (mis)education is concerned with the false images educators and educational institutions (real and mediated) sometimes perpetuate about themselves and the spaces they occupy in the lives of students. This includes continuing to link education exclusively to the quest for paid employment, the myth of an educational meritocracy of equal opportunity, and the refusal to acknowledge other types of cultural knowledge and experience that students bring to the classroom.

There is a basis for these examples of (mis)education in the real shifts taking place within North American educational systems today. Aronowitz

(1997) writes that "schools embody, for most Americans, perhaps more than any other institutions, the fulfillment of the promise of equality of opportunity." (p. 180) But he later adds that this "equality of opportunity cannot be fulfilled unless the student can see her/himself in the curriculum." (p. 182) As Aronowitz describes it, as links between education and work decline, administrators attempt to tie the two together and to insist that education is a meaningful investment in cultural capital and directly linked to the job market. Noble (1997) writes that "[T]he value of education [clearly must] be addressed independent of its alleged links to the economy and to the workplace." (p. 208) What these pedagogical theorists describe is a form of (mis)education in which the system administers knowledge to students who often see it as irrelevant to their current and future situations.

Writing in 1968, Burke said that advertisers "create a maximum desire for commodities consumed under expensive conditions." (cited in Urch, 1997, p. 215) Today, when the commodity-image is even more pervasive, education itself is a commodity to be consumed along with designer jeans and cK-One. Higher education is viewed as increasingly similar to high school, and is seen as part of a period of extended adolescence—a period of fun and exploration and (often) privileged leisure—without obvious ties to the future and employment. Media discourses often reiterate these contradictory images of education as both leisure- and employment-related.

Not much has been written about images of education in popular culture. Education has, however, been a focus of many films and television series. If Laplanche and Pontalis (1986) are correct and desire is to be understood as setting rather than object, then desire (at least youthful desire) in popular culture often revolves in and around halls of learning. Some of the films which take place on and around the college campus include *Glory Daze, PCU, Animal House, The Sure Thing, Scream II, 1969, Higher Learning, Listen to Me, The Skulls, St. Elmo's Fire, Reality Bites, Real Genius, Clerks, Slacker, Rudy, Hoosiers, The Program, With Honors, Good Will Hunting, Say Anything, Revenge of the Nerds, Candy Man, Urban Legends, Prince of Darkness, Less Than Zero,* and *Flatliners.* Television programs which feature students, teachers, and college campuses include: *A Different World, Boston Common, Third Rock from the Sun, Party of Five, Freshman Dorm, Felicity, The Fresh Prince of Bel-Air, Buffy the Vampire Slayer, Roseanne,* and several soap operas. Even if education itself is seen as somewhat irrelevant and banal, its spaces continue to evoke the promise of youth, challenge, excitement, and the future.[3]

The images of higher education that are displayed on television tend to exist within two poles: one generally anti-intellectual (in drama) and one farcical (in comedy). *Beverly Hills, 90210* is an excellent example of the former. Although its privileged teens insist on the importance of going to college, their ambitions are more vocational than academic. These residents of one of the most exclusive suburbs in the United States, whose fathers (and I say fathers intentionally) are accountants, doctors, dentists, and captains of industry, show little interest in professional or graduate work. They are completely pragmatic in their quests for employment that focus more on personal gratification than on capital accumulation. While this may be a noble sentiment and could be read as promoting a discourse that pursuing your dreams is more important than pursuing wealth, how many people have the opportunity to be actors, journalists, designers, and musicians, to run free-clinics and clubs and newspapers right out of college, and to keep living in luxury digs, driving luxury cars, and shopping on Rodeo Drive in the process?[4]

On *90210* we discover ourselves in a space of (mis)education, where learning is performed as a bastion of privilege; a space of primarily young, white, beautiful, able bodies; a place to live out late adolescence, to learn and to grow without any necessary thoughts about what comes after graduation. Giroux (1997) acknowledges "that education generates a privileged space for some students and a space that fosters inequality and subordination for others." (p. 233) By making higher education a visual space occupied by certain privileged bodies, a text like *Beverly Hills, 90210* literalizes this statement and, with it, this aspect of (mis)education. Marginal bodies, although potentially successful, never become primary players on this terrain and are always relegated to secondary, transient status. Marginal bodies are usually there to educate the main characters (and the viewer) about minority issues, although they may also attempt to undermine the hegemony of privilege.[5]

Film portrayals of college life are sometimes more complex than those of television because they are neither so genre restricted nor so rigorously governed by television's conservative censorship standards. *Higher Learning*, for example, actively engages the university as a site of contestation in such areas as race, gender, sexuality, generation, class, and location. *Rudy*, *Listen to Me*, and *Good Will Hunting* explore issues of class. *St. Elmo's Fire* and *Reality Bites* deal with the difficulty of the transition from college to "real life." Other movies, as diverse as *PCU*, *Animal House*, *Glory Daze*, *The Sure Thing*, and Richard Linklater's more subcultural *Slacker* revel in the Rabelaisian carnival which undergraduate life is supposed to be.

Television's collegiate depictions are often much more mundane. *Party of Five*'s high school graduates fly around to Ivy League orientations without a thought as to how they will pay for the next four years of college. *Roseanne* forays into the generational divide that occurs when children are the first to go to college. *Boston Common* also plays the class trope by juxtaposing over-privileged, elite Boston graduate students with a young Appalachian undergraduate and her witty, uneducated brother. *Third Rock from the Sun* gives us a farcical look at an alien posing as a stereotypical, socially inept university physics professor. The initially highly touted *Felicity* follows a California girl's social and (on occasion) academic ups and downs during her tenure at a university in New York City. Like the *90210* teens, Felicity chooses to pursue an art career instead of becoming a doctor like her father. That profession is left to her friend, an African American woman from a working-class family.

What each of these films and television shows presents, to a greater or lesser degree, is the liminality (the feeling of being at the margins) of the space between high school and "the rest of your life" for those lucky enough to have access to higher education. The diegetic (referring to a fictional universe) space of these performances becomes a space of metonymy or, as Pollock (1998) writes, "a boundary space, inviting laughter and transformation." (pp. 85–86) In or out of the classroom, *90210* offers a lens through which to view the politics of higher education. Although this text tends to be ideologically hegemonic, it does offer possibilities for resistance through which moments of tentative metonymic freedom may emerge.

Students, Politics, and Life on Campus

The Beverly Hillians are all going to college, a major plot fixation of the third season, during which the show examined the trials of SAT testing, choosing colleges, deciding whether to leave home (they all stay), and deciding whether to go to college at all (they all do). Right from the start this program makes a statement about higher education: You should go! The fact that this televised university exists makes it a participant in "the nationwide distribution system for symbols in anticipation and reinforcement of a national culture presented not only as desirable but as already realized somewhere else." (Morse, 1998, p. 119) C.U. offers a vacuum-sealed advertisement for college life as shiny and pristine as any glossy-covered undergraduate calendar. But academics on *90210* are peripheral, except when one of the characters has a problem with grades or a professor, and then it becomes an "issue." Though the issue show was a staple of *90210's* high school years and the college years proved to be more focused on the characters' personal growth (Owen, 1997), the issues remained.

The cast of *90210* all became very involved with campus life. When not running the student government and other major centers, these students did take time out to go to class.[6] Lewis (1992) writes that "the global economy depends on a certain percentage of failures, an underclass left behind, just as it depends on a certain elite class that benefits from its largesse." (p. 52) On *90210* the elite exist outside of any necessity for higher learning, and it is the lower and middle-classes who gain upward mobility this way. Unlike the working-class protagonists of many college films, these Beverly Hillians have no fear that a lack of education will keep them from their rightful places in the elite world (Traube, 1992). If school is rarely foremost in the minds of these C.U. students, it is perhaps because so many of them have trust funds waiting for them and parents willing to support them indefinitely, to set them up in the business of their choice, or to intervene on their behalf for jobs upon graduation.[7]

Who are these penultimate collegians? Steve is the scheming but sweet fraternity boy; Donna and Kelly, the somewhat vacant clotheshorses (a.k.a. the sweetie and the bitch); Dylan, whose education takes a backseat to his quest, funded by his trust fund millions, for emotional equilibrium; and David, who stays in school to avoid being cut off by his father. The characters who are more traditionally middle-class show somewhat more inclination towards professionalization or a career choice associated with class maintenance.[8] They bring to the show a discourse which equates academic success with graduation and the future job market.[9] Brenda moves to England after getting a scholarship to a prestigious drama school; Brandon is always focused on maintaining a balance between academics and extracurricular activities; Andrea, the most financially strapped of all the characters, chooses the medical profession as a vocation; Valerie, another girl from the wrong zip code, tries to find the business skills to match her ambition.[10]

There is little academic accomplishment on *90210*. Intellectual life is best expressed through moments of anxiety and the possibility of failure: themes, finally, which stay with the show through to the end of its final season. Only rarely do contradictorily constructed moments emerge which provide the potential for positive identification with intellectualism and academia. At C.U., extracurricular activities are the primary way in which students make their presence felt on campus.

Politics is one way that these characters express their newfound independence. In his first weeks at C.U., Brandon Walsh is elected freshman representative to the student senate. By the second college season, Brandon is running the primary campus political party, the Independents. In keeping with his characterization, Brandon's political style is unerringly middle-of-road, drawing criticism from the more right- and left-wing political parties and the admiration of the administration, especially Chancellor Arnold (Nicolas Pryor). Never as good at coloring within the lines as her twin brother, Brenda exercises her political muscle by becoming involved with an extremist animal-rights group. Her naive impetuousness earns her an arrest when she is implicated in the attempted bombing of a C.U. lab. Kelly and Donna, through their sorority (Alpha Omega), participate in a Take Back the Night march. Their commitment to their fellow women is challenged, however, when one young woman points the finger at Steve as her rapist.[11] Andrea, David, and Clare protest C.U.'s invitation of a blatantly anti-Semitic speaker.

This delineates a diegetic space in which resistance is possible primarily along the lines of maintaining the status quo. However, it offers the possibility of political action for the student characters and thus carries the suggestion of greater moments of resistance. The viewer may see these debates as they relate to the personal and political spaces s/he inhabits and, unlike these characters, will be unable to remain nonpartisan as important political and personal issues are raised. The positive implications of this are that it creates the possibility of response and resistance in the viewer.

Another way these students involved themselves with campus life was through the Greek system, and major themes in the first college season concerned fraternities and sororities. Although this was handled in a fairly complex manner, there was a tendency to revert to stereotypes and depict fraternity boys as homophobic, lecherous, "beer-guzzling-asshole-jerks" and sorority girls as skinny, perky blondes who live for charity work and discriminate against those who do not conform to their standards of beauty.[12] But important issues were hammered home through the trope of Greek inclusion, including date rape, anti-Semitism, homophobia, cheating, and alcoholism. Andrea, for instance, is deterred from rushing when she is chastised by the head of a sorority for displaying her Judaism by wearing a Star of David.[13] During Hell week, John Sears (Paul Johansson) forces Steve to steal Professor Randall's Jackie Robinson baseball and then calls campus security. Brandon intervenes and the fraternity brothers oust Sears from their midst in an attempt to prove that theirs is a fraternal organization and not a popularity contest. Room is created for fraternities and sororities to be read problematically and as historically constituted, exclusionary social spaces in need of reorganization if they are to continue to exist.

On occasion, the *90210* characters think about the future, and it causes them as much stress and anxiety as one would expect any student to confront when faced with leaving school for the first time in twenty-odd years. Late in the sixth season, Brandon gives up an internship and job prospect in Boston to stay with his girlfriend Susan (Emma Caulfield), only to have her leave him for a similar prospect a few episodes later. When Donna's boyfriend, Joe Bradley (Cameron Bancroft), discovers he has a heart condition and can longer play football, he drops out of school to become a high school football coach in his home town of Beaver Falls. D'Shawn (Cress Williams, one of the few African American characters to grace the college-years screen) faces a double loss when he injures his knee and loses his athletic scholarship. And Kelly seems determined to go to graduate school in New York but backs down three episodes later, presumably so she can stay with Brandon. As with many youth-oriented programs, the main characters' primary focus is on romance and relationship, not on scholarship.[14]

Students' Relations with Faculty

Maybe C.U. students are not spending time in class because they have terrible relationships with their professors. There are hardly any positive moments between students and faculty on this show, and relationships between them usually turn sour even when they start out sweet. While education has traditionally been "expected to teach vigorously the values of a society that thought it was righteous" (Noddings, 1988, p. 217), the professors on *90210* are shown to have almost exclusively their own best interests at heart and are willing to use anyone (especially their students) to get what they want.

One of the most involved storylines about student/faculty relations involved Lucinda (Dina Meyer), a feminist graduate student who became involved with Brandon. He ends their affair upon discovering that she has failed to mention her marriage to one of his professors, but resumes their tryst when she explains that divorce is immanent. Soon after, things end for good when Lucinda tries to seduce Dylan to get funding for her dissertation project, a feminist film. Dylan's rejection of Lucinda—clearly shown to be based on her use of sex rather than of her project—coincides with her expulsion from the show.

Lucinda also has problems with the female characters of *90210* when Andrea, Kelly, and Donna participate in her feminism course. The subject matter sparks interesting debates among the characters, for example when Lucinda advocates serial monogamy. But once Lucinda moves in on the *90210* men, the women feel she has exposed herself as a fraud, rejecting her and, it seems, all the empowering moments they had experienced in her class. Lucinda's refusal to conform her behavior to their community's moral standards makes her exile imperative. As I have written elsewhere (Byers, 1996/97): "[If] Lucinda's presence on the show is disruptive, then the possibility that she should be taken seriously, identified with or lauded is explosive. The only place for her character is off camera." (p. 109) Lucinda's feminism positions her on a radical pole of possibility for growth that, although mostly declined by her female students as they dismiss her personal actions, offers a new and potentially transformative discourse to the viewer.

Aside from Lucinda, most of the professors on *90210* are men, and many problems arise at the intersection of female student and male teacher. Valerie has problems with a male professor with whom she attempts to gain favor in hopes of succeeding in the business world. Because Valerie's character is constructed around her use of her sexuality to manipulate men, it is not surprising to find her flirting with Professor Hayward (Mark Shera) in an attempt to attract his attention. But in this case, Valerie is not simply trying to manipulate a man in order to get something from him; she is actually trying to do well in the class and to develop a relationship with her teacher. When she is invited to join him for a symposium, she is very excited, but this reaction proves premature. The conference takes place at a hotel, and Professor Haywood makes his intentions very clear when he invites her up to his room. Valerie declines his sexual advances and receives a D on her project. The fact that Professor Haywood is a horrible, exploitative man is made even more explicit when Valerie attempts to pursue a futile sexual harassment case against him. What is most unfortunate about this characterization is that there are no other, better professors against whom his conduct can be compared.

Val is not the only young woman to have this type of problem. Kelly has difficulties with Professor Finley (Alan Toy), a charismatic psychology teacher who has developed a cult following around C.U. He encourages his young converts to renounce their past lives and to be reborn into his community by making financial contributions and entering into relationships with older members of his flock. As Kelly becomes more involved with Finley, Dylan and Brandon work to expose his duplicity and to sever her ties with him. Eventually they are successful, Finley is exposed, and Kelly returns to her rightful suitors. Faculty members are thus demonstrated to have power over not only their students' grades, but also over their psychic and emotional selves. Like Haywood, Finley performs the professor as a position of manipulative, perverse, primarily masculine power.

Two other female characters, Andrea and Brenda, also have relationships with male faculty members. In order to ensure herself of being cast as the lead in the drama department's production of *Cat on a Hot Tin Roof,* Brenda goes to Professor Randolf's house and, the show suggests, sleeps with him. Andrea actively pursues and captures the attention of her critical English teacher and residence advisor Dan Rubin (Matthew Poretta). The difference between these two women's experiences and those of Valerie and Kelly is that they have some agency in their relationships with these older men, and they suffer few repercussions from their sexual liaisons, except for being chastised by their more moral friends. Randolf actively encourages Brenda in her role and her decision to go to RADA. Andrea breaks it off with Dan Rubin to pursue a relationship with a law student—whom she marries and has a child with before leaving the show—and Rubin is the one who moves out of their residence. In these instances Andrea and Brenda may offer images of young women who own their sexuality, refuse to be manipulated by men (even those older and more powerful), and do not need to be saved by anyone but themselves.

The male characters—though in different circumstances—also come into conflict with faculty members, specifically Professor Randall (Scott Paulin). Appealing to all the characters at first, Randall appears to be nice guy and a good teacher. His passion for sports fuels his relationship with Brandon and is instrumental in getting Brandon to tutor potential basketball star D'Shawn. The true Randall is only slowly revealed, as he demonstrates that he is invested in D'Shawn only as a star, not as a student.[15] Later, when Randall discovers Brandon has been involved with his ex-wife, he sets out for revenge and attempts to have Brandon and Steve expelled. His performance reiterates that of Haywood and Finley, tyrannical and power-wielding. He also exhibits an incredible fear of being emasculated by his students, who always have the moral upper hand.

The only faculty member who shows any support to her students is Professor Langely (Olivia Brown), Donna's fashion marketing professor, though she is depicted as being brutally tough and insensitive to the emotional stability of her students. When Donna misses a presentation and Langely refuses to let her present at an alternate time, Donna launches into a passionate speech about her dreams and desires. Langely is moved enough to admit that she has been so tough on Donna because she is the only student with the talent to succeed in design, but warns her that the fashion world is cruel and Donna will have to make work her priority in order to be successful. Donna makes her presentation and receives top marks. Although Professor Langely is portrayed in a much more positive light than any other faculty member, she also performs the role of educator as one of intimidation. Her students are terrified of her, and it is only Donna's just plea that makes her relent.

The main function the students perform in relation to their professors is that of moral guardians. What is demonstrated again and again as students and teachers perform their unique positions in the educational system is that the students (and specifically the main characters) are of a higher moral order than their advisors. In this program, professors are rarely, if ever, chosen as role models. In this diegetic space, education is conflated with arbitrary and often abusive power. However, there is no suggestion that young people should not go to university, or that it is a useless, thankless, or even dangerous, endeavor. Although there is very little room for resistance in the images of student/faculty relations, the fact that the students succeed despite these difficulties offers some hope. Because of the issue-show format of this program, we can also speculate that the characters have positive relationships with the faculty they come into contact with outside of our view.

Gender, Race, and Other Axes of Difference on *90210*

90210's characters, like those of most mainstream television shows, are young, thin, white, attractive, heterosexual, able-bodied, and upper- and middle-class. Matters of race, sexual orientation, religion, and ethnicity enter these spaces only through specific storylines. Gender, although an intrinsic aspect of the show, becomes problematic only when issues surrounding it arise. Disability is almost never discussed, unless it reflects a specific loss of ability, as in D'Shawn's case.[16] Traube (1992) writes that "[W]ithout question the dominant tendency in mass-cultural fictions is to limit and contain new possibilities . . . Still the new possibilities that are absorbed into received cultural forms continue to stretch the forms, sometimes in unexpected ways." (p. 25) It can be argued that the presence of storylines that focus on race, gender, ability, and sexuality are instances of new and emerging possibilities, but these are still strictly limited to the sidelines. By refusing marginal characters access to the central community of this program, they are destined to remain as "Other"—always on the outside looking in.

During college, the *90210* characters meet a few people who are not heterosexual. Brandon and Steve, for example, discover that the head of Steve's fraternity is gay. When he is outed, the underlying homophobia of the fraternity is put on display. Although Steve strongly supports him, it is obvious that this young man's relationship to his "brothers" will never be the same. In a later season, Kelly goes to work at an AIDS hospice and meets a young man there whom she becomes quite close to. Another short run character, Jimmy's (Michael Stoyanov) function is to educate Kelly (and through her the other characters) about AIDS and to enhance the viewer's sense of her empathy and personal growth.[17] The third gay man to be encountered is a statuesque drag queen whom Steve and later Chancellor Arnold believe to be a woman.[18]

The lesbian characters show up together in an episode in which David accidentally posts a party invitation to an e-mail group for gay women. During the party a fire breaks out. Kelly and Allison (Monica Schnarre), one of the gay women, are trapped in the basement bathroom together and are both burned (though Allison more badly than Kelly). In ensuing episodes Allison develops a crush on Kelly, but rather than explore the situation, the show depicts her as increasingly disturbed. And in the last seasons of the show, Steve makes what is to him a shocking discovery: His mother (Christina Belford) is gay. As Steve once again learns a lesson in tolerance, his mother must face the harsh realities of homophobia in Hollywood as she loses her comeback career.

On *90210*, the gay male characters are shown to be of greater risk to others than the gay females. Most strongly played is the trope of (mis)recognition, the possibility that homosexuals live in the community and that the community is unaware of them. This is performed as a serious problem when male homosexuality is at issue but is seen as less so when the persons in question are young and female (beautiful fantasy fodder). Unlike the gay male characters, who are shown disdain and evoke fear, these women—all beautiful femmes—excite the male characters' sexual fantasies. In either case, gay characters are introduced into this text only to be quickly pushed outside its frame.

While there are few minority characters on *90210*, their storylines provoke a great deal of thought about North American race relations. In an article focusing on race and *90210*, Waiters (1996) writes that "[T]he portrayal of inter-ethnic interaction on *Beverly Hills, 90210* brings peer role models within reach of diverse audiences each week."[19] (p. 213) D'Shawn is an African American athlete who comes to C.U. on scholarship—a stereotypical jock disinterested in education in the face of a lucrative career in professional sports. D'Shawn learns moral lessons from his Beverly Hills friends, who encourage him toward academic success and the class aspirations that supposedly come with it. In one episode Donna goes out with D'Shawn after having a fight with her boyfriend, and the negative reaction of her mother (Katherine Cannon) brings to the surface the underlying racial tensions of this program. It draws us toward Donna and D'Shawn and away from Donna's mother, a seemingly positive move in terms of identification. However, we never find any suggestion that Donna will pursue a relationship with D'Shawn. In the particular hierarchical structures of this show, in fact, Donna may cross class boundaries—as she does when she dates poor, white musician Ray Pruitt (Jaime Walters)—but the racial divide can never be crossed in any manner other than platonic friendship.

D'Shawn's character is tied not to relationship but to performance. His character is resistant to the superstructure his athletic ability has inserted him into, and he is there to show the flaw in that system by repeatedly attempting to use the system in the same way he sees it using him. Unfortunately, his potential for resistance is completely tied to his performance, and his inability to perform causes him to be rejected from the system.

During college Brandon meets and becomes interested in an African American librarian from Texas. Mariah (Maia Campbell) is problematically positioned because of her race and gender. Her status as the object of Brandon's desire negates the possible alliances he might have forged with a male character, as suggested by Waiters in her article. DuCille (1996) suggests that "[O]ne can be black *or* a woman, but claiming both identities places one on shaky familial ground, outside the romance."[20] (p. 61) Like D'Shawn, Mariah cannot be Brandon's love interest within the hierarchical structures of this text. Although she appears only briefly, Mariah's presence reifies notions of African American femininity as imbued with arcane spiritual knowledge diametrically opposing the C.U. students' Western ways of knowing, and she quickly exits.

Although Waiters (1996) commends *90210* for its strategic movement toward mutually beneficial interethnic friendships during the high school years, this does not keep D'Shawn, or any other "issue" character, on the show. Performances of race on *90210* are problematic and are often closed down before they can be adequately explored by the show or identified with by the viewer. The examples of D'Shawn and Mariah demonstrate the strength attributable to minority characters and their attempts to break with the traditional structures of the text. However, their transience indicates that the show attempts to resolve the issue of race relations too quickly and tends to mask this resistance; that is, the resistance of non-white characters to the traditional structures of the text. How can the viewer ever really identify with a character who is always being rushed off-screen?

Unlike other axes of difference, gender is central to *90210* from the moment the theme song starts playing. Of all the characters, the gender card is played most explicitly with Lucinda, whom I discussed earlier. Lucinda's strength, intellect, and sexual prowess, as well as her refusal to conform to traditional codes of femininity, repeatedly make her a target for social sanction. Unfortunately this also undermines the progressive discourses Lucinda introduces into the program: owning feminism, being independent, not relying on men for a sense of self-worth, enjoying one's sexuality, and not allowing oneself to be ruled by a sexual system in which there is one set of rules for men and another for women. These ideas are often in opposition to the portrayals of masculinity and femininity on *90210*.

Interestingly, Lucinda's pitch for serial monogamy is the way *90210*'s characters often operate. But by making their sexual movements incidental rather than self-motivated, the show removes any responsibility from the characters. Their change of partners is always coded as moving forward towards that final, perfect nuclear family relationship.

From the very first episode, boys and girls are created differently in the world of *90210*. The boys make mistakes as they grow up but generally they do the right thing in the end. The girls are more complicated. They are more obviously rebellious against the world they live in; they lie, cheat, steal, and use sex to get what they want; they are arrogant and moralistic and take their place in society completely for granted. While this bias may seem to favor men, it is through identifying with the female characters that the viewer is presented with the most vibrant oppositional strategies and moments of emancipation. Unfortunately, the girls face strong emotional, social, and moral sanctions for acting against the hegemonic structures of their community, and while the female characters on *90210* are diverse, they are also, as Willis (1991) describes, rather mundane commodities "on the supermarket shelf on gender possibilities." (p. 23) Although they perform some diversity, these characters conform to stereotyped images of the feminine: good and bad girl, virgin, slut, tease, or user.

90210 hammers home the idea that although college is a time for sexual exploration, a gendered division exists, as in other activities, between what is sexually acceptable for women and for men. All the characters have many lovers, but the repercussions for women and men are different. Again, the boys make mistakes and hurt people but generally learn from their shortcomings without too much angst. The women tend to be hurt more deeply and to have their friendships fractured because of their relationships. This reiterates a discourse that understands women as being more invested in their relationships than men. The women also use their sexuality to hurt each other and to get things from other people. They have HIV and pregnancy scares and one-night stands, date abusive men, and become involved with drugs. *90210*'s gendered standard for sexual acceptability is manifested by the doling out of harsher punishments for transgressions to the women than to the men.

Gender is the axis of difference most often and complexly dealt with on *90210*. This is not surprising, given that it is easier to exclude a whole spectrum of characters according to other axes of difference than to exclude women. But as the characters move toward graduation and "real" life, moments of gender transgression become fewer and further between as the characters settle into the penultimate quest for adult (read matrimonial) relationships. The insertion of nonheterosexual characters during the college years seems to broaden *90210*'s homogeneous character base (and the same can be said for all characters who occupy positions of difference), but it tends to close down obvious means for viewers to identify with them by making their characters deviant or transient occupants of the diegesis. There always exists the possibility for radical readings of these characters, but identifying with them is made extremely difficult by the marginal and punitive ways they are dealt with and the consistent refusal to grant them the status of permanent residents of the *90210* community.

As *90210*'s school days ended, so too did virtually all explorations of difference, prompting a reading that in the "real" world, life consists of homogenous social enclaves. Having African American (or gay/lesbian, disabled, Muslim, Latina/o, etc.) characters as permanent campus and *90210* residents would have made them much more complex and interesting places in which to grow up and get an education.

In the last season of *90210*, most of the characters seemed to be moving along the paths that a decade of televisual soul-searching had prepared them for: marriage and family life in Beverly Hills. In fact, season ten offers a return to an older era, as Kelly and Dylan drift back together and Donna and David finally make it to the alter (ever the correct couple, they had both a rabbi and a priest present). The long-absent Brandon, Andrea, and Valerie show up to show that they, too, are doing okay in the world of the American dream. Donna's Beverly Hills boutique is a success, and David is becoming a well-known radio D.J. Despite his decision to go back and finish his B.A., Dylan still is not sure what to do with his life, and neither is Kelly, but his trust fund should ensure that they do not have to worry too hard about it. Steve and Janet lead the pack with a baby, a minivan, the Walsh's old house, and their own business.[21] In the end, the final season of *90210* is the one most like the first, with many of the original cast moving back to their old stomping grounds and starting the next generation of Beverly Hillians on the right track.

Conclusion—(Mis)education and the Importance of *90210*

Television may offer a distorted view of the world, but it is one way in which viewers learn about experiences outside of their own immediate purview. Grossberg (1997) writes that "at least for significant factions of the population of the contemporary United States, we *live* in popular culture . . . ."[22] (p. 278) As a ninth-grader in a seminar that I ran some time ago suggested, many shows targeting late teens and people in their twenties also appeal to younger viewers because they provide a vision of the future. As such, images of education and educators in popular culture offer young people a skewed glimpse of what lies ahead. A critical interpretation of these images is an essential part of understanding what kind of discourses on education are floating around on our visual screens.

I chose to study *90210* because it occupies a particularly interesting place in television culture, having begun several years before the explosion of teen-oriented dramas that took Hollywood by storm in the late nineties. *90210* is seen by many as the show that started it all; more than any other show, it had the longevity to explore its characters' long-term relationships to education and so made statements about college life different from those that had previously been made on prime-time television.

Academics may have seemed superfluous to the show at times, but education was present throughout the first seven years of *90210*. In many ways, *90210* paved the way for other series, like *Party of Five, Felicity,* and *Buffy the Vampire Slayer,* which have made college an intrinsic part of their explorations of late adolescence. What *90210* made abundantly clear is that higher education is a performance, both social and intellectual, on the part of both students and faculty. It is these performances that I have been scrutinizing throughout these pages, their complexity and, often, their hegemonic functions. I have also tried to expose the possibility for resistance that exists within these performances and the positive potential this holds for viewers.

Whether explicitly or implicitly, *90210* tells its viewers a lot about education: who is successful, what education does or does not prepare us for, who fits in, what are important aspects of college life, what a student looks/sounds like, what educators are like, how faculty relate to students, how students relate to school bureaucracy and politics, and about the politics of difference on campus. What it often omits, for the sake of drama or hegemony, are the positive, meaningful moments of connection between students and faculty, the opportunities for connecting with new and diverse people, the exciting possibilities that come from the acquisition of knowledge and the questioning of previously held beliefs, and the difficulties of tying education to the future or, indeed, of securing the future at all. It is these omissions which delineate (mis)education as it is performed on *90210*.

90210's performances of (mis)education give us some indication of the position that education is accorded in contemporary North American society. This program often takes a strongly anti-intellectual stance, as demonstrated most tellingly by the depictions of professors as abusive power-mongers. In so doing, knowledge is made secondary to the moral lessons the students must teach and on occasion be taught. Equally important is the fact that the position of extreme economic privilege accorded these characters allows the text to override questions of educational attainment, "meritocracy," and the possible ramifications these may have on future economic situations. *90210* performs ideas about higher education that exist within the popular imagination: that it is a place of fun, adventure, and romance, where academics and intellectualism run a far second. Although they experience an onslaught of academic difficulties, students are usually successful despite the obstacles they face. Despite everything, characters on *90210* get an education.

(Mis)education in popular culture moves outward from the classroom to inflect our knowledge of politics, authority, morality, friendship, gender, sexuality, ability, race, religion, mobility, etc. Often, this results in moments of paradox, such as when the discourse insists that education is a meritocracy, while the campus is depicted as almost exclusively populated with gorgeous, young, rich, white, able people. This is similarly the case when a discourse is activated that insists on the links between education and work. In a certain sense *90210* conflates professional education with general undergraduate programs, which is demonstrated by the characters' decisions to study fashion, journalism, and theater, and their ability to actually work at these professions. This does not reflect most undergraduates' experience, and because this slippage is not explicit, the relationship between education and work is concretized.

90210 is quite successful at demonstrating some of the breadth and complexity of university life. Its major shortcomings arise from its insistence on portraying middle-of-the-road politics, authoritarianism, moralism, and the omission of difference from campus life. Despite this, moments of resistance occur and, with them, possibilities for radical critique not only of this one program but of images of higher education everywhere.

The future of education appears to be increasingly tied to mediatization: the inclusion of media structures in the classroom and the growing critiques of education in popular culture and of popular culture in the academy. Television, often a conservative medium, demonstrates which ideas about education can be deployed in the public sphere. Often, we learn just as much from what is left outside the frame as what is placed inside it, from what cannot be shown or said; these things are more easily taken up by students of pedagogy and popular culture or by filmmakers. But outside of the academic sphere, television, and programs like *90210*, continue to educate and (mis)educate us about performances of education and educators today and to suggest what performances will be necessary in the future.

Notes

In the time since this article was originally written, a great deal of literature dealing with mainstream television series has emerged from academia. Much of this work has focused on gender in relation to television texts featuring "tough girls" and "women warriors" (Inness, 1999; Helford, 2000; Early and Kennedy, 2003; Heinecken, 2003), which can be linked to a growing interest in studying girls and young women more generally (Inness, 1998; Baumgardner and Richards, 2000; Gateward and Pomerance, 2002; Driscoll, 2002; Dicker and Piepmeier, 2003). While many shows, such as *Xena: Warrior Princess*, have provoked a great deal of interest, *Buffy the Vampire Slayer* is the series most closely associated with the current growth in television studies (Kaveney, 2002; Wilcox and Lavery, 2002; South, 2003). While the author is certainly familiar with this literature, the time needed to make the revisions that would have been necessary to include the new literature in this work was not available. However, the new literature should certainly inform ongoing discussions of television and youth culture today.

1. As Jenkins (1992) writes: "I have found approaching popular culture as a fan gives me new insights into the media . . . When I write about fan culture, then, I write *both* as an academic . . . and as a fan." (p. 5)

2. Although it might be suggested that these fantasies lessen the desire for higher learning, declining enrollment rates are more likely attributable to increased tuition, lack of symmetry between getting an education and procuring employment, and the abolition of programs that encourage minority students to enter and stay in post-secondary education.

3. Davies (1996), in discussing *Stand and Deliver*, concedes the difficulty of presenting images of classroom interaction between teacher and student in popular culture. It remains to be seen what this means when images of education and educators are co-opted by the media in order to sell lifestyle, the future, and (mis)education.

4. Just for a laugh, the cars these collegians drove included an Acura NSX, a Range Rover, two BMW roadsters, a Corvette, and a Mustang. Until he left the series, Dylan (Luke Perry) drove an antique Porsche.

5. It should be acknowledged that other television shows, for example, *The Fresh Prince of Bel-Air* and *A Different World*, have focused on college as a site of privilege that is nonwhite. Like *90210*, however, they also show college as a space of privilege of class, location, beauty, and ability.

6. My thanks to Stephanie Roy for pointing out during my criticism that it is hardly unusual for one group of people to run a lot of major events in a university (especially a small one). *90210*'s main characters ran the radio station, newspaper, drama club, and television station, as well as political office.

7. Other television programs aimed at similar population demographics do show more diverse ranges of education and employment. There are of course the doctors and nurses of *E.R.* and *Chicago Hope* and the lawyers of *Ally McBeal* and *The Practice*. But even a show like *Friends* is more diverse: Ross has a Ph.D. and works at a museum, his ex-wife Carol is a teacher, and her girlfriend Susan makes television commercials; Monica is a chef; Joey is an actor; Chandler is a business executive; Phoebe is a massage therapist; and Rachel goes from being a waitress to working as an assistant buyer for Bloomingdale's. Although there is no time to look at this in depth here, it is also interesting to look at the parents of these characters. Like *90210*, the *Friends* fathers are professionals: doctors, dentists, accountants, and businessmen. Most of the mothers are homemakers, with the exception in *90210* of Kelly (a former model) and Steve's (an actress) and in *Friends* of Chandler's (a best-selling author of romance novels).

8. Ehrenrich (1990) describes how many middle- and upper-class aspirants have abandoned the professions for more lucrative endeavors.

It is possible that many of *90210*'s students do not have the life experience to put in the time (in hours and in years) required to attain professionalism. Many of them have surpassed that level of financial success just by being born (which reflects a general tendency to view wealth as the ultimate goal of everything, including education). The problem with this is that they do not relinquish the discourse of working for their success, and so the viewer exists in a contradictory space between discourses of work ethic and of inheritance.

9. It is Brenda, Brandon, Clare, and Andrea who worry on a regular basis about their grades and about succeeding in their classes. The other characters' scholastic anxieties tend to be motivated only by imminent failure.

10. Other characters who joined the show after the college years did not offer a much wider spectrum of professional and intellectual achievement. Though there was Kelly's ambivalent lawyer suitor Matt Durning (Daniel Cosgrove), most of the other characters recapitulated the ambivalent relationship to professionalism and intellectualism already described, including Gina Kincaid (Vanessa Marcil) an almost-pro skater turned personal trainer, Noah Hunter (Vincent Young) an Ivy League pretender turned alcoholic club manager, and Janet Sosna (Lindsay Price) an intellectual writer who ends up working for a tabloid.

11. Of course his name is cleared, and the viewer learns that not all women who accuse men of rape are telling the truth. Kelly's admission that she was date-raped in high school is an attempt to level this problematic storyline.

12. Quoted from Winona Ryder's character Veronica Sawyer in *Heathers* (1989). New Line Cinema. Directed by Michael Lehman. Written by Daniel Wakrs.

13. It is later exposed that this girl is also Jewish and that she is the only sorority sister who has issues with the display of Judaism. Problematically, this becomes an exclusively "insider" issue, making anti-Semitism an issue only among Jews.

14. The secondary characters have no such luck unless they happen to snag onto a long-term relationship with one of the main characters. All of them are discarded in some way, during these seasons in particular, often through failure and bodily injury.

15. The theme of universities using minority and inner-city youth as athletic stars (and often abandoning them if they are injured or dismissing their academics) has been a theme of numerous films, including *Hoop Dreams, He Got Game, The Program*, and *Higher Learning*.

16. McKinley (1997) does devote a chapter segment to the discussion of talk about the character of Holly (Sydney Browne), a visually impaired musician (pp. 225–234). Holly is one of the very few characters with disabilities who appear on *90210* and on mainstream American television more generally.

17. Jimmy is the first sexually active gay character that we encounter in the *90210* diegesis, and it is unfortunate that he appears so briefly. It is also unfortunate that he allows this disease to be coded as homosexual, especially in a text where the characters have so many sexual partners. At the end of the eighth season, Valerie took an AIDS test after having unprotected sex with a stranger who turned out to be an I.V. drug user. She tested negative.

18. And who is actually portrayed by a woman, Canadian model Monica Schnarre.

19. Emphasis in the original.

20. Emphasis in the original.

21. Janet becomes the only visibly racialized cast member in this last season, but this is never made a part of the storylines in which she performs. There is an underlying suggestion that her parents do not approve of Steve because he is not Asian, but this is never clear. The fact that Steve's father is initially ambivalent about their marriage, but then quickly relents (more quickly than Janet's parents) also makes problematic the question of where prejudice usually lies.

22. Emphasis in the original.

References

Aronowitz, S. "A Different Perspective on Educational Inequality." In *Education and Cultural Studies: Towards a Performative Practice,* edited by H. A. Giroux and P. Shannon. New York: Routledge, 1997: 119–139.

Baumgardner, J., and Richards, A. *Manifesta: Young Women, Feminism, and the Future.* New York: Farrar, Straus, and Giroux, 2000.

Byers, M. "Constructing Divas in the Academy: Why the Female Graduate Student Emerges in Prime-Time Television Culture." *Higher Education Perspectives* 1 (1996/97): 99–118.

Davies, J. *Educating Students in a Media-Saturated Culture.* Lancaster, PA: Technomic Publishing Company, Inc., 1996.

Dicker, R. and Piepmeier, A., eds. *Catching a Wave: Reclaiming Feminism for the 21st Century.* Boston: Northeastern University Press, 2003.

Driscoll, C. *Girls: Feminine Adolescence in Popular Culture and Cultural Theory.* New York: Columbia University Press, 2002.

DuCille, A. *Skin Trade.* Cambridge, MA: Harvard University Press, 1996.

Early, F. and Kennedy, K., eds. *Athena's Daughters: Television's New Woman Warriors.* New York: Syracuse University Press, 2003.

Ehrenreich, B. *Fear of Falling: The Inner Life of the Middle Class.* New York: Harper Perrenial, 1990.

Gateward, F. and Pomerance, M. *Sugar, Spice, and Everything Nice: Cinemas of Girlhood.* Detroit: Wayne State University Press, 2002.

Giroux, H. A. *Disturbing Pleasures: Learning Popular Culture*. London: Routledge, 1994.
———. "Is There a Place for Cultural Studies in Colleges of Education?" In *Education and Cultural Studies: Toward a Performative Practice,* edited by H. A Giroux and P. Shannon. New York: Routledge, 1997: 231–249.
Grossberg, L. *Dancing in Spite of Myself: Essays on PopularCulture*. Durham, NC: Duke University Press, 1997.
Heinecken, D. *The Warrior Women of Television*. New York: Peter Lang, 2003.
Helford, E. R., ed. *Fantasy Girls*. Lanham, MD: Rowman & Littlefield, 2000.
Holland, D. C. and Eisenhart, M. A. *Educated in Romance: Women, Achievement, and College Culture*. Chicago: The University of Chicago Press, 1990.
Inness, S. *Tough Girls: Women Warriors and Wonder Women in Popular Culture*. Philadelphia, PA: University of Pennsylvania Press, 1999.
Inness, S., ed. *Delinquents and Debutantes*. New York: NYU Press, 1998.
Jenkins, H. *Textual Poachers: Television Fans and Participatory Culture*. New York: Routledge, 1992.
Kaveney, R., ed. *Reading the Vampire Slayer*. New York: Tauris Parke Paperbacks, 2002.
LaPlanche, J. and Pontalis, J.-B. "Fantasy and the Origins of Sexuality." In *Formations of Fantasy,* edited by V. Burgin, J. Donald, and C. Kaplan. London: Routledge, 1986.
Lewis, J. *The Road to Romance and Ruin*. New York: Routledge, 1992.
McKinley, E. G. *Beverly Hills, 90210: Television, Gender, and Identity*. Philadelphia, PA: University of Pennsylvania Press, 1997.
Morgan, R. "Television, Space, Education: Rethinking Relations Between Schools and Media." *Discourse* 16 (1995): 39–57.
Morse, M. *Virtualities: Television, Media Art, and Cyberculture*. Bloomington and Indianapolis: Indiana University Press, 1998.
Noble, D. D. "Let Them Eat Skills." In *Education and Cultural Studies: Toward a Performative Practice,* edited by H. A. Giroux and P. Shannon. New York: Routledge, 1997: 197–212.
Noddings, N. "An Ethic of Care and its Implications for Instructional Arrangements." *American Journal of Education* 96 (1988): 215–230.
Owen, R. *Gen X TV: The Brady Bunch to Melrose Place*. New York: Syracuse University Press, 1997.
Pollock, D. "Performing Writing." In *The Ends of Performance,* edited by P. Phelan and J. Lane. New York: NYU Press, 1998: 73–103.
South, J. B., ed. *Buffy the Vampire Slayer: Fear and Trembling in Sunnydale*. Chicago: Open Court, 2003.
Traube, E. G. *Dreaming Identities: Class, Gender, and Generation in 1980s Hollywood Movies*. Boulder, CO: Westview Press, 1992.
Urch, K. "Fighting Academic Agoraphobia: Self-Help Books for Cultural Studies' Fear of the Marketplace." In *Education and Cultural Studies: Toward a Performative Practice,* edited by H. A. Giroux and P. Shannon. New York: Routledge, (1997): 213–230.
Waiters, E. D. "*90210* in Black & White and Color: Inter-Ethnic Friendship on Prime Time Television." In *Pictures of a Generation on Hold: Selected Papers,* edited by M. Pomerance and J. Sakeris. Toronto: Media Studies Working Group, 1996: 205–214.
Wilcox, R. W. and D. Lavery, eds. *Fighting the Forces: What's at Stake in Buffy the Vampire Slayer*. Lanham, MD: Rowman & Littlefield, 2002.
Willis, S. *A Primer for Daily Life*. New York: Routledge, 1991.

5

Rap (in) the Academy: Academic Work, Education, and Cultural Studies[1]

TOBY DASPIT AND JOHN A. WEAVER

Can I get a Witness?

(Public Enemy, 1989)

He [the academic] bears witness: he is objective;
he guarantees the clarity and purity of objects. His
subjectivity is his objectivity. (Haraway, 1997, p. 24)

A choice of a song that contains objectionable content will result in
an F for this project.

Student Teacher, University of Akron

Academia on the Periphery of Life

Public Enemy asks if it can get a witness as it stands for the rights of post-industrial capitalism and against modernist rules of copyright laws. In the recent past, academia has come to rap's defense. We are not just talking about Henry Louis Gates and his testimony at the 2 Live Crew's trial in Miami-Dade County, Florida, but also about the flourishing publishing industry on rap/hip-hop culture(s). Yet, when Public Enemy shouts out for a witness, all we give them is Donna Haraway's modest witness. Their cries for passion, emotion, noise, and radical change are meet with cool reason, scholarship, and strange looks. The problem is while Public Enemy and other rap groups are responding to the crises of our postmodern society with their hybrid mix'n, unsolicited sampl'n, and radical mess(age), academics can respond to these crises only with modernist retorts limited by the artificial disciplines and stifling methodologies they have created. The academy comes to the scene as a modest witness who knows how to construct human subjects, probe these subjects, analyze their conditions, respond with moral panics, frame rap with distant prose, and package all of this by denying that they are constructing, framing, and panicking in the first place. The academy cannot respond in the rhythmic, scratch'n, mix'n, and flow'n way in which rap demands to be treated. Yet, the academy purports to be a bastion of diversity and academic freedom.

I, Weaver, place this tempest on academic work on the margins because in relation to rap and other cutting edge-cultural movements, it plays no role. Academic work is in crisis, and rap and hip-hop culture(s) highlight this crisis. While rap and hip-hop artists like Public Enemy, DJ Spooky, KRS-One, and others explore new territories, break old rules (and establish new ones), highlight the experiences of urban youth, and define postmodern capitalism, academics respond with stifling methodologies that are more concerned with fitting the world into categories and boxes than understanding what is going on. The modest witness with his internal/external validity, laws of generalizability, carefully demarcated disciplines, and confessionary/missionary methodologies is a powerful fictional character who has captured our attention in academia and held our imaginations hostage for over a century. He has banished women from science, stringently defined what is knowledge, and carefully guarded the gates of the Ivory Towers so no one who fails to meet these standards is permitted to enter.

In the meantime, the world has changed. Rap has responded, but the modest witness hasn't a clue. Urban centers have become schizophrenic, as one city block resembles the burnt-out streets of Dresden or London in 1945 (not from bombings but from modernist city planning; see Rose, 1994a, pp. 76–77), while the next is a symbol of revitalization and recovery from the deep wounds of deindustrialization and suburban sprawl. The city has become a hybrid; that is the source and mirror for the music of rap as rap blends these experiences with its sampl'n and mix'n techniques. As American cities have crumbled, the academy confines itself to principles of purity and essentialism as it seeks to protect its disciplinary boundaries and methods. The academy has become a modernist hideaway for those who do not wish to deal with the hybridity of postmodern life, where freaks with implants, prosthetic limbs, and memory chips are the norm; mutants with tattoos and body piercing are the fashion trend setters; and distortion is the truth of all knowledge and realities. Academic work has become a fiction where academics can construct and order their own world without dealing with the ambiguities and uncertainties of the postmodern world(s).

The purity of the modest witness and the hybridity of postmodern life enter into the classroom as they clash everyday over what knowledge and culture(s) will be sanctioned as important and legitimate. The modest witness, somewhat uncharacteristically, transforms itself as teachers and administrators interpret what they learn in the academy and impose it upon public schools. Like the academic, they try to mold—forcefully if need be—students into clones of what they think they should be. The cultures of the students are ignored and outlawed from the school grounds as the colors they wear, the styles they choose, the music they listen to, the language they speak, and the experiences they share are all regulated in order to control and manage the student. When the students' cultures are invited into the modest witness' probing grounds called public schools, it is always with stipulations and permission. The modest witness makes sure that the student knows that, in their current form and mindset, they are mere guests in the sanctuary of the academy and are unacceptable the way they are. At any time, when their cultures are permitted to exist within schools, students who transgress the regulations and stipulations the modest witness has imposed upon them run the risk of getting an "F." The modest witness tries to tame the cultures of students through F's, expulsions, and Foucauldian surveillance—take your pick.

But students revolts against the panopticon gaze and the taming powers of the modest witness in many ways. They create their own localizing space within schools where they can talk about nothing, smoke, do drugs, and listen to the noise of rap. It is the noise of rap that is most annoying to the modest witnesses of public schools. Whereas the students can talk, smoke, and snort without entering the space of teachers and administrators, the noise of rap penetrates and transforms anything that is within its decibel range. The noise tells the modest witness that he may be eager to construct an enclave of purity and innocence, but the sounds and shapes of rap will penetrate his fictions and remind him that the messages, issues, and concerns of postmodern life cannot be wished away by rules and regulations, standardized tests, clean methodological approaches, and safe forms of knowledge. The noise of rap is the nemesis of the academy, and refusing to deal with it is impossible. Like urban centers, schools are the probing grounds of rap, and the modest witness has to admit that the pristine illusion he struggled so hard to create is evaporating before his eyes. The only solution is to accept the hybridity of life, the messiness of academic work, the insanity of objectivity, and the fiction of the modest witness. The only solution is to accept rap as the messiah of the postmodern mess(age).

All is not lost in the academy, and the modest witness is not as dominant as I let on above. The studies movements, in particular for this essay cultural studies, but also women's, black, gay and lesbian, and subcultural studies, have challenged many of the premises of the modest witness and modernity. In the academy, cultural studies is like rap: It is in tune with the hybridity of life, it understands the ambiguity and fluidness of everyday experiences, and it deconstructs the counterfeit reality academic work tries to create. Because of its ability to understand and deconstruct, it is noise to the academy. Cultural studies breaks almost every rule the modest witness lives by and values the subjectivity and creativity of everyday life; therefore, it is outlawed in most institutions (asylums?) of higher learning, like Boston University, and is unknown by others. Cultural studies movements echo the words of DJ Spooky when he shouts, "At school (Bowdoin College), I ran into this segregation between academic disciplines . . . and I didn't see any need to have barriers between any of them." (Ferguson 1996, p. 10) Cultural studies has been asking the same question for decades now. It is for these reasons alone that cultural studies is an important movement for education to understand better and get involved in. Like rap, cultural studies provides possible solutions to the problems and concerns students and teachers face in their postmodern lives. We need only to break through the artificially constructed and highly inflated barriers we have erected to distance ourselves from the knowledge, standards, and values of the world and see the importance cultural studies has for education.

For me, the influence of cultural studies comes in at least five forms: the articulation of Hall; the ruptures of Grossberg; the anti-essentialism of Gilroy; the subcultures of Hebdige; and the techno-feminism of Plant. Each of these cultural critics offers us new insights into the theoretical constructs that invent our worlds and presents opportunities to reconfigure and reinvent educational processes. If we are committed to understanding the minds, needs, and desires of our students, we will embrace cultural studies as a vibrant alternative to the problems modern, scientistic scholarship has created.

Hall's concept of articulation, like E. P. Thompson's notions of historical developments, rescued British Marxism from the reductionist, predetermined theoretical tendencies it logically constructed in the twentieth century. For Hall, articulation is any linkage between two subjects or objects that are united by this linkage. "The two parts are connected to each other," Hall (Grossberg 1996) speculates, "but through a specific linkage that can be broken. An articulation is thus the form of the connection that can make a unity of two different elements, under certain conditions. It is a linkage which is not necessary, determined, absolute, and essential at any time." (p. 141) With his work on articulation, Hall transformed cultural studies into a multidisciplinary endeavor that was still committed to political issues, but not in the realm of historical determinism and universal laws. By abandoning such traditional Marxist core foundations as the inevitable march of historical forces in favor of the proletariat and the tacit belief that all proletariat acts are by nature progressive, Hall shifted the interests of cultural studies away from the meta-level of culture to the everyday level, where certainty and clarity are replaced by ambiguity and unpredictability. Hall's theory of articulation reshaped the research agendas of cultural critics as they began to focus on the everyday experiences of subcultural groups such as punk rockers, rap artists, television watchers, Elvis impersonators, and the like. By the 1980s, the cultural tastes of everyday people were the interest of cultural critics as they discovered that they do indeed construct complex worlds out of their cultural habits.

After Hall's attempts to decouple the articulation between cultural studies and historical determinism and universal laws, other traditional articulations were soon to be questioned. Grossberg, following Hall's work on articulation, warned about the elitist and reductionist tendencies of cultural studies to construct popular culture into a binary relationship with so-called mainstream culture. Binaries, as they were constructed, often placed popular culture embodiments into a subordinate position in which their meaning was limited to their relationship to dominant powers. As Grossberg (1997) states, "I have always felt uncomfortable with models that locate power in an economy of domination and resistance and that see cultural practices as immediately resistant." (p. 14) Such a theoretical stance is another form of historical determinism that is used to dismiss the complexity of uncertainty of cultural movements. It dismisses the possibility that cultural movements either support dominant powers or exist independent from dominant powers. For Grossberg, the power of cultural studies lies in its ability to rupture not only the traditional theoretical assumptions Hall exposed in his work but also in our ability to break stifling theoretical binaries that construct the way we see the worlds of cultural movements. We have to begin to see cultural movements as fluid, complex, and capable of reinforcing, resisting, or ignoring the abilities of so-called mainstream cultures to define meanings, tastes, standards, and values.

Combined, Hall and Grossberg constructed theoretical mappings that invited a whole new generation of cultural studies scholars to look into offbeat and iconoclastic movements that not only provided insights into the development of cultural movements but also questioned traditional notions of taste and academic work. By the 1980s, the funky, tasteless, and freaky were legitimate sites for research. Romance novel readers, soap opera watchers, comic book readers, punk rockers, and teenage hackers were acceptable for tenure committees. A revolution of taste(lessness) had begun.

Some of the more innovative work from this new generation has come from Paul Gilroy, Dick Hebdige, and Sadie Plant. Gilroy's (1993) work has been a conscious effort to encourage cultural studies to question its essentialist notions of identity and ethnicity. For Gilroy, identities are hybrids, and the norm is not perfection or purity but imperfection and mutation. Russell Potter (1995) points this out about Gilroy's work on identity and cultural formations:

> Too often, as Paul Gilroy has demonstrated, cultural formations which move across multiple borders are nonetheless treated as isolated national phenomena. Gilroy has shown . . . that what he calls the 'black Atlantic' is a densely interconnected cultural formation which, despite and in some cases because of discontinuities, continues to mobilize, encode, and transmit cultural matter . . . Gilroy does not capitalize 'black,' and in this way marks his difference from the kinds of conservative and essentialistic conceptions of 'black' that have formed and fueled some black nationalist movements (p. 19).

Because of Gilroy's work, cultural studies is seen as a hybrid in which the vitality and sustainability of any cultural movement is in its ability to sample, mix, and blend different parts of other cultural movements and thereby morph into something it never intended to develop into. In this sense rap, like situational comedy television shows that morph with other sit-coms, is a quintessential example of the type of cultural movement that I think Gilroy has in mind since its lifeline to continued development is in its ability to sample, mix, and blend with previously recorded songs and musical traditions.

Hebdige's contribution to the cultural studies movements rests with the ways in which we look at and interpret subcultural movements. As Hebdige uses the term, subculture is not meant to imply dependency or subordinance but rather stubborn and overt independence. Hebdige (1988) theorizes a subculture as a cultural movement that forms "up in the space between surveillance and the evasion of surveillance" and "is neither simply affirmation or refusal, neither 'commercial exploitation' nor genuine revolt." (p. 35) For Hebdige, subcultures hide in the light. They emerge and develop in the very terrain in cultural politics that dominant or mainstream cultures cannot see—the space right in front of them. In fact, it is the ability of subcultures to exist in the midst of mainstream cultures that makes subcultures more imaginative and creative than mainstream cultures. When cultural critics place subcultures within a theoretical binary of subordination, cultural studies loses sight of the fact that when it comes to constructing or inventing cultural movements, it is the dominant or mainstream cultures that are placed in a reactionary position. Dominant cultures are too busy constructing standards of taste and policing these standards to be interested in understanding how subcultures emerge and develop in the light. Instead, they can only react to these subcultures with a moral panic, public relation campaigns of condemnation, or coopting aspects of the subcultures. For example, dominant or mainstream cultures do not know where the body piercing and tattoo art movements emerged and developed. They could only react to these movements and adjust their standards to allow that body piercing and tattoos are now more socially acceptable than they ever were.

A final force in the cultural studies movement that is pertinent to my ideas is Sadie Plant. Plant is one of the first cultural studies scholars to venture into the worlds of cyberspace and information technology. Her work not only attempts to see how information technology reconfigures such issues of feminism, gender, history, psycho-analysis, and politics but also academic writing. In *Zeros + Ones: Digital Women + The New Technoculture*, Plant demonstrates how information technology is transforming the way we write and think about cultural studies. Her style is swift, abrupt, and open. She combines an efficient economy of writing with a general economy, maximizing the possible meanings of her words with the fewest words possible. Moreover, she demonstrates how information technology is not the latest instrument for utopian thinking in which all our earthly and physical problems like sexism, racism, homophobia, and social class discrimination are suddenly wished away. Instead, these concerns are mutated and reconfigured by the new mediums of information technology. To make her point she highlights some of the ways in which academic writing remains dominant but at a different plateau. She notes how even with information technology, we continue to value certain details, styles, methods, and forms of authority over others that are relegated to the back pages of endnotes or erased altogether. Plant (1997) suggests:

> Distinctions between the main bodies of texts and all their peripheral detail—indices, headings, prefaces, dedications, appendices, illustrations, references, notes, and diagrams—have long been integral to orthodox conceptions of nonfiction books and articles. Authored, authorized, and authoritative, a piece of writing is its own mainstream. Its asides are backwaters which might have been—and often are—compiled by anonymous editors, secretaries, copyists, and clerks, and while they also connect to other sources, resources, and leads, they are also sidelined and downplayed (p. 9).

When we in education ignore cultural studies and the cultures of students and teachers, we sideline, erase, and relegate to the backwaters these people while giving ourselves the authority to speak to what is needed in education and how reform will take place in education. Rap is no exception. We sideline it when we treat it as scholarship. We treat it as an endnote, reference, or something we can probe and analyze—authorizing our voice while erasing the voices of rap artists and others who make up the cultures of hip-hop. Our work in the middle column is not scholarship. It is better than that. It mutates rap as we write about it, but we do not mutilate it in a violent act that traditional scientific scholarship often performs on popular culture. Traditional scientific scholarship forces popular culture into its norms, standards, styles, and preferences, all along assuming that popular culture is inferior. We are writing about rap not to explain it; rather we are using rap to transform the academy, to educate the academy. The challenge is not for rap artists to explain themselves to the academy; the challenge is for scholars to overcome their limitations and to ask themselves how heterogenous the academy is and how much freedom it offers. Our task is to test those limits and to show that we have academic freedom only within strict parameters. If we choose to "research" a subject within these parameters, we are free. If, however, we transgress those limits, we no longer have freedom. We are relegated to the realm of non-scholarship. We are exiled. We want to be exiled because, just as modernity has failed to answer many of the questions we have today, the academy has stopped being a vibrant and dynamic place. It is too closed, too conservative, and too cautious, while the world around us, whether in the recording studio, cyberspace, urban street corner, or elsewhere, is mutating into a dynamic, limitless place where opportunities are begging to be invented. Scholarship needs to be transformed, and cultural studies can provide us with some insights into how this process can take place.

Rap: In the Center of Academic Discourses

In the past decade, rap has enjoyed or suffered through an increased interest from those who call the academy home. While political pundits and ideologues like William Bennett or Charlton Heston construct rap only as a haven for "gangsta" activity, cultural critics often envision rap at worst romantically or at best as a counter-hegemonic force responding to the (white) moral panic embedded in the dominant conservative discourse of the 1990s. We contend that rap is more than "gangsta" rap, romance, and resistance. Rap is a totalizing discourse, and reducing it to one or all of the three responses above is to reveal nothing about rap and everything about the political and cultural agendas of those who try to co-opt rap for their own purposes.

On the romantic front, Andrew Ross (1991) describes the hip-hop and rap movements in this way:

> the hip-hop aesthetic is devoted to bringing color, style, and movement into inner-city environments, transforming bleak backdrops by graffiti that speaks to the act of creative landscaping, rather than urban decay. . . . hip-hop's leading musicians and producers have emerged as important organic intellectuals within the black community (p. 144).

For us, Ross's prose ironically conjures up images of the traditional Western myth of the self-made man. Instead of a rags-to-riches story or a frontier story, Ross presents the urban youth as emerging from the ashes of urban decay, collecting the rubble that lies around them to create a new sound, and through this new sound, rejuvenating the urban centers. Ross's story erases other dimensions of rap that do not fit the story of organic intellectuals, Gramscian politics, and urban renewal, including the fact that many rap artists like those who grew up in the Hollis neighborhood of Queens never experienced a life of urban blight.

Then there are those who try to force rap into the story of dominance and subordination, power and resistance, occupation and opposition. Henry Giroux (1994), with his own form of romanticism, writes:

> rap music offers him [Quincy from the movie *Juice*] the opportunity to claim some 'juice' among his peers while simultaneously providing him with a context to construct an affirmative identity along with the chance for real employment. Music in this context becomes a major referent for understanding how identities and bodies come together in a hip-hop culture that at its most oppositional moment is testing the limits of the American dream (p. 294).

Our stance fits more in line with, but not completely as we will demonstrate below, Peter McLaren's take on rap as a form of cultural politics. "In recent years," McLaren (1997) admits, "I have grown to greatly appreciate gangsta rap as an oppositional political practice, but despite its possibilities for articulating an oppositional performative politics, gangsta rap remains, in some senses, a problematic cultural practice." (p. 154) McLaren, in part, recognizes the dynamic and problematic dimensions of rap. However, we are still troubled by the way rap is being framed within the current cultural and political discourse of academia. There are oppositional tendencies within rap, but it is not happening in the manner Giroux or McLaren imply. Rap artists do not construct themselves within a dichotomous framework of dominance and subordination, hegemony and opposition. We submit that the only time rap becomes a form of traditional, Western-style opposition is when rap invades suburbia and (white) middle class young adults adopt and construct their own form of hip-hop culture in order to revolt against the dominance of middle class values. We join Johnathan Scott (1995) when he suggests "something interesting and complicated is going on" within hip-hop culture and rap, "and one will find very few answers by looking to categories like 'oppositional' and 'counter-hegemonic.' Hip-hop is hegemonic and refuses to be treated as a minority culture—as disadvantaged and excluded." (p. 170) Binaries like dominance and subordination and hegemonic and oppositional limit the power of rap and ignore the fact that rap is not resistant to consumer capitalism and the American Dream. Like the geeks and nerds of the techno-culture of hacking and software creation, rap artists want access to consumer capitalism with no strings and stipulations attached in order to construct their own version of the American Dream.

Moreover, labeling rap as oppositional places it in a position in which rap artists are capable only of reacting to the plans, policies, and decisions of other groups. Oppositional dichotomies strip rap of its creative powers to transcend the efforts of hegemonic powers to erase and ignore its existence in deindustrial urban and suburban centers. If rap is oppositional, it can be found in its ability to ignore hegemonic powers that promote moral panics within mainstream America while going about its business of utilizing the mechanisms of capitalism and post-industrialism that were originally reserved for the traditional (white) middle class affirmative action and preference programs that manifest themselves in the form of corporate welfare, nepotism, and alumni admissions policies, and to build recording empires and create the next generation of music. The power of rap is in its ability to build its own world without asking permission. Rap's power in this sense is in its ability to package itself as the raw, uncut . . . the real of life.

As stated above, we see rap as a totalizing discourse. A totalizing discourse contains moments of romance and resistance in it, but it is more. A totalizing discourse is a self-contained system of affective experiences and inventions about the world but is not hermetically sealed. It contains seeds of radical change but also kernels of dominance and repression. More important, a totalizing discourse is heteroglossic. It is capable of absorbing any reading, whether invited or uninvited. By absorbing a new reading, however, it is inextricably transformed into something more than it ever intended to be. In this light, to understand rap as a cultural movement we have to look not only at its "controversial" messages, especially as these messages are filtered through numerous mediums and perceived by (white) middle class American eyes, but also its embracing of corporate capitalism; not only its sexism but also its concern for creating memories of African American history; not only its urban roots but also its middle-class American roots; not only its "gangsta" genre but also its techno genre; not only the commentary of rap artists but also the commentary of cultural (and academic) critics. To ignore all the dimensions of rap is to subordinate it to causes that it might not be willing to support or endorse.

To look at rap as a totalizing discourse is also to see it not as a traditional efficient economy of meaning but as a general economy. Lawrence Grossberg (1997) notes that "too much of cultural studies" is mired in an efficient economy of meaning in which clarity and a correspondence theory of interpretation (one true interpretation) reign uncontested. As a result, cultural critics often

> locate popular culture within two binary normative economies, on the one hand, the popular (as poaching, fragmented, contradictory, bodily, carnivalesque, pleasurable) versus the legitimate (as reified, hierarchical, intellectual, etc.) and on the other hand, the popular (as stylized, artificial, disruptive, marginal, resisting) versus the mainstream (as naturalized, commonsensical, incorporated, etc.) (Grossberg, 1997, pp. 2–3).

Our reading and sampl'n of rap is not based on an efficient or normative economy of cultural studies; rather, it is based on a general economy of meaning. We co-opt this term from Georges Bataille via the work of Arkady Plotnitsky (1994), in which a general economy of meaning is an acceptance that an apparent condition of life is that "excesses of energy are produced, which, by definition, cannot be utilized. This excessive energy can only be lost without the slightest aim, consequently without any meaning." (pp. 1–2) In relation to rap, a general economy recognizes the dynamic condition of rap as a cultural phenomenon. Given that rap, like any cultural phenomenon, is a general economy of meaning, there is no interpretation of rap that can capture its meaning or significance. However, those interpretations that focus on moral panics, romance, and resistance are mired in traditional academic discourses that are based in efficient economies of meaning and limit the significance of rap to academic concerns and political issues while ignoring the fact that rap exceeds academic readings and is a totalizing discourse.

So when rap scholars like William Eric Perkins (1996) suggest that there is not enough "serious scholarship" done on "rap music and hip hop culture"(p. 2), we approach such statements with extreme caution. It is too often serious scholarship that tries to reduce the general economies of cultural movements like rap into efficient economies of meaning in which cultural movements can be controlled, probed, and manipulated. It is our contention that scholarship should stay away from rap and cultural studies unless it is willing to follow Grossberg's lead and recognize the dynamic uncertainty of cultural movements and the stifling tendencies of academic work. In this sense, scholarship has to become like rap. Whereas scholars try to control with their discourses on methodologies, token commentaries on ethical issues, and illusions to objectivity in order to transform rap into something it is not and does not want to be, rap is alive with the emotions and passions of everyday life. We say this not because we feel rap is some-how beyond academic writing or that it contains some mythical innocent essence that academic writing will corrupt. It is that academic writing is too staid, too clean, and too innocent, while rap contains the hybridity of life and the fluidness of experience.

Rap is a site where cultural studies and education can converge. Yet, few people are willing to transcend their academic cultures. It is this lack of transcendence and understanding that causes many of the problems in public schools today. While students see the value and significance of rap and other cultural manifestations like films, comic books, and fashion, pro-fessors, teachers, and administrators, with their inflated hierarchies of knowledge, dismiss these sites as insignificant and interpret these sites as proof of the malaise youth today embrace. The tendency of adults is to quickly condemn youth cultures like hip hop and then blame the youth for being too pessimistic and aimless. Yet, it is with our brutal efficiency that academic work and schooling murders the general economy of meaning in rap and other cultural movements.

What follows in this middle column will be a look at how rap is a totalizing discourse with a vibrant general economy of meaning. We will focus on the issues of sampl'n, mix'n, corporate capitalism, recombinant texts (hybridity), and techno-culture. What follows is our (academic) rap on cultural studies, hip-hop, and education. We are attempting, in this part, to capture rap on its own (shifting and unstable) terrain, but at the same time, we are rewriting and redefining rap as we let it flow into the (illusory and too self-confident) terrain of academia. By doing this, we are trans-forming both rap and academia because each are alien to the other not in any essentialist way but by choice (or in the case of rap, no-choice). Rap disses science for distancing itself from the real world, and science, in turn, disses rap by trying to force rap into the language and culture of academia, never accepting rap on its own terms and assuming it is infe-rior to science.

Rap, Mix'n, and Recombinant Textuality
"Rap is dj (disc jockey) and MC (Master of Ceremonies or Microphone Controller) music . . . (I)t relies on pre-recorded sounds. . . . The hip hoppers 'stole' music off air and cut it up. Then

they broke it down into its component parts and remixed it on tape. By doing this they were breaking the law of copyright. But the cut 'n' mix attitude was that no one owns a rhythm or a sound. You just borrow it, use it and give it back to the people in a slightly different form . . . you just *version* it."

Dick Hebdige (*Cut 'N' Mix*, 1987, p. 141)

"(H)ip hop was not just the product of . . . different, though converging, black cultural traditions. The centrality of 'the break' within it, and the subsequent refinement of cutting and mixing techniques through digital sampling which took the form far beyond the competence of hands on turntables, mean that the aesthetic rules which govern it are premised on a dialectic of rescuing appropriation and recombination which creates special pleasures and is not limited to the technological complex in which it originated."

Paul Gilroy (*The Black Atlantic*, 1993, pp. 103–104)

"Mixer man cook 'em in a pot like gumbo."

N.W.A. (*Straight Outta Compton*, 1988)

Although Rose (1994b) argues that rap cannot be understood in a purely postmodern context (what can?), rap artists, like the cyberpunks that Larry McCaffery refers to in the following, exhibit a "postmodernist spirit of free play (*jouissance*) . . . (and) delight in creating cut-ups and collages . . . in which familiar objects and motifs are placed in startling, unfamiliar contexts" (1991, p. 15) Any previously recorded sound or beat might be "sampled" and recombined in the "mix." Technology is appropriated and utilized, as Gilroy notes, but the effects of this mix exceed its origins. "The previous meanings," DJ Spooky (1996) writes, are "corralled into a space where the differences in time, place, and culture, are collapsed to create a recombinant text or autonomous zone of expression" (p. 14)—a "zone" of hybrid selves, hybrid cultures, hybrid conversations. A rich, spicy gumbo, with origins in African diasporic traditions, recombined continually through collisions with cultures and technologies.

Rap as Slippery History

" . . . I've tried to show how the roots (of Caribbean music) themselves are in a state of constant flux and change. The roots don't stay in one place. They change shape. They change colour. And they grow. There is no such thing as a pure point of origin, least of all in something as slippery as music, but that doesn't mean there isn't history."

Dick Hebdige (*Cut 'N' Mix*, 1987, p. 10)

"In the electronic milieu . . . the DJ is a custodian of aural history. In the mix, creator and re-mixer are woven together in the syncretic space of the text of samples and other sonic material to create a seamless fabric of sound that in a strange way mirrors the modern macrocosm of cyberspace where different voices and visions constantly collide and cross fertilize one another. . . . The mix, in this picture, allows the invocation of different languages, texts, and sounds to converge, meld, and create a new medium that transcends its original components."

DJ Spooky ("Flow My Blood the DJ Said", 1996, p. 10)

Greil Marcus (1995) suspects, he says, "that we are living out history, making it and unmaking it . . . all of the time, in far more ways than we have really learned." (p. 3) Rap embodies this suspicion, mobilizes it aurally. The illusory dichotomies between artist and audience, artist and text, and text and audience are all exposed as DJs harness previously produced beats and mix in other sound shards, and MCs rap the new poetry over this sonic melange—all the while with a localized audience that is technologically capable of taking rap music and re-mixing it, perpetuating the infinite possibilities of hypertextual realities. Robert Cantwell (in Marcus 1995) notes, "Where orders of meaning have vanished entirely, and the sign erupts in its incandescence onto the cultural surface, we begin history anew and call our epoch by new names. . . . We are all doctors and fortune tellers." (pp. 3–4)

Rap as (an underground, Lo-tek)Techno-Culture

Rap is post-industrial urban creativity denied access and left for the dead.

"Nighttown pays no taxes . . . The neon arcs are dead, and the geodesics have been smoked black by decades of cooking fires. . . . We'd been climbing for two hours, up concrete stairs . . . past abandoned gantries . . . We'd started in what looked like a disused maintenance yard . . . Everything there had been covered with that same uniform layer of spraybomb graffiti . . . gradually thinning until a single name was repeated at intervals. LO TEK."

William Gibson (*Johnny Mnemonic*, 1986, p. 14)

"All of these artists [DJ Kool Herc, Grand Master Flash, etc.] found themselves positioned with few resources in marginal economic circumstances, but each found ways to become famous as entertainers by appropriating the most advanced technologies and emerging cultural forms."

Tricia Rose (*A Style Nobody Can Deal With*, 1994a, p. 79)

Erased by choice theories, denied access by unequal (free market) economics and school policies, steamrolled by suburban sprawl and (mostly) white flight, urban youth are still resilient, tapping into new advances in information technology and co-opting these creations for their own purposes and agendas. Rap artists symbolize Gibson's LO TEKs. They do not have the power to decide how funds will be used to allocate resources in our post-industrial, information-technologically based world, but they force their way in, hacking their way into the system, demanding to be heard on their own terms. Rap is the LO TEKs weapon of choice in a "free" market society.

Technology + Information Reconfigured as Meaning = Techno-Culture

"DJ culture—urban youth culture—is about recombinant potential . . . Each and every source sample is fragmented and bereft of prior meaning . . . The samples are given meaning only when represented in the assemblage of the mix."

DJ Spooky ("Flow My Blood the DJ Said," 1996, p. 7)

"Information is transmitted in packets [CDs?] which rarely take the same route twice, and may take many different routes to a destination at which they weave themselves together again. Maps [samples?] of the network cannot be stolen, not because they are closely guarded, but because there is no definitive terrain."

Sadie Plant (*Zeros + Ones*, 1997, p. 49)

Information technology has flooded our airways, classrooms, homes, and communities with an unlimited amount of information that comes with no guide and no directions. We have to construct the meaning and those who do will not be branded plagiarists, thieves, or hacks but imaginative, creative, and ingenious. Rap artists are leading the way.

Rap Is an Authentic Copy

"In the beginning was the copy"

Donna Haraway (Simians, Cyborgs, and Women, 1991, p. 216)

"Rap technology . . . There is 'sampling': taking a portion . . . of a known or unknown record . . . and combining it in the overall mix . . . 'yo, man I hear Ellington, but you done put a new (w)rap on it!'"

Houston Baker ("Hybridity, the Rap Race, and Pedagogy for the 1990s," 1991, p. 201)

In a techno-culture the copy is the original. The key is what you do with the copy and how imaginatively you create another copy. In rap, sampling is sport but in bio-genetics, implant surgery, educational testing, advertising, politics, and economics, sampling is reality. In academic work we pretend to do original work, but our work is merely a copy of previous work.

Our creativity is not in our ability to patent or copyright something; this only stifles our potential. Our creativity is found in our ability to interpret.

Cyborgs/Rap Artists

"(C)yborg bodies can take pleasure in machine skill and thus have embodied reasons not to demonize it in favor of some mythical organic origin or unity . . . The cyborg . . . is . . . some human-machine, some machine."

> Chris Hables Gray and Steven Mentor (*The Cyborg Body Politic*, 1995, p. 230)

"Discotechnology was hybridized through the human hand and ear . . . The conversation produced a rap DJ who became a postmodern, ritual priest of sound . . . A reverse cyborgism was clearly at work in the rap conversation."

> Houston Baker ("Hybridity, the Rap Race, and Pedagogy for the 1990s," 1991, p. 200).

"About 10 percent of the U.S. population [by 1990 standards and definitions] are cyborgs, including people who have electronic pace-makers, artificial joints, prosthetic limbs, and artificial skin."

> N. Katherine Hayles (*Chaos Bound*, 1990, p. 276–77).

The cyborg is the norm today. Men and women strive for the perfect artificial body, parents seek out high-tech memory gimmicks for their children to enhance their learning capabilities, the drugs of choice are safe and bio-chemically synthesized, and techno-nerds and geeks search for ways to lose their "meat" in order to become one with cyberspace. Rap artists are just a different manifestation of the cyborg as they blend with their technology to form a vibration and sound that forms hip-hop culture. Rap is (an underground) techno-culture. Uncensored, beyond mainstream control, untamed, and rebellious. As much as adult, white, middle-class America hates it, they have to live with it because they have no choice. The noise is here to stay because it has latched itself to the future: information technology, cyborgs, and post-industrial life.

Rap as Post-Industrial Capitalism: The Rebellion Only Goes so Far

"It's been said that the Wu [Tang Clan] Enterprise or the Wu conglomerate is like an octopus; it reaches out with many tentacles."

> Kronick (*WU* issue, Fall 97, p. 29)

"The axis of competition is shifting from nations to these corporate alliances, and so is economic initiative and power."

> Chris Hables Gray and Steven Mentor (*The Cyborg Body Politic*, 1995, p. 233)

> "For unlike Punk, rap is less about rejecting the [multi-national] culture industry than demanding a place within it on its own terms."
>
> Tim Brennan ("Off the Gangsta Tip," 1994, p. 679)

Rap is as much a product of the shifting economic order of the world as it is a techno-culture. Like a multinational corporation, it transcends traditional barriers and reaches to control, manipulate, and profit from all that is within its grasp. A difference, though, between Nike, Ford, IBM, and other multinationals and rap artists is that rap artists and their recording companies are taking initiative and power to spread their influence on their own terms and rules. And Charlton Heston, William Bennett, Wal-Mart and the other boys don't like the fact that they are not playing by the "rules."

> "When personal consciousness is the single determining factor in social change, then all social problems . . . are seen as the result of personal failures and shortcomings."
>
> Andrew Ross (*Strange Weather*, 1991, p. 70–1)

In a multinational corporate world, individual responsibility, free will, and choice reign supreme. Action need not be taken; one need only make the right choices and will oneself to success. Rap artists embody this logic as they preach to the urban masses to pull themselves up and ignore the fact that the rest of the nation has abandoned them. If they can visualize themselves as rich, then it will happen. In a multinational corporate world, mainstream infomercial motivation speakers like Tony Robbins and Richard Simmons utilize the medium of television and video, and underground urban motivators utilize rap. Both accept consumerism as salvation: for $300 you can buy Robbins' tapes and for $15.95 you can have KRS-One's latest CD. If you believe in yourself, you might even will them into your possession.

The choice is yours

Vampires, Anti-Theory, and Style in the Ivory Tower

I suspect it's no coincidence that, as I neared the completion of my doctorate, I became obsessed (again, dredging up childhood/adolescent fascinations) with vampires. Ostensibly I was doing research. My dissertation focused on cultural studies and curriculum theory—vampires seemed particularly relevant with the television series *Buffy the Vampire Slayer* exceeding cult status and its star, Sarah Michelle Gellar, on the cover of *Rolling Stone*. "One of the real special things here," comments Gellar as she explains the show's popularity, and its relation to my work, "is that all the horror comes from high school, and let me tell you, high school is a very horrific place." (quoted in Goods, 1997, p. 3)

Accompanying this obsession were weekly tapings and screenings of *Buffy* (research!), increasingly frequent runs to the video store (research has its price), and the obligatory trip to my parents house to search for memorabilia from my youth that might prove useful (genealogical and archaeological excavations). And conversations. I think I queried everyone I encountered about their relationship with vampires in film and literature (one of my former students actually claims to be a member of a vampire clan!). One of the members of my doctoral committee even suggested that I explore the metaphor in relation to teacher education via evening course work—a day life of practice in the schools (slumbering time for real vampires), a pasty-faced netherworld of theory in night school. Fodder for a paper, for academic writing.

After all, vampires *do* relate to my academic work, even in (*especially* in) our postindustrial, postmodern world. "Vampires, " Gordon and Hollinger (1997) tell us, are "one of the most powerful archetypes bequeathed to us from the imagination of the nineteenth century" and are "a late twentieth-century cultural necessity." (p. 1) Hollinger (1997) continues by elucidating some of the "ways in which some vampire texts 'mirror' aspects of that peculiar human condition which has come to be termed 'postmodern,' since postmodernism is one of the more productive—and challenging—paradigms through which contemporary Western reality is currently being conceptualized." (p. 199) Noting that "certain previously sacrosanct boundaries—political, philosophical, conceptual, ethical, aesthetic—have tended to become problemitized" in postmodernity, Hollinger explains that

> (t)his deconstruction of boundaries helps to explain why the vampire is a monster-of-choice these days, since it is itself an inherently deconstructive figure: it is the monster that used to be human; it is the undead that used to be alive; it is the monster that *looks like us*. For this reason, the figure of the vampire always has the potential to jeopardize conventional distinctions between human and monster, between life an death, between ourselves and others. We look into the mirror it provides and we see a version of ourselves. Or, more accurately, keeping in mind the orthodoxy that vampires cast no mirror reflections, we look into the mirror and see nothing *but* ourselves (p. 201, emphasis in original).

I even discovered, with a tip from someone who had just finished her Ph.D., via someone at the same stage as me, a film that drives a stake through the heart (sorry) of vampirism and the academy, Abel Ferrara's (1995) *The*

Addiction. The film centers around a New York philosophy doctoral student who becomes a vampire while completing her dissertation. Roger Ebert (1995) succinctly summarizes the relationship between "real" and academic vampirism, noting

> On campuses, where *The Addiction* is likely to find an underground audience, the climax of the film may be wickedly popular. Kathleen passes her oral PhD exam, graduates, and leads fellow vampires in attacking the faculty party afterward. The white wine and philosophical chatter are replaced by a pulsating feeding frenzy. As a metaphor for campus student-teacher relationships, it will do (p. 2).

See, I told you I was doing research.

But this "research" posed problems, dilemmas of all sorts, from the beginning of my doctoral work. One of the reasons I entered a PhD program was to attempt to not only untangle the thorns that I had wrapped myself in during six years of high school teaching, but to do so without falling into the trap of academic elitism and exclusion that had previously led me to proclaim (loudly, I might add) that I would never pursue this terminal degree. In one of my first reaction papers in my doctoral work, I wrote the following about bell hooks' (1994) *Teaching to Transgress: Education and the Practice of Freedom*:

> I am intrigued by hooks' notion of "theory as liberatory practice" which she articulates in chapter 5. I believe that her indictments of academic alienation (from genuine social struggle and change) are valid. Theoretical thought is often nothing more than a . . . power game of word play that reinforces the very constructs it should be challenging. Western, linear, bifurcated epistemological modes privilege not only certain types of knowledge, but also how this knowledge is discussed (i.e., written, AND with a supposedly sophisticated vocabulary and style) . . . I guess I want to focus on the possibilities of developing an emancipatory praxis in schools with pedagogical possibilities perhaps emerging from the terrain of popular culture (rap/hip-hop music seems particularly relevant).

Right before beginning the official writing of my dissertation, I wrote these late night "notes," ideas for a future paper:

> *I wonder if we have lost our nerve, lost our way.*
> *Theory near the apocalyptic shimmers of a new millennium (which is an artificial construction/re-construction of time of course) seems uncertain of itself, perpetually adductive, and not always in an interdisciplinary, generative sense—but often formulaically, forging the facade of rigorous academic work. We prop up our ideas with words*

*culled from others—who perversely, and consciously or not, we attrib-
ute with "original" thoughts. Serres (1990/1995) says of this situation,
"Don't you laugh at learned articles in which each word is flanked by
a number, whose corresponding footnote attributes that word to an
owner, as though proper names were soon going to replace common
nouns" (p. 81)?*

*I wonder if we have lost the "working from within" that Pinar
(1994, pp. 7–11) articulated early in his writings—not the need for it,
but the re-presentative powers of it.*

*Theory, which of course is potentially "freeing," for all who
encounter the text(s) and its traces/lineages—we are "dreamt into existence by others" (Pinar 1994, pp. 235–252), right?—might also, in the
"teaching machine" (Spivak 1993), smother under its own pretenses—
smother us.*

And all in the name of the ironic "progress," of post-modernity.

*Even in the midst of unlayering, perhaps moving toward disman-
tling, historically oppressive notions like "rites of passage," we enact
them, we embody them (try moving through any academic field without a "working knowledge" of figures, individuals—not only concepts
and ideas—perhaps the author is not dead, never has been).*

*We theorize, we experiment, we move to undertake to expose the
"taken-for-granted"—all the while frequently oblivious to the "taken-
for-grantedness" of our theorizing, our movement.*

*Chilean poet Nicanor Parra (1985) recognized a similar malaise in
the poetry of the 1950s, writing and (with the assistance of Pablo
Neruda) publishing, Poems and Antipoems in 1954, declaring that for
the "old folks" poetry "was a luxury item," but for his generation, "It's
an absolute necessity." (p. xi)*

*I need not extrapolate any conclusions. Anyone interested in the his-
tories of ideas should find something in Parra that resonates (unless
there are still those noblesse out there who honestly feel that we only
exist to perpetuate an academic elite). Parra's "antipoetry was an open
challenge to those who believed that poetry should be rhetorical,
obscure, and dignified." (Unger, in Parra, 1985, p. ix)*

*Time to confront ourselves, our writings. "Rhetorical?" "Obscure?"
"Dignified?" Or hoping to achieve such status?*

*Edward Hirsch (1997) in his essay on post-war Polish poetry, "After
the End of the World," contends that "Every major Polish poet shows
an absolute distrust of any political creed or ideology," (p. 9) opting
instead to "keep human beings in full view." (p. 10) In fact, Hirsch
argues, humans actually fall out of sight, out of existence, if the violence
of language, an epistemic exclusion, precludes understanding. For
post-war Polish poets, who witnessed or in their writings bear witness
to that ultimate of human tragedies, genocide, "stylistic clarity is a
form of ethics . . . a response to ideological obfuscations." (p. 10)*

> *Serres again: "I don't like jargon . . . Technical vocabulary seems*
> *even immoral: it prevents the majority from participating in the con-*
> *versation, it eliminates rather than welcomes, and, further, it lies in*
> *order to express in a more complex way things that are often simple"*
> *(p. 25, emphasis in original).*
> *When we lose our nerve, when we hide behind the grandiosity of*
> *theory—what are we obfuscating?*
> *I'm not sure, and the longer I go on, the more I tangle myself in the*
> *thorns of theory, even if desiring an anti-theory.*

I don't know if it's really anti-theory that I'm after. But what I am looking for in my academic life/work is certainly, in cultural studies' terminology, "anti-disciplinary." (Nelson, Treichler, and Grossberg, 1992, p. 2) And yet "(i)nformed use of the term 'cultural studies,'" Edgerton (1996) contends, "is still a rare event in colleges of education." (p. 18)

Cultural studies, in its movement, in its inter- and anti-disciplinarity, and in its theoretical perspectives, undertakes to disrupt traditional, highly policed, academic boundaries. Specifically for the purposes of this essay, it serves to reconfigure that which lurks, as Pinar (1997) notes, in "all our scholarship" (p. 87)—namely reason. Regimes of reason are of course entrenched throughout the Western world and its institutions—it is as Foucault (1972) contends, the Western episteme, its "gaze," regulating each of us in complex ways. Cultural studies attempts to make use of reason in new ways (or make a new reason), ways that work within its institutional regimes to destabilize the center—the white, heterosexual, male world that for too long was considered "natural." Rap music epitomizes the fluid spaces that might point us toward new modes of knowing, new means of relating to the world.

Michel Serres (1983/1991) uses the metaphor of the "termitarium" to address the manners that "reason" has been narrowly construed, noting that reason is actually tripartite. The reason he invokes is "harmony" and "noise," as well as the "amalgam" of the two (p. 6). Working within his metaphor of the colony of termites, Serres notes how what initially appears to be the random placement of clay balls eventually begins to take the shape of the "termitarium." That is, the "effect of attraction" (p. 2) serves to order the termite activity—many still seem to randomly sow their clay balls, away from the center, but the attraction produces an increasingly larger (and powerful) pile. Thus, a regime of truth is established—the center appearing natural and progressive, the "others" marginal. The "dream of our reason," Serres writes, is to "weave together the stochastic sowing and the law of harmony, murky chance and clear necessity, order and dissemination." (p. 2)

But in spite of what may seem a tyranny of order, of attraction, of a naturalized center (a reason), there are possibilities. Serres notes:

> I am sure that here and there, all around, several individuals always continue to deposit their balls on the ground, while the Tower of Babel rises. These termites are the guardians of the possible. They sow a time of waiting, while the crystal next to them solidifies law and repetition (p. 3).

Reason has been narrowly conceived and appropriated for a multitude of hegemonic purposes. Serres writes, "A certain rationalism . . . took pleasure in eliminating or filtering multiplicity and confusion, holding onto a little less than a third of what it called the truth." (p. 6) It is time, Public Enemy (1988) tells us, to "bring the noise" so that we might witness the emergent knowledges of the "other" two-thirds of Serres' equation. Cultural studies, I believe, does this.

Cultural studies epitomizes Serres' vision of the cross-breeding of intellectual disciplines, which he views as a more appropriate mode of existing in and relating to the world. As such, it "possesses neither a well-defined methodology nor clearly demarcated fields of investigation" (During, 1993, p. 1), except, of course, for "culture understood as the texts and practices of everyday life." (Storey, 1996, p. 2)

One particularly generative approach to cultural studies is Edgerton's (1996) "notion of a cross-cultural 'conversation' that neither reduces one culture to the concerns of another, nor proliferates into infinity the 'multiplicities' or 'pluralities' of human concerns." (p. 15) This approach is generative because it acknowledges both the "political" nature of cultural studies (also see Storey, 1996, p. 2) and the "hybrid" nature of some popular culture. Rap is an excellent example of a post-colonial sense of "creolization" (see Brathwaite, in Ashcroft, Griffith, and Tiffin, 1995) not only in its aesthetics but also in its peculiar dialectic of performer and audience. Largely consumed by white suburbanites, rap is certainly appropriated, but it is also transformative—the very nature of engagement and "conversation" leaves text and audience altered. As Edgerton notes, "encounters between cultures shape and transform those cultures . . . neither exists as pure and unmediated—outside a conversation." (pp. 15–16)

Pinar (1994) elucidates some of the curricular implications for a new "architecture of self" that are quite germane to cultural studies in his reading of Foucault (mindful of the complex relationships between bodies, space, power, and knowledge). In identifying Foucault's alliance with "possibilities, exclusions, repressions (through) language and discourse" (p. 213), Pinar articulates the "subversive" nature of Foucault's positioning. For educational theorizing, we must imagine the realities and possibilities of language and relationality, that, at first blush are unimaginable. These might include, for instance, the meditative rather than the calculative, the intuitive rather than the rationalistic, the imagistic rather than the conceptual . . . The excluded and marginalized elements become central, and the discursive formation that is the political present is perverted (p. 214).

Rap/hip-hop aesthetics might nudge us toward such possibilities. In fact, hip-hop (which is in large measure revealed through its physicality, its gestures, its non-verbal postures) is especially concerned with the "horizontal plane" of the body as a site of discursive practices (Pinar, Reynolds, Slattery, and Taubman 1995, p. 463). But placing such practices under the panoptic gaze of Western logocentrism ignores and debases the localizing powers exerted in the development of such cultures. Additionally, one might question how the privileging of language discounts sound and aesthetic sensibilities as possible discursive sites, thus recentering language.

Potter (1995) locates as a site of possibility much of rap music's "attitude towards the police," noting the resistance evident in the "postcolonial urban landscapes described by KRS-One, Paris, or Ice Cube." (p. 87) Rose (1996), elaborates in her essay, "Hidden Politics: Discursive and Institutional Policing of Rap Music," that the "struggle over access to public space, community resources (etc.)" is "policed" institutionally in a "complex and interactive process," and that this struggle has "profound potential as a basis for a language of liberation." (p. 253) Although I agree that rap's counterdiscourses are significant to political action, I believe that the real issue at hand is indeed a struggle over modes of knowing. When N.W.A. snarls "Fuck Tha Police;" when Paris (1994) explores his fantasy of destroying the "ghetto Gestapo;" when Boogie Down Productions (in Rose, 1994b, p. 107) asks "Who Protects Us From You?" of the police, we are witnessing more than simply a resistance/rebellion against the physical presence and racist practices of urban police officers. We are seeing, and maybe more importantly hearing, a challenge to the Western episteme that cannot simply be formulated in terms of resistance. It is the splendid cacophony that Serres says has always been fundamental to knowledge but has hitherto been silenced or filtered elsewhere.

Cultural studies thus provides possibilities for movement in the "currere of marginality" of which Edgerton speaks. The gaze of reason, Pinar (1997) reminds us, subjugates in complex manners. But by identifying and exploring the marginal spaces, or more appropriately, the subterranean caverns where cultural forms like rap music dwell in all of their thunderous, pulsing intensity, we might find "passages out of the center toward the margins and from the margins toward the center" where we might "be" in the "body" as "breathing, desiring bodies moving with others through lived space." (Pinar, 1997, p. 105)

It might sound, as Boogie Down Productions (1988) says, a little "unrational," its timbre unrecognizable or "noisy" to the Western ear.

And cultural studies might, in its treacherous navigation against the maelstrom of academic disciplines, infuse the academy with what the poet Charles Bukowski (1975) calls "style." "To do a dangerous thing with style," Bukowski says, "is what I call art."

It's what I call living in academia.

Note

1. Previously published in *Taboo: The Journal of Culture and Education*, 5(2), 103–131. Used by permission.

References

Ashcroft, B., Griffith, G., and Tiffin, H., eds. *The Post-Colonial Studies Reader*. New York: Routledge, 1995.

Baker, H. "Hybridity, the Rap Race, and Pedagogy for the 1990s." In *Technoculture*, edited by A. Ross and C. Penley. Minneapolis, MN: University of Minnesota Press, 1991.

Boogie Down Productions. *By All Means Necessary*. New York: Zomba Recording Corporation, 1988.

Brennan, T. "Off the Gangsta Tip: A Rap Appreciation, or Forgetting about Los Angeles." *Critical Inquiry*, 20 (1994): 663–693.

Bukowski, C. *Style. On Poems and Insults*. San Francisco, CA: Bitter Lemon Records, 1975.

DJ Spooky. An excerpt from a recombinant text entitled: "Flow My Blood the DJ Said." In the notes for the compact disc *Songs of a Dead Dreamer*. New York: Asphodel, 1996.

During, S., ed. *The Cultural Studies Reader*. New York: Routledge, 1993.

Ebert, R. Review of the film *The Addiction*. *The Chicago Sun Times*. (Online), 1995. Available at http://www.suntimes.com/ebert_reviews/1995/10/1003731.html

Edgerton, S. H. *Translating the Curriculum: Multiculturalism into Cultural Studies*. New York: Routledge, 1996.

Ferguson, J. "The Dialectics of Dance." *Huh*, 10 (June 1996).

Ferrara, A. (Director). *The Addiction*. October Films, 1995.

Foucault, M. *The Archaeology of Knowledge*. Translated by M. Smith. New York: Pantheon Books, 1972.

Gibson, W. "Johnny Mnemonic." In *Burning Chrome*. New York: Ace, 1986.

Gilroy, P. *The Black Atlantic: Modernity and Double Consciousness*. Cambridge, MA: Harvard University Press, 1993.

Giroux, H. "Doing Cultural Studies: Youth and the Challenge of Pedagogy." *Harvard Educational Review*, 64(3), 1994: 278–307.

Goods, L. "Sarah Michelle Gellar: Cult of the Vampire." *People Profiles Online*, 1997. Available at http://www.pathfinder.com/people/profiles/gellar

Gordon, J. and Hollinger, V. (Eds.). *Blood Read: The Vampire as Metaphor in Contemporary Culture*. Philadelphia, PA: University of Pennsylvania Press, 1997.

Gray, C., and Mentor, S. "The Cyborg Body Politic and the New World Order." In *Prosthetic Territories: Politics and Hypertechnologies*, edited by G. Brahm, Jr., and M. Driscoll. Boulder, CO: Westview, 1995.

Grossberg, L. *Dancing in Spite of Myself: Essays on Popular Culture*. Durham, NC: Duke, 1997.

———. "On Postmodernism and Articulation: An Interview with Stuart Hall." In *Stuart Hall: Critical Dialogues in Cultural Studies*, edited by D. Morley and K-H. Chen. New York: Routledge, 1996.

Haraway, D. *Modest_Witness @ Second_Millenniun—FemaleMan_Meets_OncoMouse: Feminism and Technoscience*. New York, Routledge, 1997.

————. *Simians, Cyborgs, and Women: The Reinvention of Nature*. New York: Routledge, 1991.

Hayles, N.K. *Chaos Bound*. Ithaca, NY: Cornell, 1990.

Hebdige, D. *Hiding in the Light*. New York: Routledge, 1988.

————. *Cut 'N' Mix: Culture, Identity, and Caribbean Music*. London: Methuen, 1987.

Hirsch, E. "After the End of the World." *American Poetry Review*, 26 (2), March/April 1997: 9–12.

Hollinger, V. "Fantasies of Absence: The Postmodern Vampire." In *Blood Read: The Vampire as Metaphor in Contemporary Culture*, edited by J. Gordon and V. Hollinger. Philadelphia, PA: The University of Pennsylvania Press, 1997.

Hooks, B. *Teaching to Transgress: Education as the Practice of Freedom*. New York: Routledge, 1994.

Kronick. *The underground chronicle*. Hollywood, CA: Meshack Blaq, 1997.

KRS-ONE *I Got Next*. New York: Jive, 1997.

Marcus, G. *The Dustbin of History*. Cambridge, MA: Harvard U. Press, 1995.

McCaffery, L. "Introduction: The Desert of the Real." In *Storming the Reality Studio: A Casebook of Cyberpunk and Postmodern Fiction*, edited by L. McCaffery. Durham, NC: Duke University Press, 1991.

McLaren, P. *Revolutionary multiculturalism: Pedagogies of dissent for the new millennium*. Boulder, Westview, 1997.

Nelson, C., Treichler, P. A., and Grossberg, L. "Cultural Studies: An Introduction." In *Cultural Studies*, edited by L. Grossberg, P. A. Treichler, and C. Nelson. New York: Routledge, 1992.

N.W.A. *Straight Outta Compton*. Hollywood, CA: Priority Records, 1988.

Paris *Guerilla Funk*. Los Angeles: Priority Records, 1994.

Parra, N. *Antipoems: New and Selected*. New York: New Directions, 1985.

Perkins, W.E. *Droppin' Science: Critical Essays on Rap Music and Hip Hop Culture*. Philadelphia, PA: Temple University Press, 1996.

Pinar, W. "Regimes of Reason and the Male Narrative Voice." In *Representation and the Text: ReFraming the Narrative Voice*, edited by W. G. Tierney and Y. S. Lincoln. Albany, NY: SUNY Press, 1997.

————. *Autobiography, Politics, and Sexuality: Essays in Curriculum Theory, 1972–1992*. New York: Peter Lang, 1994.

Pinar, W., Reynolds, W., Slattery, P., and Taubman, P. *Understanding Curriculum: An Introduction to the Study of Historical and Contemporary Curriculum Discourses*. New York: Peter Lang, 1995.

Plant, S. *Zeros + Ones: Digital Women + The New Technoculture*. New York: Doubleday, 1997.

Plotnitsky, A. *Complimentarity: Anti-Epistemology after Bohr and Derrida*. Durham, NC: Duke, 1994.

Potter, R. *Spectacular Vernaculars: Hip-Hop and the Politics of Postmodernism*. Albany, NY: SUNY, 1995.

Public Enemy. *It Takes a Nation of Millions to Hold Us Back*. New York: Def Jam Recordings, 1988.

————. "Caught, Can We Get a Witness?" On *It Takes a Nation of Millions to Hold Us Back*. New York: Def Jam Recordings, 1988 (b).

Rose, T. "Hidden Politics: Discursive and Institutional Policing of Rap Music." In *Droppin' science: Critical essays on rap music and hip hop culture*, edited by W. E. Perkins. Philadelphia, PA: Temple University Press, 1996.

————. "A Style Nobody Can Deal With: Politics, Style and the Postindustrial City in Hip Hop." In *Microphone Fiends: Youth Music & Youth Culture*, edited by A. Ross and T. Rose. New York: Routledge, 1994 (a).

————. *Black Noise: Rap Music and Black Culture in Contemporary America*. Hanover, NH: Wesleyan University Press, 1994 (b).

Ross, A. *Strange Weather: Culture, Science and Technology in the Age of Limits*. New York: Verso, 1991.

Scott, J. "Critical Aesthetics on the Down Low." *The Minnesota Review* (43,44), 1995: 164–171.

Serres, M. *Rome: The Book of Foundations*. Translated by F. McCarren. Stanford, CA: Stanford University Press, 1991. (Original work published 1983.)

Serres, M., with Latour, B. *Conversations on Science, Culture, and Time*. Translated by R. Lapidus. Ann Arbor, MI: University of Michigan Press, 1995. (Original work published 1990.)

Spirak, G. *Outside in the Teaching Machine*. London: Routledge, 1993.

Storey, J. *Cultural Studies and the Study of Popular Culture: Theories and Methods*. Athens, GA: University of Georgia Press, 1996.

2

The New Vocationalism and the Marketing of Higher Education

6

Selling the Dream of Higher Education: Marketing Images of University Life

PAUL FARBER AND GUNILLA HOLM

Introduction

Institutions have a history; they change over time. The modern university is not what it was, nor is it what it will become. But in the midst of change, there are deep interests expressed in efforts to identify what is of value in the institution that has arisen in its current form, as well as in efforts to evoke a sense of where it is headed (or, for that matter, to head off further change or its possible demise). Such interests take many forms, including various kinds of formal pronouncements and official publications concerning particular universities, as when a university president gives an address about the state of the institution. But there are other ways to communicate notions about universities today, ways that in fact reach a much wider audience than any particular address might do. These include the variety of ways that universities now engage in marketing campaigns.

Some university marketing is highly selective. Fund-raising efforts target people with money. Other campaigns deal more broadly with the public image of the university. It is the broader campaigns, particularly in the familiar form of the 30-second TV promo, that are the focus of this paper. What aspects of the modern university are distilled for the purpose of conveying an impression of what is admirable about universities today?

The Political Context of Marketing Campaigns

The modern corporate university encompasses a variety of purposes and seeks to satisfy a variety of real and perceived needs. From the most general and detached societal perspective, large universities are entrusted with the task of advancing important domains of knowledge, as well as fostering the skills, capabilities, and desirable attitudes of students. Particular interests generate a variety of perspectives. Business and professional interests expect the university to maintain a flow of skilled workers and useful ideas and techniques. From the perspective of alumni, the continued good name and positive standing of their alma mater remains a concern. From the perspective of students—as well as potential students and their parents—the university is a site of promise, excitement, and concern; it is both a springboard of future plans and a place where diverse cultures intersect, one or more of which appeals to most who choose or seek to attend. One formulation of this latter insight includes the academic, collegiate, vocational, or rebel cultures (see Sperber, 2000). That is, the university is a place to study and gain knowledge, to party and socialize, to pick up the credentials and training necessary for particular career paths, or to explore and engage in forms of life contesting the beliefs and values of mainstream culture. Given such a diversity of wants, the potential for dissatisfaction is high when viewing the university from any particular perspective.

This inherent instability is disconcerting, especially given the fact that universities exist in a competitive environment. Declining degrees of public support from the states paired with the large number of colleges and universities, including many either founded or greatly expanded following the G.I. Bill and the arrival of the baby boomers, intensify the competition. New threats have emerged in recent years with the ascent of virtual programs, distance education, siteless universities, and related entrepreneurial approaches to specific domains of study and training.

The university is pulled in multiple, sometimes contradictory, directions. High profile research—and researchers—is a costly priority, especially when set against the demands for high quality, student-centered undergraduate teaching. Entrepreneurial programs are designed to create new markets for students but draw funds from traditional programs that, in order to flourish, need also to grow. Accommodating the interests and needs of students concerned with careers and credentials creates a climate that is frustrating for those in academia seeking intellectual stimulation (including, of course, faculty members themselves, given their own academic predilections). And the pursuit of a campus culture stimulating for collegians—the "beer and circus" approach—drains budgets for academic and scholarly pursuits.

Universities are, in short, seething, anxious, and contentious places. Louis Menand, writing about academic politics in the famous nineteenth century Dartmouth case, characterized the politics of the dispute in a way bound to register with readers familiar with academia today: "the issues were myriad, they were interrelated in arcane ways, and they were fantastically petty." (2001, p. 239) They are sites of intercultural turmoil, where uncertainties about direction and a fundamental ambiguity of mission erode trust, keep everyone wary, and frustrate on a daily basis the diverse dreams people hold as to what the university ought to be. Seeking to be many things, the university is never enough of any one of them to suit the diverse and necessarily partial preferences of those involved.

Despite the frustration, so much is invested in universities by so many that they continue to achieve part of each of their diverse promises and remain vitally important institutions in contemporary society. But the frustrations do take a toll, and in order to survive, let alone to flourish, universities struggle on several fronts. Among these are the internal and external political battles: the wrangling within university administrative circles for shares of the total budget and the competition externally for state funding and private gifts. Universities must also compete for students (and the support of prospective students' families) through a variety of school contacts and admissions department activities. Finally, and related to all of these others, is the public relations battle to create and maintain positive public perceptions of the university. This involves focused efforts to augment the reputation of particular universities and the marketing of their name and what they provide. This will be our focus here.

Managing the public image of the modern university is fascinating, in part, because of the way it is affected by and in turn bears on all of the struggles alluded to thus far. The image must convey something of the multiplicity of university pursuits and missions—the variety of things those involved want the university to be and to do. But given the competitive environment, both for funds and for students, the public image must elide the internal strife and contradictions and convey instead a grand harmony of diverse ends. The ability to do so, to manage public perceptions about the university's capacity to be all things that its diverse participants, supporters, and "customers"—current and potential—want it to be is unmistakably important.

How is this done? By what magic are the ambiguities and contentiousness, the bitter cross-purposes and in-fighting, converted to the common dream of a high status institutional profile? One prominent example of this magic is the 30-second, made-for-TV promotional spot. We explore the way that makers of these commercials address a seemingly daunting task. It is daunting because, on the one hand, a university is, as we have indicated, actually a loose confederation of competing, and sometimes conflicting, cultures, programs, units, and purposes. And on the other hand, the similarities of universities, within the broad general categories, are substantial; their distinguishing characteristics are few compared with overriding common features of structure, organization, size, and so on. The university's effort to manage public perceptions thus faces a dual challenge. Each seeks both to harmonize the conflicts and to distinguish itself from its competition, i.e., to underscore common perceptions of "essential" aspects of what a university is, while highlighting its own "unique" qualities.

In examining how this is done, we hope to capture something of the guiding desire that propels large universities today. What dreams are awakened? What desires are promised satisfaction? What goods are harmonized in the dense text that results when universities advertise themselves on TV?

Public Interest Promos

This study is based on a sample of some 45 university promos aired during the college football season of 1997, up to and including the end-of-season bowl games.[1] The advertisements in question were provided by the various universities in fulfillment of a part of network agreements supplying airtime for public interest promotional spots. Clearly these spots are meant to cast the various universities that created them in a good light. The question is, what does the spot do (or at least what is it intended to do) in that regard? What images and themes provide (or at least are believed to provide) a satisfying message about the institution composing it for that purpose? In what follows, we will attend first to the explicit messages conveyed in particular spots and explore their unifying and organizing slogans. We will then turn to consider certain identifiable tensions that the set of commercials, taken as a whole, bring into view.

Proclaiming Merits: Slogans of Pride and Virtue

"A future of unlimited potential!"

"Where the world turns for big ideas"

"Skills for the global marketplace"

"Taking you anywhere you want to go"

"Meeting the challenges of our world"

"Where big ideas come in small classes"

"Bringing dreams to life"

"From here everything is possible"

"Education for the future"

And so on. University budgets include a line for those churning out slogans like these, to say nothing of the slick packaging in which they are framed for wide dispersal. It is not difficult to let such efforts slide past along with "Coke is it!" or Nike's "Just do it" (to say nothing of Dow Chemical's reminder that "Dow brings good things to life"). The comical possibilities have also been tapped, as in George Felton's wry commentary in the *Chronicle of Higher Education* where, for example, one college's slogan about a "Unique Alpine setting" is taken as an academic way of saying "Tahoe, baby, ski your shins off.." (Felton, 2001, p. B5) The advantage of irony is that it relieves the feeling of being slightly soiled by earnestly manipulative and misleading marketeering or of worrying too much about the soul of a place that would devolve to pandering.

But there's a suitably academic response possible as well. Let's analyze the phenomena a little more closely. One way to view the promos is to see them individually in relation to the particular categories of desire to which they speak. There is an identifiable pitch evident in each of the short works in question, often built round a particular unifying slogan. The pitch typically reflects, and in turn reinforces, certain perceived goods that can be associated with institutions of higher education. This is the thematic core of these concentrated, often visually busy texts. And in this, universities are simply working to secure their place in a world made up of, among other things, a large number of corporate entities that are more or less associated with particular goods or services, about which we have been encouraged to have a vaguely positive feeling.

In the case of university promos, the slogans all serve to proclaim and highlight particular merits of the universities in question and, by way of standard advertising synecdoche, attach each university's good name to the satisfaction of particular desires. The promos we viewed may be grouped by the kinds of desire they evoke.

One category of desire is rather mundane and pragmatic in nature. It is the desire that universities repay the investment made in them by enhancing the public good. Some schools focus their operative slogans on aspects of the public good and offer explicit reminders of the kind of benefits that follow from public support of the schools in question. Auburn is, for example, "A university putting knowledge to work." This is an instance of a university pursuing the line some private corporations have taken in promoting their reputations over and above particular products. This involves reference to the way the public benefits from the organization's expertise. Hence, some of Auburn's "most important victories" include the jobs it has created and the drinking water it has brought to Alabama. Similarly, the University of Missouri links itself to the image of "little Sam," an infant saved by some unspecified procedures and expertise at the University hospital (presumably), another example of how "great beginnings happen at MU."

Missouri's ad cleverly links the public service message with a second prominent category of desire, one focusing attention on the university's perceived role in launching students on their way in the world, the aspirations of individuals (students and potential students, as well as their parents). Consider Michigan, for example: "From here everything is possible." Universities have a long tradition, evident in countless commencement addresses—for example, of celebrating in general terms their capacity to act as a springboard for the young pursuing a dream or a job. Michigan uses a famous alumnus, Mike Wallace of CBS *60 Minutes* fame, to express the sentiment in verse. His reading ends with these lines, "you're on to big things and it's your turn to try, life is a journey so set your sites high." With less flare, Big Ten opponent Purdue spells it out in more prosaic terms, "A future of unlimited potential," in this case because of Purdue professors who care about your success. This category of sloganeering most clearly reflects the need for schools to market themselves and to compete for qualified students. The university's pitch is in effect an elaboration of "ring around the collar," where the brighter future follows from making wise choices today.

But what is it that makes the future bright for those enrolled in particular schools? In most cases, like those above, vocational success and security are the principal concern. Numerous ads tout the careerist advantages that certain university programs provide. But an offshoot of this calls attention to a different kind of aspiration also associated with higher education. At the center of this is the desire of those whose academic ideal centers on the promotion of intellectual activity. Take Northwestern, for example, "Where big ideas come in small classes." Some portion of higher education is occupied by those who think of it in terms of intellectual activity, the life of the mind, and devoted teaching. It may, as Murray Sperber (2000) suggests, be a small part, but it's there, and it does get touted by schools that want to highlight their alignment with more selective private institutions. In the Northwestern spot, diverse fields of study are suggested in images of concentrated engagement. Likewise, Michigan runs an ad focused on teaching and open-ended learning, where one student praises a teacher for "getting me to question myself," another for ideas that "I'm going to take with me the rest of my life."

Another offshoot from the family of spots addressing individual aspirations is a small number of promos that center on desires that have to do with reaching out to a wider, more mysterious, and intriguing world. Some university ads feature slogans proclaiming their standing with respect to more global ambitions, stimulating global perspectives. An example is Notre Dame: "Our classroom is the world." This ad, filmed at Notre Dame's campus in Israel, is a prominent example of the desirability of being situated in the global community, of offering a link between the known and the unknown, the other. Michigan State puts it more crassly: "creating skills for the global marketplace," though its piece evokes the wonders of travel to exotic places, locating wide-eyed Spartans in Kenya, El Salvador, and Nepal.

Another category of evoked desire centers on the standing of particular universities themselves. Some of the ads call attention to the fact that university reputations are arrayed hierarchically in most people's minds. Many schools use their advertising dollars in an effort to secure a loftier standing by way of spots that are designed to tout specific competitive accomplishments. Clemson University, for example: "Building a national university through national caliber people." In some cases it seems that institutions, too, can have a chip on their shoulder. We learn about Kansas State's record of scholarship winners, New Mexico's $200 million in research support, and Oklahoma's National Merit Scholars. As a selling point, these accomplishments cut two ways, of course. The reported accomplishments are impressive in themselves, but at the same time the announcement of them serves as an implicit reminder that these schools are striving to be seen in the big league with places that no doubt could list more than a few accomplishments of their own. As happens with individuals as well, schools trying too hard to demonstrate their standing run the risk of exhibiting the conceit of the also-ran.

A strong contrast is evident in a curious set of promos that evoke a most general, amorphous desire—the wish to stand apart, to be unique. Particular promos are organized around a slogan addressing the desire that universities, that is those speaking for and associating themselves closely with universities, have to distinguish themselves from higher education in general. Slogans evoke the aura of uniqueness that certain places claim for themselves. Hence, "There's no place like Nebraska." In the spot culminating in this slogan, we see pictures in the collection of the university's art museum (apparently) and are "reminded" that Nebraska, too, is singular and fine, a place apart. There's no need to try to convince or persuade; the narrator (Dick Cavett) already knows and softly exclaims the obvious. Promos such as this one are imbued with confidence, constructed to function like a reminder of the special glories of certain places, even if many or most of those viewing the piece have never been there. Indeed, the spot works on that very difference; if you've been there, you know it's true, and if you haven't, no particular information would be sufficient for you to understand. When, in one Ohio State spot, the speaker intones, "I'll always be a Buckeye," the point is that really only one who is one could possibly understand his full meaning. In spots such as these, vague allusions to place signal and seek to satisfy the desire to identify with something unique, a place apart.

In summary, particular university promos address any of a number of particular kinds of desire. These include the desire to achieve (or at least be perceived as achieving) worthwhile results benefiting the public, the desire to be a springboard for individual aspirations, the desire to gain rank in the hierarchy of university reputations, and the desire to be regarded as uniquely dear. When universities advertise themselves, these desires generate the themes that recur. This is not surprising, though it does seem rather meager. Taken individually, university promos tend to play it safe, highlighting winning themes and avoiding the myriad issues that constitute institutional life. These distinct messages run together, however, in ways that are more revealing.

Enduring Tensions

Viewed collectively, university promos suggest a set of intriguing, interlocking tensions at the center of university life today. We will focus on three thematically central issues that the promos, taken together, suggest and highlight.

Theme 1: Entering into a Tradition of Service and Gaining a Competitive Edge

The first theme centers on the fact that for some time, higher education both has provided an important point of entry into various kinds of meaningful, tradition-bound work, including most professions, and has served as a springboard for diverse kinds of personal ambition. Universities help one to fit in and break out, or better perhaps, they help most to fit in and some to set themselves apart in various domains of expertise.

The promos pick up this theme. University promos often intimate that attendance brings one into some line of meaningful work, preparing one to enter the larger community and serve it well. The vocational usefulness of university studies is a common theme. Scenes of earnest study are commonplace, as are applied forms of activity. At the University of New Mexico, for example, the focus is on "meeting the challenges of a new world." Niches are conveyed, opportunities evident. At Colorado "learning takes place inside the mind and outside the classroom," for example, "helping neighborhood children learn in school . . . meeting the needs of an evolving workplace." These kinds of references align, of course, with the strongly vocational ways of thinking about higher education that currently predominate. There's a place for you, too, to fit in, the ads suggest, and join the tradition of university-grounded work. This theme generates a welcoming and reassuring tone in many of the promos, with the emphasis on coming on board and finding one's place.

The vocational concern leads in some cases, however, to an emphasis on the competitive structure of opportunity, the need to gain an edge, and the role particular universities can play in providing that advantage. Purdue, for example, places students in contact with "professors who care about your success" and delivers the "cutting edge-knowledge" that success depends upon. At Michigan State, students study abroad, "creating skills for the global marketplace." In promos of this kind claims about the capacity of certain schools to give students a competitive advantage imply doubts about traditional programs and play to viewer concerns about getting ahead. The first tension then reveals a kind of vocational ambiguity, whether one turns to higher education to find a calling to which one can give oneself over or finds some training that can propel one ahead.

Theme 2: Teaching the Young and Exploring the Horizons of Research

A second tension centers on university faculty. What is central to the role of professor? Commitment to the practice of teaching is one thing often valued, even expected. But so, too, is the idea, long rooted in the academic profession, of work on the frontiers of knowledge. As Mark Schwehn (1992) comments in *Exiles from Eden*, many university professors today, when asked about their work, scarcely think of teaching, interactions with students, service, and so on; instead, they identify their work as the things they do at the edge of their academic specialization, the things that most distinguish them as unique.

This tension emerges also with respect to the image of the professor in the promos. On the one hand, there are the reassuring reminders of the classroom setting, familiar, close, and personal. At Michigan, a student speaks of "a great teacher . . . he allowed me to get closer to my dreams." For another student, the teacher helped him "to question myself, to question who I am." While yet another encountered "ideas I'm going to take with me the rest of my life." At Ohio State University, a physics professor comments about her teaching role with undergraduate students: "it's my passion." In one other Big Ten school, we find "that big ideas come in small classes" and see Northwestern professors attending to 6 students in a lab, 15 in a drama class, and 30 learning their biology from someone who has developed a flu vaccine. Finally, at Florida State University the point is summed up this way: "to be a professor is to bring ideas to life, to enrich young minds and gently guide, pondering ancient verities and finding new truths, it is making the world a better place by sharing what we know."

On the other hand, the classroom gives way to the laboratory, and the image of path-breaking research accomplishments is foregrounded. Purdue's faculty are "blazing the research trail," for example, while Penn State ranks first in the nation in faculty Fulbright scholars, second in industry-sponsored research. UCLA puts the point in a somewhat more enticing form, asking "where was the internet first created?" and "who is a leader in the battle for a cure for AIDS?" The exciting thing about university faculty is their work at the cutting edge, especially when it concerns problems that are widely comprehensible. So come to a place, some promos maintain, where faculty work on the farthest fringe of specialized research; look for the signs of how well they distance themselves from the mainstream and ordinary work in their diverse fields.

Theme 3: Coming Home and Leaving on a Journey

While each of the tensions above has to do with what universities and the people in them do, a third has more to do with how they are understood to be. Universities generate for many people a sense of belonging, a valuable part of their identity. But higher education is also, at least part of the time, about leaving provincial viewpoints and local understandings behind, of breaking away. This theme, too, the promos underscore.

Whatever one was before arriving at a university, it seems, being there, and having been, transforms one's identity (or so it seems). "I'll always be a Buckeye." This phrase captures a notion widely evoked in these pieces to the effect that one's identity is bound up with belonging to the evoked community of the university. Going to college is a kind of coming home, finding oneself and belonging. In one ad, Badgers—young and old, men and women, black and white—stand on the steps and sing Wisconsin's Alma Mater. It's an affecting piece, partly for the faces, partly the setting. They are arrayed on the steps of an elegant, pillared building on campus and thus convey physically the unity of feeling centered on their stately home.

The visual metaphors of sacred space recur often. More than any other image of campus or campus life, university promos feature some select towered, well-pillared, or monumental building, often from on high or lit up at night. The evocation is of sacred, long-standing presence. It's been here a long time and will stand proudly into the future. Football stadiums, leafy walkways, and various kinds of labs featuring highly focused engagement in an atmosphere of hushed attentiveness are also familiar accoutrements of enduring, sacred space. This is the place to be, many promos suggest, and once you have arrived, it will be part of you always.

On the other hand, the university is a springboard, a place for stepping out, a release to the pursuit of one's dreams. In the Michigan spot featuring Mike Wallace's reading of the poem, "Life is a journey . . . ," images depict scenes of young people leaving their separate homes and heading out. The university conveys them *from* home in this instance. In this view, the university is instrumental but incidental to the search for oneself and one's dream. Uncomfortable associations with being tied down to a place and its traditions are replaced with images of adventure, a world beyond.

A most vivid example comes from the University of Southern California, a spot composed of continuously overlapping images suggestive of a multicultural melange of faces and artifacts that beckon a new millennium in which USC is for "people who like tomorrow more than yesterday, hard questions better than easy answers," and so on. This exemplifies the theme of transcending specific locations, traditions, identifications, and one's circumstantial home and roots. The university is just the ticket.

In these three ways then, university promos exhibit some of the enduring tensions of higher education. Universities extend a nexus of countervailing hopes, wishes, and needs. Taken together, university promos hint at the kind of ambiguity that universities continue to embody.

Putting Promos in Perspective

All three of the tensions we have introduced underscore a deeper ambivalence about what is most wanted and appreciated about universities. Admired for their reassuring, stable, and familiar traditions of teaching and support for those who come to belong there, universities are admired, too, for their restless capacity for launching journeys, breaking down barriers, and exploring horizons. This ambivalence is not going to vanish any time soon, and perhaps that's a good thing. There is room in the world for both kinds of institutions, as well as institutions managing both kinds of role. The small window that the promos open to view this ambivalence suggests the range of considerations that must be managed: how to build upon thick traditions of belonging, identification, and responsive teaching while providing institutional support for individual efforts to break with tradition and fixed frames of reference.

But while manageable, this ambivalence complicates satisfaction of the diverse kinds of desire to which universities attend. The simplistic kinds of desire that frame the way many people view the university, some of which are highlighted in one or another of the promos, often are frustrated by the way universities manage their inherent complexities. And to the extent that university promotional campaigns succeed in selling certain ideas about the good that particular schools will bring about, they probably enhance the difficulty of supporting the full range of goods that particular institutions pursue. Consider, for example, the way a school's marketing based on vocational results (or big-time sports) undercuts the efforts of those, say, seeking to engage students in rigorous general education in the humanities. It is just those aspects of higher education that are least popular that are likely to be undercut, or altogether marginalized, as a result.

The issue is important when one reflects upon the kinds of things that university promos do minimize in the portrayal of higher education. Where, for example, is the practice of liberal learning (the vision Martha Nussbaum (1998) represents, for example, in *Cultivating Humanity*) and teaching the conflicts (as in Gerald Graff's [1993] *Beyond the Culture Wars*)? Absent also are the kinds of opportunities universities present to encounter cultural difference and living issues concerning the politics of recognition and difference (see Charles Taylor, *Multiculturalism*, 1994). Universities are inherently complex with respect to the goods they seek to bring about, many of which are remotely related, if at all, to those characteristically presented in the promos. To the extent that promos cultivate certain kinds of expectations about university life, their tilt away from some of the more contentious, demanding, and disconcerting goods that universities sometimes deliver undercuts those goods still further.

These particular concerns point to a more general one concerning the possibility that universities may be compromising a core value of modern higher education by engaging in marketing campaigns. The issue encapsulates the particular kinds of distortions mentioned above. The idea is this: Fundamental to the conception of the university, and in particular the profession of university teaching and scholarship, is the notion that it is in the public good to support of open-ended, rigorous inquiry. The struggle to establish the modern tradition of academic freedom was grounded on this idea. And the acid test of it is the continued sanctity of the university with respect to the pursuit of obscure, unpopular, contentious, or otherwise unsettling ideas and ways of thinking.

This is not to deny the other roles that universities have come to have, vocational skill-building, the development of particular forms of expertise, traditions of socialization, and so on. But of these roles, the most distinctive and vulnerable role is that of protector of just those lines of thought and inquiry that are most challenging of received ideas and opinion. Perhaps our personal orientation here emerges all too strongly, but as we see it, what the university provides those of us who now inhabit it as professors is the freedom to pursue difficult ideas wherever they lead (within the constraints of whatever disciplinary or other limitations we bring to the matter). Clearly such freedom and security is questionable, and much of what universities do with respect to the development and application of specialized kinds of marketable expertise can survive its elimination. The institution may evolve in just that way, with commercialization conceivably a contributing factor. Ideals concerning the pursuit of difficult and unpopular truths are far removed from practices centered on the manipulation of public opinion. From the perspective of concern about the future of academic freedom in universities, there is something disconcerting about the penetration of marketing techniques into the world of higher education, selling certain promises of satisfied desire as the basis of the institution's value. Image management and marketing slogans seem fundamentally concerned to portray an academic world that comfortably satisfies the needs and wants of the consumer. Professors have a stake in preserving an academic world that would allow for such wants to be consistently overridden by their various professional commitments and understandings. With each new instance, then, as university promos endeavor to boost their sponsoring school, they undercut certain institutional values of higher education as a whole and set more than a few academic teeth on edge.

In the end, the play of images regarding the features and future of institutions of higher education will continue to fascinate, and sometimes frustrate, those who tune into them. For our part, it is the larger vision of the institution in its full complexity that needs to be sustained over and against the particular marketing strategies that remove ambiguity in the interests of sharpening the pitch. Universities are both tradition bound and barrier breaking, home and journey, places of teaching and of research. They satisfy popular desires of certain kinds, but not only those. In particular, universities still provide an almost singularly protective site for the pursuit of rarefied and unpopular ideas. Particular promotional ad campaigns capture a piece, but never one that succeeds in standing in for the whole of the place. But seen together as a collage, the diverse promotional ads that universities produce do a decent job of characterizing the institution in its perpetual state as the nexus of unsettled, often contradictory, yearnings.

Note

1. Altogether 45 promos, representing 33 universities are included in the study. For the most part, the schools included are those that appeared on the major college football networks. Big-name (athletically prominent) schools thus predominate.

References

Felton, G. "How to Write a Great College Slogan." *The Chronicle of Higher Education*, January 19, 2001: B5.

Graff, G. *Beyond the Culture Wars: How Teaching the Conflicts Can Revitalize American Education.* New York: Norton, 1993.

Menand, L. *The Metaphysical Club.* New York: Farrar, Strauss and Giroux, 2001.

Nussbaum, M. *Cultivating Humanity: A Classical Defense of Liberal Education,* Cambridge, MA: Harvard University Press, 1998.

Schwehn, M. *Exiles from Eden.* New York: Oxford University Press, 1992.

Sperber, M. *Beer and Circus.* New York: Henry Holt, 2000.

Taylor, C. *Multiculturalism.* Princeton, NJ: Princeton University Press, 1994.

7

In Just Six Short Weeks, You Too Can Be a Truck Driver, a Teacher, or a Preacher ... a Doctor, Lawyer, ... or Engineer

KAREN ANIJAR

Pariahs into Paragons

We have all seen the advertisements during daytime and late-night television: "In six short weeks you can be a truck driver, a nurse's aide, a medical assistant, or a computer programmer." These advertisements tout that by training at a particular school for a "high paying, high prestige career," the "good life" will be yours. All you have to do is pick up the phone (now) and call 1-800-*whatever* (you can begin almost immediately because classes are always forming).

The perpetually forming classes, replete with "guaranteed career placement," are held at what are known as proprietary institutions. Proprietary schools are profit-driven institutions, which over the past thirty years have been the subject of continuous media exposés; reports by local, state, and federal agencies and the FBI; lawsuits; and ultimately, a series of congressional hearings (in 1990, 1992, and 1995).

The exposés, hearings, and lawsuits precipitated a crackdown on the industry. The crackdown was overseen by several government agencies, including the U.S. Department of Education. In an effort to circumvent the highly aggressive marketing and recruitment practices and the flagrant abuses of student financial aid (which caused student loan default rates to soar in the early 1990's due to loans given out in the 1980's), the government attempted to impose stricter controls on the proprietary school industry.

Considering the publicity surrounding the government' investigations and media exposes of the student aid scandals, you might think that the forces of justice and civic responsibility would have prevailed over the forces of greed and that the industry would have crumbled. To the contrary, "creeping vocationalization and subordination of learning to the dictates of the market—has become an open, and defining principle of education at all levels of learning." (Giroux, 1999, p. 152) The university has become a "consumer-oriented corporation." (Readings, 1996, p. 2) Privatization has precipitated a complete transformation of the university, to the extent that the proprietary school industry has emerged like a phoenix from the ashes of scandal and become a model for contemporary educational policy, politics, and practice.

Autobiographical Frame and Some Notes on Method

In this chapter I use several narrative research approaches to investigate the proprietary school industry. The narratives come from a variety of sources (face-to-face interviews, government testimony, radio and television transcripts, field notes, newspaper and magazine articles, and Internet postings). They take place over a somewhat erratic 17-year period, from the early 1980s until 2001. I theorize around the dominant themes arising from all of the narrative artifacts collected. In order to protect the anonymity of the speakers, all the names I use are pseudonyms (unless otherwise specified). In order to protect the narrators, myself, the editors of this book, and our publisher, many of the names of schools have been removed. I have 17 years of narrative documentation because of an incident that transpired in my life during the early 1980's, when I first became aware of the proprietary school industry.

At the time I was a young single parent. I needed to find a job—and find one *fast*. I looked in the *Miami Herald*, my local paper. I saw an advertisement. I answered it. I got the job and began work the next day.

The position was as an admissions counselor at a technical college associated with a larger chain of colleges nationwide. Jaime (not her real name) was going to "train" me. Jamie's personal mantra: "money talks and bullshit walks." Jaime confided in me, telling me she had recently gotten out of prison for having involved herself in a "boiler-room operation" selling vitamins. I asked (and I cannot believe I was ever that naïve) "Were you guilty?" "Yeah," she replied, "I made a killing on vitamins."

For a couple of hours, I thought it was wonderful that the "college" would hire someone who had served time, and "paid" her debt to society. Then I listened a bit more closely to what Jaime said on the phone and what Jaime did to admit students. After about four hours, I began to feel uncomfortable about everything. Jaime was doing the same type of hard sell she did in the vitamin scams. Sitting in my cubicle, I (quite by accident) heard a student complain about student loans and "sit"[1] days. This was *not* like the college I had attended. In fact, this was unlike any college I had ever heard of.

I thought (because this was a Fortune 500 company), "The training director and the dean probably did not have knowledge of what was transpiring in admissions and financial aid." I went to see them. "Is this standard practice?" I asked. Nobody would supply me with answers; they spoke around the issues I raised. (I was told later on by another admissions representative that the executives felt I might have been a "plant" sent by the government). I quit.

Angered by the whole situation and scheme, I wanted to expose the place to the press. I did research and uncovered a much larger "can of worms." I recorded the narratives of students, former students, and admissions counselors. I had my five seconds of fame appearing on talk shows and being quoted in the local press (which, given the corruption in the industry, was something I did not want). How could I have known at the time that the mercenary can of worms I encountered would become a model for education?

Higher Education Transitions

There are some that continue to have a hostile attitude toward the schools that I represent.
— *Omer E. Waddles; quoted in Burd, 1997 http://www.chronicle.com*

The passage of The Higher Education Act of 1998 represented a tremendous shift in governmental policy. The law afforded proprietary schools (as institutes of *higher learning*) more nearly equal status with "traditional" colleges and universities. The Higher Education Act also heralded a new boom in the proprietary-school industry. The Internet (i.e., the digital technological revolution), globalization, and what is labeled as the "new economy" exacerbated the boom.

As reported in Burd, 1997 (http://www.chronicle.com), Omer E. Waddles said, "We've seen a fire across the prairie, and that fire has had a purifying effect. As our sector has weathered the storms of recent years, a stronger group of schools is emerging to carry, at a high level of credibility, the mantle of training and career development." As Burd explains, Mr. Waddles spent thirteen years working in Congress, six of them as "as staff counsel for key (educational) committees and for the Secretary of Education. Mr. Waddles helped to develop virtually every piece of legislation affecting higher education." He knows the in's and out's and nuances of all government agencies dealing with higher education. Mr. Waddles was instrumental in drafting legislation directing the Department of Education to expel institutions that had high default rates from the student-aid programs. That was *before* Mr. Waddles accepted a position as a lobbyist for the Career College Association, described by Burd as "a group with a reputation for its bare-knuckled defense of unscrupulous trade schools."

Mr. Waddles is not alone in his career move. His predecessor at the Career College Association, Stephen J. Blair, worked on student aid programs for the federal government from 1981 to 1985. The list of goes on and on and reads like a 'Who's Who of the Office of Post-Secondary Education. As Richard Hastings, executive vice president of CareerCom in Lemoyne, Pennsylvania, himself a former director of student loan collections for the federal government, stated: "If they (the US Government) keep pay scales what they are, more are going to do it." (Cooper, 1989, p. A-21) *It* means jump ship to join the forces of the industry that these individuals were supposed to regulate. As Mahlon Anderson, a department of Education spokesman, explained, "that knowledge and understanding of how it works over here can save a lot of money" for business and the proprietary industry (Cooper, 1989: A-21).

So ... What Else Is New?

I contend that a premeditated strategy has been pursued by a juggernaut of business-minded, profit-driven forces. Although I want to resist conspiracy theorizing, these business forces have been extraordinarily successful in creating a ruse and diverting attention away from the real issue: the victory of global, multinational capital in an increasingly undemocratic sphere—higher education—which is one of many cultural sites ripe for privatization.

> Thus, it is essential to reconsider the changing conditions of economic production and cultural reproduction because mere training is increasingly becoming confused with real *education* in a context where the latter is becoming increasingly abstract, irrelevant to everyday life and tied to the particular ideological agenda of the managerial state (Luke, 1998, p. 15).

In the *managerial state*, schooling is redefined in terms of marketable technologies and work skills (Noble, 1997; Shumar, 1997). "Learning becomes a particularized process of acquisition . . . logical sequential objective means to an end" (Atkinson-Grosjean, 1998: http://www.sociology.org/vol003.003/atkinson.html). The end result (as has been said so many times before in so many different venues) is a form of utilitarian essentialism concerning preparing employees for a global market.

This attitude sacrifices Aristotelean ideals of educating citizens for lives of ethics and politics through leisurely learning, in favor of honing their skills of subjection to the clock or of devoting their talents to an essentially mechanical training. The wisdom of UPS (learning how "to move at the speed of business") and the teachings of Lexus (accepting "the relentless pursuit of perfection") displace Plato and Aristotle as the privileged codes for constituting social individuality. Aristotle's plea to impart the wisdom of statesmen to citizens falls on deaf ears as job markets, parents, and tax-payers demand more and more techne needed to function in the globalized marketplace. (Luke, 1998, p. 6)

Demanding Skills—Educational Incentives

"It's more important to align . . . education programs with the needs of the employer rather than to educate people for education's sake."
— *Head of Michigan State Jobs Commission (Cole, 1996; quoted in Larabee, 1997, p. 23)*

Alan Greenspan, speaking to a congressional committee on April, 11, 2000, stated: "The U.S. system of higher education must remain the world's leader in generating scientific and technological breakthroughs and in preparing workers to meet the evolving demand for skills labor", adding that the effort "also requires that we strengthen the significant contribution of other types of training and educational programs, especially for those with lesser skills." (Greenspan, 2000) Greenspan's use of the phrase "lesser skills" is (not too skillfully) coded language, constructed on a scaffold of race, ethnicity, gender, and social class.

In the hypercapitalist "order," everybody and everything (or every body as a thing) is transformed into objects of relative value. As objects and as commodities, each *thing* is assigned market value in real and symbolic polit-ical economies (hence the interchangeable expressions "post-Industrial era," the "Information Age," and the "era of human capital"). All objects have use value (of one type or another), which can be exploited for what *really counts*. And what counts is profit. Schiller (1989) notes that we have entered a second phase of Taylorism. The control of capital subsumes and consumes everything in its path as aesthetics, subjectivity, knowledge, and human beings (ourselves) all become materials for the explosive growth of business. In the managerial state, society becomes one long uninterrupted moment of production as business disguises "its hegemony and interest in exploitation . . . pass[ing] off its conquest . . . as being in the general interest." (Dyer-Witherford, 1999, p. 51)

A reform movement that views education as a business . . . underlies the call for privatization. Proprietary institutions of higher education, otherwise known as "education corporations," are the engine driving the education revolution.

Gregory, a student at a proprietary school, stated: "Why should I worry about all the classes? I get life experience credits. I don't have to write a dissertation, and I will have the same degree that you do." I contested: "How can it be the same degree? Graduate school provides the opportunity for in-depth study on something that you care about deeply." He replied: "It is better to get out and get practical experience as a professor or something than to waste time reading books, or engaging in theory that does not really matter in the real world."

Sean felt, "Hey, I can get out in six months rather than two years. Schools will hire me as a teacher much faster; they don't care where you got you degree from." I asked, "Are you afraid that you will be unprepared to work with young people?" "No," he replied, "the professors have practical experience, that is why they never use full time instructors,[2] besides, you learn on the job when you teach in public schools. Face it, the university is a dinosaur."

Joseph J. Charles posted the following on Epinons.com:

A graduate degree is a recipe for higher salary! It makes perfect sense that this university would tap into this huge market. How many heads of family, friends, colleagues and bosses do you know who would like to pursue their education? I am sure that many of them have been baffled or disappointed by the way the higher education system has been working. If any of them manage to close their eyes on other aspects of their family and professional lives to pursue their educational goals, they often do it at the cost of many sacrifices in the end. This is why despite the complaints of some former students and the soaring tuition, many professionals find themselves attracted to the _____ (name of proprietary school). http://www.epinions.com/content_28159086212/tk_~CB001.1.7

I asked Gregory about Mr. Charles' comment and he answered:

He is right. Traditional universities are out of step—too many requirements and the classes are not convenient. Why do I need to take all kinds of filler classes, just give me what I need and get me out there working.

Similarly, DeVry Institute, a part of a much larger corporate structure, touts in flyers that

> The DeVry information technology degree is an accelerated program with weekend classes . . . based on a very simple and pragmatic philosophy: Understand and define the current needs of business and determine the kind of program that will meet those needs. (DeVry institute flyer, 2000)

Reduced to prescriptive formulas, the terrain that we now negotiate is that of the "education industry." The education industry, supplicant to multinational corporate interests, highlights a peculiar hegemonic terrain in which there is an ever-widening gulf between the powerful and those without access to the fundamental "unit of measure" in this brave new all-Fordist (all-the-time) educational system, which converts education into marketable, tradeable, and commercially viable products that are sold on the stock exchange and purchased by labyrinth-like corporations and their subsidiaries. Because wealthy and powerful stockholders will *still* send their progeny to elite schools, it is a system that sustains an exploitative exchange (of both real and symbolic capital) of domination and oppression, which benefits the wealthy and the powerful. The mode of production in the information age, as well as the product, becomes increasingly obscured under the false banner of educational democratization.

Educational supra-corporations, corporations create the courses, the books, the tests, and which like snowballs rolling down hills are part of larger corporations. Knowledge, like many other intangibles, is recreated into some *thing*, a thing of value that can be bought by and sold to the highest bidder in the marketplace. As "KrispyKreme" (his online name) posted to Epinions.com,

> While I am extremely happy to have achieved this level of education, I do not feel that the University _____ has contributed and/or expanded my knowledge base in the business industry. . . . It is a very expensive school that feeds you a "Quantity Education not Quality Education." I am thoroughly convinced that the institution is satisfied to remain status quo as long as you pay your way, and the accreditation is not repealed. After all, _____ is a private institution with the primary goal to make money . . . not advance American education. ("Krispy Kreme," 2000)

The question remains: How can Krispy Kreme feel proud to have achieved a level of education when he admits he learned nothing and put nothing into his schooling? Gregory answered the question as follows: "What counts is the degree, nothing else." Reynaldo, a former proprietary school student, said: "This form of schooling is concerned only with the bottom line and the profit of stockholders." "What did you learn?" I inquired. "It is not about learning, it is about getting a piece of paper," Reynaldo replied. "And," he continued smugly, "I have my piece of paper which puts me on the same plane as any other college graduate."

Darian, a stockholder in a large educational corporation, exclaimed:

> I am not in love with _____ and what they do. But I still invest and watch this company. Why? This is a rock solid company, a cash cow. It has strong conservative management and is one of the few companies that can tell you what it wants to be doing in 5 years. If people want to react emotionally, well fine, who cares. Name me a CD at a bank that can give you 25%. This company has not even scratched the surface of e-commerce or the market overseas.

Krispy Kreme would counter Darian's argument. He sees a tremendous amount of waste in the system:

> The finance and accounting department has the worst professional staff in America. They are rude, obnoxious and incompetent. My account was in error every-other-class due to the administration's error. To finally resolve one payment problem, I had to remain on the phone for 4 hours while the accountant searched my personal account history. (Just to let you know. If you choose this school, always pay with a credit card so that you retain records of payment). The Administration's problems are deeply rooted in the fact that they hire their own graduates. ("Krispy Kreme," 2000)

To Market, to Market, to Buy Me Some School

To sum up, more schools, more new students, more continuing students and more graduates, along with greater margins, should lead to strong growth in earnings per share
    — *Taylor, a corporate executive for a proprietary school:*

The stock market doesn't care how companies earn their money. The stock market doesn't care that 1/2 of _____ [the school's] recruits can't speak English or count to ten. What the stock market cares about is that these students are paying $4000/semester until these students fail out. Let me settle it at this . . . is _____ stock a dog—NO . . . is _____ [the school] . . . the institution a dog—YES . . .
    Student Narrative

Proprietary schools were explicitly singled out in a harshly worded report issued by the General Accounting Office. "Some proprietary school operators have enriched themselves at the expense of economically disadvantaged students while providing them little or no education in return." (Quinn, 1989, p. 8D) The report reads, "faced with large debts and no new marketable skills, these students often defaulted on their loans." (Quinn, 1989, p. 8D) As Mary June Malus, director of Louisiana's Center for Displaced Homemakers explains,

> My experience with graduates of the for-profit trade schools has been horrifying . . . We see women who proudly announce that they are an executive secretary, and upon being tested are found unable to type 15 words a minute." (Quinn, 1989, p. H-15)

Proprietary school tuition is more often than not paid through government student loans and government grants. In a series of hearings beginning in 1990 and culminating with a report in 1991, the United States government cited "overwhelming evidence that the Guaranteed Student Loan Program, particularly as it relates to proprietary schools, [was] riddled with fraud, waste, and abuse, and is plagued by substantial mismanagement and incompetence." (Eaton, 1991, p. A-19) What happened to government funds was appalling.

The Culinary School of Washington, for example, received more than $18 million in student aid between 1982 and 1990. Though the school offered such programs as "international buffet catering," its main classroom site was the basement of a closed public school. At another site, training consisted of operating a cafeteria at a waste-water treatment plant. The school declared bankruptcy and closed in 1990, one day before a search by investigators. A 1992 report from the U.S. Department of Education's inspector general concluded: "An alarming number of individuals are draining funds out of the schools, seeking protection under bankruptcy laws and locking out thousands of students without their promised training." (Toch, 1993, p. 56)

What happens when a student drops out or is unable to pay is far more troubling than the waste of tax dollars. Even if the student does not pay, the school still receives the cost of the course from the government, and the student is still liable for the funds.

> For-profit schools are the worst abusers of the student-aid system. About 900,000 of the 14 million students in higher education attend 4,500 for-profit vocational schools. But these students make up 24 percent of federal-loan recipients and are responsible for 41 percent of unpaid loans. Many of the schools are clearly designed to make money from the student aid program rather than to educate students. In one case, three Texas trade schools inflated the length of their training for aspiring security guards to about 300 hours. It enrolled 2600 students and received $7.4 million in student-aid payments. Security experts told the department's inspector general

that the 2600 students could have been trained to industry standards in a 30-hour course for $100 per student, or $260,000. The owners of USA Training Academy, a Delaware truck-driving and secretarial school that defrauded the student-aid system of $350 million over 15 years, created computer software that automatically added courses to students' transcripts and changed failing grades to passing to maintain students' eligibility for the aid. "We've made millionaires out of a lot of people," says an Department of Education staffer, referring to trade-school operators. The losers are students, who frequently are saddled with large debts and little or no marketable training." (Toch, 1993, p. 58)

Given all the current hyperbole surrounding for-profit education, have these practices changed since the early 1990's? "Yes," said a student, "something has changed: Students are afraid to say anything at all. We all know fraud is illegal." "But," as another student explained, "people who take _____ [the for-profit university] to task confront their well paid, well staffed legal force." Said still another ex-student, "I was ripped off . . . local government agencies don't want to face their legal A-Team, so they never contest what happens." "What about Congress? Let's go tell this to Congress!" a different student wailed. "Well," said one more ex-student, "most of them are lawyers too. This is a big time scam, and the student always loses." Natalia, who was exasperated and exhausted, felt:

> It is impossible to do anything at all. I tried to get to the bottom of this. But so many people are involved. I think there are people in the Congress and the Senate who are involved as well. I bet many of them own stocks in the companies. The lobbying groups for this industry are unbelievable. You can not change it on the state level either because as far as I can determine the situation is the same; it is the same old pork barrel with Political Action Committees and lobbyists, and our representatives all feeding off the same trough.

Jeff, an ex-administrator for one of the larger proprietary schools in the nation, recalled:

> Almost every full time student on my campus collected some form of financial aid, mostly student loans. Sadly, most of the students (who are usually from minority SES groups) incurred tremendous amount of debt only to drop out . . . a horrible disservice to this population and the schools do so without the slightest hint of regret.

Robert, another ex-school administrator, described his conglomerate Fortune 500 school as a training ground for advancement, the advancement of its staff. You know what I mean, aggressive business people ready to lock onto your money and pull with Caterpillar-truck like force . . . look on the inside and you see students who are disgusted and demoralized. You see mostly African Americans and Hispanics and poor people, having their one chance nixed.

Nestor, another ex-proprietary school functionary, felt:

They teach people all right . . . how to use flashy advertising to bait and lock people into a contract with deceptive fine print. It's just like bullying, taking kids' lunch money, and nobody protects or stands up for them and it keeps on going on.

Ted, a corporate stockholder, stood steadfast: "Hey, you know what, I don't care. The stock is profitable. The bottom line is money talks and bullshit walks."

I *have* heard that before.

Easy Targets

Several unlicensed computer schools in Brooklyn pitch their training toward the growing community of immigrants from the former Soviet Union. The courses are popular because they're taught in Russian and offer the potential of landing jobs with starting annual salaries up to $60,000. (McCoy, 1998, p. 5)

Our review of IADE American Schools revealed that IADE engaged in a pattern of abusive practices designed to attract low income, poorly educated, immigrant students. In the first instance, it did so through the use of a deceptive advertising campaign that offered potential students a "free education." From 1990 until 1993, IADE spent over $2 million running promotional advertisements for its school on Spanish-language television and radio stations in the Los Angeles area. According to former IADE students, this advertising promised potential students a free education that would lead to a high-paying job in the fields of computers, truck driving, or auto mechanics. Because IADE's target audience was composed primarily of unskilled, uneducated laborers employed in minimum-wage jobs and living at or below the poverty level, these advertisements were ultimately quite successful in attracting large numbers of new students.

Miguel Garcia also enrolled in IADE as a result of the school's advertising campaign. He stated that when he went to the school for an interview, he was promised that upon completion of his training he would be given a set of mechanic's tools and placed in a job at $15 per hour. He was then given papers to fill out and sign, which he was told were for a government grant to pay for his tuition. Mr. Garcia had no real understanding of the papers he was signing because of his limited command of the English language. It was only after he had completed his courses at IADE that Mr. Garcia learned that he had signed applications not only for a Pell Grant but for a guaranteed student loan as well (U.S. Senate Subcommittee hearings, 1995).

Admissions counselors were and continue to be the immediate targets for complaints because they are the corporate representatives with whom students have direct contact. Moreover, educational corporations can blame abuses on aggressive admissions counselors (although corporate policies pay admissions representatives' commissions). "It is not corporate policy, but the individual functionary," Hector, an administrator for a proprietary school, explained with deadpan seriousness. "Admissions counselors should not admit everybody." I asked: "Are admissions counselors educators or school psychologists?" "No," Hector said. "Are they paid a salary or commission?" "He answered, "They are paid salary against commission."

At the now-closed American Career Training Corporation in Pompano Beach, Florida, admissions representatives "won cash prizes and TV sets for signing up students. In 1988, the school employed 109 recruiters and 70 financial-aid officers but just 23 instructors." (Toch, 1993, p. 56) I asked Hector if it is "the responsibility of the admissions representatives to generate admissions." He answered, "Of course; that is how they get paid—per student that they enroll." Persisting in my line of questioning, I queried: "Do you see any sort of conflict of interest in this arrangement at all? Could admissions representatives enroll unqualified students to get larger commissions?" He did not answer.

He asked me to leave his office after I brought up the 1995 Senate Subcommittee hearings that described the ways in which admissions representatives would sign up displaced homemakers, welfare clients, the mentally retarded, high school dropouts, and people who could not read, write, or understand English. The counselors promised potential students a bright, financially successful future and often labeled student loans scholarship money (or free money) given out by the United States government in order to train people for a variety of jobs.

Within the corporate order, however, admissions representatives (also labeled as counselors) remain expendable personnel. As Darleen, a disgruntled ex-admissions counselor stated: "Not everyone ought to have been in our programs. I didn't want to admit everyone. I don't think some people understood what they were getting into. I was fired for not making my sales quota."

Post-Fordist economies requires a panoply of techniques in order to market goods and services. Discussions surrounding capital previously focused on the mode of production, on how to manufacture and produce tangible goods. The focus has shifted completely now, to how to market or sell products (both tangible and intangible). Economic exigencies have created a scenario in which the center of gravity of the economic system has shifted from production to sales and finance. , One needs sales in order to make a profit. Salespeople will always try to make sales. It is what they were hired to do and what they are paid to do.

Linda Sax, vocational counselor at a shelter for mentally retarded adults, reported that trade schools were luring her impaired clients with promises of glorious jobs. People with IQs of 64 and 65 were told they had passed qualifying tests for business schools and travel-agent courses. "None of our mentally retarded clients ever reported that they'd failed the admissions test," she said. Once in school, they were given textbooks they couldn't read and put into courses they couldn't begin to understand. Nor did they realize that they had borrowed money to go to school. They signed the papers for guaranteed student loans. (Quinn, 1989, p. 8-D)

In a hearing before a committee of the New York State Assembly, stories abounded concerning

> hopeful students signed up on street corners, at welfare offices, at prison-inmate and drug-rehabilitation centers, and through newspaper ads. The ads are placed by "counselors" who falsely advertise jobs available, when what they are really selling is a place at a sleazy trade school. Angelo Aponte, commissioner of New York City's Department of Consumer Affairs, told of Spanish-speaking students recruited for computer courses taught in English. A former prison inmate, trying to put his life back together, was promised a job as an accountant although he had only fourth-grade understanding of math. A course for auto mechanics had no cars to work on unless a student's car broke down (Quinn, 1989, p. 8-D).

Another fraudulent school operated in Florida:

> Sold on dreams of better lives as medical assistants, high school dropouts and single mothers from depressed neighborhoods in the Tampa Bay area signed up for loans at the school in the Town 'N Country section of Tampa. When they quit, Bell forged their signatures on the loan checks and stole the money. "He lifted them up with hope and kicked them down," said W. Grant Purdy, a federal investigator who investigated Bell for the Department of Education. They cannot get credit cards or finance cars because their credit ratings have been ruined. The former students cannot return to school

because no one will offer them financial aid. "It's hard enough for me as it is," explained Earline Ruffin, a single mother with three children. "And to have something like this happen, it's holding me back." Thousands of students around the country face similar problems. The idea of alerting hundreds of collection agencies is dizzying. Meanwhile, the collectors' letters and phone calls keep coming. "The students face a lifetime of pain for this," said Assistant State Attorney Judy Hoyer, who prosecuted Bell. For 53-year-old Betty Island, the nightmare began one sunny August morning in 1987. A well-dressed former insurance salesman knocked on her door in Central Park Village in Tampa. He told an incredible story about a wonderful school: Free courses designed to train medical, dental and pharmaceutical assistants. No high school diploma required. "He talked so nice you couldn't turn it down," recalled Island, who was unemployed and had reached only the eighth grade in school. "I always wanted to learn something. He said if I enrolled I would get $ 4,000 like money I had in the bank." So the next day, Island visited Bell's school at 8318 W Hillsborough Ave. She enrolled and signed up for government loans. After taking classes for about three days, she quit. "I didn't understand it too good," Island explained. She asked school officials to cancel her loan and found a job ironing clothes in a factory. Six months later, the bills started coming. "It made me sick," she said. "I don't owe no loan." Bell deliberately targeted people who are hard to find, they said. Recruiters canvassed low-income neighborhoods. They looked for people who moved frequently and who probably could not complete the curriculum (Swarns, 1990, p. 1)

At ACT, once a large nationwide chain of proprietary schools, recruiters outnumbered instructors 109 to 23:

Management held contests promising cash or color televisions as incentives to generate loan applications. It offered tips: "Food stamp offices leave referral cards," advised a memo a sales supervisor distributed to recruiters. "Drive through large housing projects SLOWLY with door sign on. Best times are Friday afternoons and Sunday afternoons."

Two former students testified that they did not even know they were obligating themselves to federal student loans. "I asked if I could set up a cash payment plan," said Andrea Lynn Merritts-West. The recruiter "talked me out of this idea." "They are making almost $3,000 off me for nothing," said Angela M. Jones, who did not receive instruction beyond a second set of lessons. "I would not have signed for a government loan." Another witness testified to seeing one owner and his managers falsify aid forms for students not qualified to receive loans. "I refused to alter the records," said Brenda Ann Brandon, formerly the school's chief financial aid officer. "Joseph Calareso did this on several occasions in my presence." (Vick, 1992, p. 1-A)

According to Harold Goldsmith, who headed the New York State Education Department's Bureau of Proprietary Schools,

> There are a lot of schools violating the law, targeting the non-English-speaking community and charging students a lot of money for what in some cases is training of questionable value . . . Some of them are really horrific." (McCoy, 1986, p. 5)

In a list-serv posting, Clarice, a former proprietary school administrator, expressed:

> I think they misrepresent themselves at every level. _____ (the school) does not provide education, it is a money making enterprise. . . . I witnessed first hand the underhandedness of the administration and their lack of ethics and concern for students. Education is about learning in a supportive environment. _____ (the school) does not represent either. At the campus where I work student worked with antiquated equipment, cheating was rampant and instructor were low quality. As for a supportive environment, _____ (the school) put NO money into improving the campus and making it a place conducive to studying. I tried to support _____ (the school) and after 5 years I had to get out of there, there were destroying my belief in higher education. There admit underprepared students and then do nothing to help these students succeed. I remember when I worked there that they censored the student newspaper for fear someone may actually learn the truth about the company!!! Let me just state for liability purposes, these comments are only my opinion, nothing more.

With more than a modicum of regret, Charles, another ex-administrator for a proprietary school, wrote in a bulletin board post on a different Internet site:

> It was my first "real" job after graduate school, and I lasted about 13 months. Had some trepidation's about taking the job at _____ (the school) when it was offered to me, but I saw it as a challenge. From nearly the first day I began my new position, as an associate dean, I was utterly dismayed at what went on. As many have noted _____ (the school) is a money making enterprise—and really nothing more. Yes, graduates do find jobs after completing their

education at _____ (the school), but these are fairly entry-level positions that offer little in the way of substantial advancement. I cannot help but be amused by the admissions representative who wrote (on a web board) that _____ (the school) was a superior option to MIT. I don't know of many students who if given the opportunity to attend MIT, its high tuition notwithstanding, would opt instead to go to _____ (the school). Speaking of representatives, these folks were utterly devoid of ethics. Their goal is to "write" applications, convince students to attend _____ (the school), and then struggle to keep them enrolled for a mere 30 days (which is the criteria for collecting the commission). The notion of someone receiving a commission to enroll a student is so antithetical to the basic tenets of higher education. Not surprisingly, once students had lasted 30 days the so-called "rep." wanted nothing to do with his or her student. Advocacy at such as it is, is driven solely by a desire to collect the commission. How could this possibly be in the student's best interest? This question is especially important given the thorough unpreparedness of the student body. Sure, we had on our campus some good students (many of whom left in frustration), but by and large those admitted had no business attending a baccalaureate institution, let alone one that specializes in technology fields. Almost every last full-time student on my campus collected some form of financial aid, mostly student loans. Sadly, many of those students, most of whom are minorities, incurred large amounts of debt only then to drop out or flunk out of school. In these cases, which were many, _____ (the school) has done a horrible disservice to this population—and it does so without the slightest hint of regret. Well, I could go on and on and on.

And so could I. I have hundreds of pages of transcripts and hundreds of news stories, and each story flies in the face of any sense of ethics. Dan's story exemplifies this:

When you first go to the school to see a technical representative BEWARE! They will lie and say whatever they can to get you to sign up to the school. I know it happened to me and many other students. They will lie about your schedule, about what they teach and how good their job placement is. I originally went to _____ (the school) under the impression that I will be learning what is necessary to be a computer programmer in the business world. What they really teach you, is how to be a corporate secretary!!!! If you want to be a secretary go to _____ (the school). The representative and the catalog both said they teach people to be programmers, but once you take the courses by incompetent Professors, you will see that you can never get a job as a programmer. Most people who get a job who went through the Computer Information System (CIS), get a very low paying job as a helpdesk, or technician, because they do not have enough knowledge to make it in the real world as for example, a Visual C++/Unix programmer. They don't even teach real Unix. _____ (the school) says that businesses do not even use it as much anymore. Who are you kidding? Well, I went to confront the Dean of CIS on how I felt at _____ (the school), to hopefully improve the education. Do you know what he told me, if you do not like it here go someplace else!!! He could care less. He told me maybe what the representatives said was a little bit of exaggeration, but he said we still get you jobs. Yeah, jobs that are very low pay in what we do not want to do. I have it all on tape to prove it!!!

Ricky, a former proprietary school student, wrote "I have tapes, but I can not take them to court, they are one of the largest corporations in the world. If I drop out I still owe money." To which a shareholder and administrator at the "university" responded, "don't be such a cry-baby, you signed the contract!"

Where There Is a Will to Profit, There Is a Way

Stockholder 1: Well I can see why they are disgruntled ... I would be pissed if I had a graduate professor providing grade-school quality handouts. It's not like a public school where you just accept what you get and assume they are doing the best they can ... When the school is making a profit the expectations are much higher! I'm a little scared about the callous way _____ (the proprietary university) is taking towards obeying the laws ... Although petty, they are probably opening themselves up if the allegations of fraud (charging for things the U said would be free), and charging excessive fees is true. If the scanned-in materials I have seen are indeed true, it appears to me they are in violation of a couple laws; albeit petty violations. Probably nothing to worry about.

Stockholder 2: I don't think it will interfere with profits in the long run. Vouchers are gaining a positive outlook in K–12 education, and I think a couple of petty little legal violations will go unnoticed.

As I stated before, the focus of part of the proprietary school industry has changed. Proprietary schools, which were once exclusively trade schools, now offer degrees at the undergraduate and graduate levels. The University of Phoenix has 60,000 students and in 1997 had profits of $33 million; DeVry, Inc., with 48,000 students, had $24 million in profits; and ITT, Education Management, and Strayer Education, Inc., had 26,000 students, 19,000 students, and 10,000 students, respectively. These "institutions of higher learning" "are "glamour stocks on NASDAQ, rivaling

Internet companies. The University of Phoenix's price/earnings ratio was 50."
(Winston, 1999, p. 12) The University of Phoenix is now the largest private
university in the country.

There is something going on that speaks to more than material transformation if, as Winston suggests, the success of each of these institutions
is "fed by the nation's disenchantment with traditional colleges and universities and [the nation's] infatuation with 'privatization' and 'the market'"
and "these schools . . . will harness the limitless powers of free enterprise to
mend a failed higher education institution stuck in the past." (Winston,
1999, p. 12) The title of Berliner and Biddle's book "The Manufactured
Crisis" (Berliner and Biddle, 1996) comes to mind. The crisis runs parallel to the arguments for charters and vouchers in K–12 schools, having
more to do with intensified capital reaching into previously untapped
markets.

Intercourse of Marketability

Colleges and universities are turning out insufficient numbers of graduates
for the new economy, and corporate America can't keep its employees
properly up-to-speed on technological change. Education may seem to be
in crisis and decline, but therein lies opportunity: Scores of entrepreneurs
and companies sense a chance to make money by doing better (Melcher,
1999)

David J. Collis, a business strategist who serves on the faculty of
Harvard's Graduate School of Business Administration and is a guest lec-
turer at Yale's School of Management, issued a wake-up call to educators:
"Competition is about to get a lot tougher. Successful institutions must
make difficult strategic choices—sooner rather than later." This is true,
Collis warned, because higher education is a good (i.e., profitable) industry
in which to compete. This is a tough message for educators and the business and finance officers charged with keeping higher education institutions afloat. "One day we're a learned profession in the apocryphal ivory
tower; come the following season, we're down in mammon's muck and private sector entrepreneurs are eyeing us as lunch." (Grills, 2000)

> For the market to exist, there have to be buyers. Who's buying and
> why? First among reasons for private-industry success is widespread
> dissatisfaction with the current systems, both at the K–12 and the
> post-secondary levels. But there are other forces at work as well.
> Companies like Apollo and Sylvan are taking advantage of a trend con-
> comitant with the rise of the knowledge economy: while the premium
> paid for intellectual capital is at an all-time high (ask Bill Gates), many
> are questioning the value of formal academic credentials (again, ask

Bill Gates). Michael Prowse, writing for the Financial Times in November 20, 1995, argues that "Higher degrees serve a function akin to that of the exotic plumage of birds: they are primarily a means of attracting attention, of signaling that you deserve special attention." In today's world, as Sylvan Learning Systems knows well, "simple tests of cognitive ability can be administered in less than 30 minutes. Such tests, which can be tailored to the needs of particular companies, are a better guide to job performance than academic degrees (Garber, 1996, p. 57)

Anti-intellectual populism and corporate relations intertwine in an intercourse of marketability. Amy Snider of the VIS Corporation writes:

The University of Phoenix has been an important innovator in higher education, but the real trailblazing has been taking place within corporate education. Because corporations place a premium on efficiency and are free of the blinders of educational tradition, they have become leaders in the development of new approaches to education. (Shapiro, Brann, and Snider, 2000, p. 13)

Corporations optimize and capitalize on formulas that focus upon more *efficient* ways to teach with respect to pragmatic, quantified outcomes. Marketing to historically situated populist sentiments, the proprietary industry can and has positioned itself as a change agent, a crusader against waste, extravagance, and irrelevance. So, during the 1999 House impeachment hearings,

Judiciary Committee Chairman Henry Hyde revived the cluelessness-of-the-eggheads stereotype before the Senate a few weeks later, referring to the "parade of professors" the House had endured and suggesting that the Senate might be in for a similar fright. "You know what an intellectual is?" he folksily asked his audience. "Someone educated beyond their intelligence." The senators responded with a collective belly laugh. (Shea, 1999)

And we also have

former National Endowment for the Humanities Chairman Lynne Cheney's continual complaints that humanities professors have betrayed the Enlightenment and practically keep busts of Lenin on their desks; mix in the economic lure of a booming economy, and the result is a recipe for the irrelevance of the liberal arts. Is it any wonder that more and more students are thinking: Hello, network technician certificate; no thanks to Thucydides, Ben Jonson and

Wittgenstein? Students may be inclined to skirt the culture wars by skirting culture. (Shea, 1999)

So it ought not to be surprising that University of Phoenix founder John Sperling celebrates that "[t]here's not a leaf of ivy or a single sports team at the country's largest private university. No dorms, no frats, no place to play Frisbee". And what does its leader think of a liberal arts education, with its great books and late-night philosophical debates? "It's a luxury." The focus on certification and accountability (actually accountancy), replete with attendant organizational discourses and practices, leaves no room for "*frivolous, useless luxuries*." Philosophy is impractical; reflection is a waste of time. As the Nike commercial says, "Just do it," and that is precisely what the proprietary-school industry has done. Civic responsibility; social justice; independent, critical, and creative thought: These are sticky little extravagant excesses.

Held Hostage

More and more companies are creating their own colleges or asking for-profit institutions like the University of Phoenix to train their employees because traditional colleges and universities are deemed too slow to respond to these corporations' needs.

> Dennis Jones, the CIO of Federal Express, told what his company is doing about it: "To begin to address the needs of the corporation, FedEx convened a task force called the Internet Curriculum Consortium, which includes representatives from Hewlett-Packard, Informix, Netscape, Sun Microsystems, Sybase, and the University of Memphis" (DeLong, 1998)

In his column "The 21st Century Work Force," Jones asserted

> Corporations must step up to the plate and assist their local universities as they implement these ideas and curricula. We may have to assist our educational institutions in financing these changes and to lend some of our current workers to help train the students. . . . After reading the white paper, request a meeting with the dean of your local college or university. Discuss the white paper and then ask how your company can help improve the curriculum at the school." (cited in DeLong, 1998)

Academia is held hostage through a variety of university/business collaborations (in publishing, in grants, in high technology—a process that really began to take hold during the Cold War).

Rick Worthington, professor of public policy at Pomona College, called attention to the controversial link between U.C.L.A. and the strictly for-profit Home Education Network. "Why would this firm be interested in the university?" he asked. "The reason is clear: U.C.L.A. is a good brand!"

Another arrangement between business and the university . . . was the California Education Technology Initiative, a sweetheart deal announced in December 1997, linking the entire California State University system to a consortium of information technology firms—Fujitsu, Hughes, Electronics, GTE and, of course, Microsoft in the group first announced. The plan involves a $300 million upgrade of the CSU digital "backbone" and the transfer of the $80 million a year that CSU budgets for computing services to the new CETI monopoly.

University administrators see the plan as a convenient way to improve information technology services within the college system. . . . Students and faculty at the Harvey Mudd conference blasted the scheme as a corruption of the fundamental purposes of a public university, renaming it the "Corporate Education Takeover Initiative." Several speakers voiced fears that CETI corporate partners would begin to control the content of courses, reducing professors to a distinctly secondary role. One faculty member from a CSU campus reported that in the original CETI contract, professors were expected to become members of an active sales force, hawking products of the corporate partners to the 365,000 students on CSU's twenty-two campuses. [It's worth noting that as campus protests about CETI roiled this spring, Microsoft and Hughes Electronics withdrew from the negotiations . . .] (Winner, 1998)

"Should we allow commercial forces to determine the university's educational mission and academic ideals?" asked Eyal Press and Jennifer Washburn, in an *Atlantic Monthly* cover story (Press and Washburn, 2000). In the academic–industrial marketplace-complex, corporate interests have come to play an increasingly important, perhaps even dominant, role in determining the nature and range of learning experiences that colleges and universities provide and the kinds and quantity of research they supply. "Did you think that knowledge was not a commodity? If so than you are really misinformed, misguided, or just plain stupid," said Ralph, an administrator for a large proprietary university. I protested: "There is public purpose to higher education. There is public obligation as well. "The public purpose is simple," Ralph continued, "to keep America number one in the world economically and technologically. You can't do that studying art history, not with the Japanese breathing down our necks."

Jamie, you recall, had a mantra: "money talks and bullshit walks." The mantra I read for higher education is "streamline:" minimize capital expenses, reduce operating costs, and maximize profit above everything. Education is just one more commodity, like shirts, sneakers, or washing machines.

But What about the Students?

Don't to go to the University _____ [school's name]; think twice! Don't let those TV ads to fool you. This is what _____ [corporate CEO] believes: to lie to the people and get their money! Like _____ [another student] says, we saw that after you gradu-ate from _____ Information Systems there is no "Get ahead!" _____ [school's name] IT is rusted! I know many students who have _____ [school's name] BS and now they are working for low paid minimum wage jobs trying to pay back student loans.

— *Student narrative*

The _____ [proprietary university] does not have a library. It does not have a tenure system. It did have a six-million-dollar fine from the U.S. Department of Education for misusing student-aid funds. The misuse of student-aid funding, which in the past would have been cause to question the motives of the institution, is not ever discussed. The proprietary institution in question is celebrated as a model for education.

— *Student narrative*

University faculties have not been willing to address non-traditional learners. Because they haven't . . . those learners have been addressed by entrepreneurs and administrators who have created a whole par-allel education system which they now control . . . (Andrew Feenberg quoted in Winner, 1998)

The very notion that the business of education is business ought to raise cautionary flags throughout the nation. But years of marketing and a tra-dition of anti-intellectualism reinforce "the complaints about clueless, arrogant, pedantic professors and all the tension between the public and the ivory tower." (Shea, 1999) Nevertheless, one thing is certain: "The elites who are most clamorous in the bashing of liberal arts professors won't be sending their own kids to stripped-down colleges like Phoenix." (Shea, 1999)

So when the University of Phoenix President Jorge Klor de Alva (formerly a professor of ethnic studies and anthropology at the University of California at Berkeley) discusses his commitment to working class students, I wonder. His intention is to give "them a substantial education to take back their communities by helping them in their jobs." (Klor de Alva, 2000, p. 59)

I am not too sure about Dr. De Alva's use of pronouns. Who are "they" taking back their communities from? How can people take back their communities if we present them with an uncritical practical education? Is his reaction really against "the self-referential, politically correct theorizing in the top liberal arts departments" (Klor de Alva, 2000, p. 37)? Giving back to the community means more than getting a job (especially a minimum wage job, or a part-time job without benefits). In many communities there are no jobs. You cannot make something appear out of thin air. You cannot develop the political understanding necessary for rebuilding a local economy together if you are being (de)skilled through inadequate training.

> "We don't want edutainment," Maria Quintero exclaimed. "What we want is people to inspire or infuriate us." Another of the students, Julia Baker, spoke as a leader of the revolt against CETI in the California State University system. Ms. Baker pointed to the destruction of the partnership between students and professors . . . Suggesting that the problem was ultimately one of corporate domination of education. . . . she announced that a "revolution in consciousness" is on the horizon, one quite different from the educational revolution corporate managers and university bean counters have in mind, an uprising that would bring students to renew their commitment to social justice and ecological principles. "When the revolt arrives," she asked, "will the faculty stand with us?" (Winner, 1998)

I wish I could answer in the affirmative. But given the fact that academe has been proletarianized by the same proprietary forces and by business-minded bottom line sensibilities, I really don't know. Nicky, a college freshman, says, "Our future is at stake, and I read *Brave New World* and *1984* and unless we do something, that is what you are doing in the name of corporate profit, foreclosing my future."

"Look what happened in New Jersey," Jonathan, a college junior at a large state university, proclaimed: "The University of Phoenix was not let in. . . . DeVry was kicked out of Canada . . . we need to take matters into our own hands."

Anita, a first year MA student, tells me, "_____ (the proprietary university) was successfully sued in California this way for misleading advertising. I can give you contacts and the case file if you like."

But she cautions that this does not always work.

In Canada . . . a judge threw out a class action against _____ (the proprietary university) because (he wrote) . . . a class action would take too long to hear with all the complaints that were filed. I was and am still involved with this case. The judge wrote, and I have the papers, that other legal avenues would be more proper. So we are splitting the ex-students into small claim actions and general division actions which when completed will really screw up _____ (the proprietary university).

— *Student narrative*

Cassandra, another student, feels that ultimately the efforts of Anita, Jonathan, and other students like them do not matter in the long run:

They (the proprietary university) had to pay a fine of $6.9 million dollars up here for loan fraud because of the actions of our group. My friend has worked closely with the lawyers and media here and has collected evidence that proves _____ (the proprietary university) misrepresented themselves. _____ (the university) claims that the $6.9 million was not a big loss to take.

— *Student narrative*

Nevertheless, Sal maintains that suits and complaints against proprietary schools and universities are not working toward his and other students advantage.

Don't ruin it for us . . . we know it's a crock . . . but we can make more money, by kissing the asses of these ridiculous professors." No one says, " _____ (the proprietary university) is a God-send . . . I've got classmates in the graduate program who brag about never having cracked a text book, yet maintain a 3.50 or better GPA. Truly, I can see why some responses have been so angry . . . they feel that if you tell the world what a joke it is . . . well, then they might have to really work at their education. As for me, I just want to graduate before everyone realizes that we're all buying our education instead of earning it.

What still nags at me is that after years of investigations for nefarious practices, financial aid abuse, and more, proprietary schools have triumphantly become the standard against which higher education is measured. Jorge Klor de Alva may have a vision when he sees education moving towards

The certification of competence with a focus on demonstrated skills and knowledge—on "what you know" rather than "what you have taken" in school—more associations and organizations, who can prove themselves worthy to the U.S. Department of Education, will be able to gain accreditation. Increased competition from corporate universities, training companies, course-content aggregators, and publisher-media conglomerates will put a premium on the ability of institutions not only to provide quality education but to do so in a way that meets consumers' expectations. In short, as education becomes more a continuous process of certification of new skills, institutional success for any higher education enterprise will depend more on successful marketing, solid quality assurance and control systems, and effective use of the new media and not solely on the production and communication of knowledge. This is a shift that I believe UOP is well positioned to undertake, but I am less confident that many . . . traditional academic, institutions will manage to survive successfully. Those that cannot or will not change will become irrelevant, will condemn misled masses to second-class economic status or poverty, and will ultimately die, probably at the hands of those they chose to delude by serving up an education for a nonexistent world (Klor de Alva, 2000, p. 59).

But, I keep saying to myself, nothing is completely determined. I decide to take a break from writing, thinking of a hopeful note to end this chapter. I pick up a magazine from the dining room table. It is the *California Teacher*. Throughout its pages, "shorter, more condensed, tailored to the needs of the working student," and advertisements abound. Finding no respite in its pages, I turn on the television and an advertisement comes on: "We understand your needs and your lifestyles . . . you can get your bachelor's degree in just one year!" Although I began this chapter with a tongue-in-cheek statement—"you can be a teacher, preacher, etc. . . . in just six short weeks"—it is not an exaggerated comment—at least not anymore.

Notes

1. "Sit days" are a prespecified number of days written into the small print of a proprietary-school contract. For example, after five days of classes, a student owes one hundred percent of the tuition for the course. Admissions counselors try to ensure that students stay in school for the prespecified number of days so that they will be paid their commission.

2. The proletarianization of faculty has often been discussed, in a variety of different venues. It certainly costs the corporation, the college, or the university a lot less to pay part-time labor than it does to hire tenured or tenure-track personnel. This is one of the many bottom-line business sensibilities that have transformed academia.

References

Armstrong, L. "Distance Learning: An Academic Leader's Perspective on a Disruptive Product." *Change* 32 (2000), 20–27.

Atkinson-Grosjean, J. "Illusions of Excellence and the Selling of the University: A Micro-Study. *Electronic Journal of Sociology* 3 (1998). Available at http://www.sociology.org

Berliner, D., and Biddle, B. *The Manufactured Crisis: Myths, Fraud, and the Attack on America's Public Schools.* New York: Perseus Press, 1996.

Blumenstyk, G. "Company That Owns the U. of Phoenix Plans for a Major Foreign Expansion." *The Chronicle of Higher Education,* August 11, 2000. Available at http://www.chronicle.com

Burd, S. "Former Aide in Congress Raises Eyebrows over Trade-School Job: Omer Waddles Changes Roles as Lawmakers Prepare to Revise Student-Aid Programs." *The Chronicle of Higher Education,* February 28, 1997. Available at http://www.chronicle.com

Christie, J. Apollo Launches Education Overseas. August 17, 2000. Available at http://www.red-herring.com

Cole, K. "The Price of Learning: Engler Puts Adult Education on '97 Endangered List." *Detroit News,* June 4, 1996.

Cooper, K. J. "Ex-Officials Turn to Trade Schools: Under Education Department Scrutiny, Industry Seeks Insiders' Knowledge." *The Washington Post,* December 26, 1989 (Final Edition, p. A21).

DeLong, S. "As Long as It'$ Green: Imagining the Sense-and-Respond University for the 21st Century." Electronic document, March 1998. Available at http://hawk.fab2.albany.edu/$green/green.htm

Dyer-Witherford, N. *Cyber-Marx: Cycles and Circuits of Struggle in High-Technology Capitalism* Springfield, Illinois: University of Illinois Press, 1999.

Eaton, W. "Student Loan Program Called a Failure." *Los Angeles Times,* 1991 (Home Edition, p. A19). May 21, 1991.

Garber, M. P. "Wall Street Ph.D." *National Review* 48, September, 1996: 57–72.

Giroux, H. "Vocationalizing Higher Education: Schooling and the Politics of Corporate Culture." *College Literature* 26(30), 1999, 147–162.

Greenspan, A. Remarks at the U.S. Department of Labor National Skills Summit, Washington, D.C., April 11, 2000. Federal Reserve Board document available at http://www.federalreserve.gov/boarddocs/speeches/2000/20000411.htm

Grills, C. "Lead or Bleed: Colleges, Universities and the e-Universe." *Business Officer,* April 2000 (magazine of the National Association of College and University Business Officers).

Hood, J. "Ante-freeze." *Policy Review* 68 (1994): 62–68.

Klor de Alva, J. "Remaking the Academy in the Age of Information." *Issues in Science and Technology,* 16 (2), Winter 1999/2000: 52–59.

———. "Remaking the Academy." *Educause Review,* 35 (2), March/April 2000, 32–39.

KrispyKreme [electronic alias]. "UOP: 'Pay Your Way, Get Your A.'" Review of University of Phoenix posted to Epinions.com on June 26, 2000. Available at http://www.epinions.com/educ-review-7033-5A98514-3957EF51-prod1/tk_~CB001.1.5

Larabee, D. *How to Succeed in School Without Really Learning: The Credentials Race in American Education.* New Haven, CT: Yale University Press, 1997.

Luke, T. "Miscast canons? The Future of Universities in an Era of Flexible Specialization." Telos, issue111 (Spring 1998): 15–32.

McCoy, K. "Hopes Dashed in School Sham." *Daily News* (New York), March 30, 1986, p. 5.

Melcher, R. "1999 Education Prognosis." *BusinessWeek,* January 11, 1999. Available at http://www.businessweek.com/1999/02/b3611127.htm

Noble, D. *America by Design.* New York: Alfred A. Knopf, 1977.

———. "Digital diploma mills: The automation of higher education." Essay written in October, 1977. Available at First Monday, 3(1), Online journal. http://www.firstmonday.dk/issues/issue3_1/noble/

Press, E. and Washburn, J. "The Kept University." *The Atlantic Monthly,* 285, no. 3 (March 2000). Available at http://www.theatlantic.com

Quinn, J. B. "Schools for Scandal." *The Washington Post,* April 30, 1989 (Final Edition, p. H-15).

———. "Ticks: Schools Ripping Off Taxpayers." *St. Louis Times Dispatch,* May 9, 1989 (THREE STAR Edition, p. 8D)

Readings, B. *The University in Ruins.* Cambridge, Mass. Harvard University Press, 1996.

Schiller, H. *The Corporate Takeover of Public Expression*. Oxford: Oxford University Press, 1989.

Selingo, J. "For-Profit Colleges Aim to Take a Share of State Financial-Aid Funds." *The Chronicle of Higher Education* 46(5), September 24, 1999: A41–A43.

Shapiro, H.T., and Brann, E. "Higher Education." *Issues in Science and Technology*, 16(3), Spring 2000: 12–16.

Shea, C. "The Gap." *The Washington Post*, April 11, 1999, p. W14.

———. "Visionary or 'Operator'? Jorge Klor de Alva and his Unusual Intellectual Journey: Controversial Anthropologist Gives Up a Chair at Berkeley to Lead the U. of Phoenix." *The Chronicle of Higher Education,* July 3, 1998p. A8. Available at http://chronicle.com/data/articles.dir/art-44.dir/issue-43.dir/43a00101.htm

Shumar, W. *College for Sale: A Critique of the Commodification of Higher Education*. Washington, D.C.: The Falmer Press, 1997.

Snider, A. (2000). "Higher Education." *Issues in Science and Technology*, 16(3), Spring 2000: 12–16.

Swarns, R. "Loan Scam Leaves Former Students in Debt." *St. Petersburg* (Florida)*Times*, July 29, 1990 (Brandon Times Edition, p. 1).

Toch, T. "Defaulting the Future." *U. S. News and World Report* 114 (24): 56–61.

U.S. House Committee on Appropriations. Subcommittee on Labor, Health and Human Services and Education. Statement of Thomas R. Bloom, Inspector General, U.S. Department of Education, March 20, 1997. Available at http://www.ed.gov/about/offices/list/oig/auditrpts/dempi.pdf

Vick, K. "Florida Trade School Probed for Loan Abuse." *St. Petersburg* (Florida) *Times*, February 27, 1992 (City Edition, p. 1A).

Webster, M. (1995). Federal Document Clearing House, Inc. July 12, 1995, Wednesday

Federal Document Clearing House Congressional Testimony. Testimony, July 12, 1995, Mark Webster U.S. Senate Permanent Subcommittee on Investigations fraud and abuse in student grant programs.

Winner, L. "Report from the Diploma Mills Conference," *NETFUTURE: Technology and Human Responsibility*, no. 72 (1998). Available at http://www.praxagora.com/stevet/netfuture/1998/Jun0298_72.html

Winston, G. "For-Profit Higher Education." *Change* 31(1), January/February 1999: 12–20.

Wolfe, A. "How a For-Profit University Can Be Invaluable to the Traditional Liberal Arts." *The Chronicle of Higher Education,* December 4, 1998, p. B4. Available at http://www.chronicle.com

8

"Meritocracy" at Middle Age: Skewed Views and Selective Admissions

JOHN G. RAMSAY

Meri-what-cracy?

"Meritocracy" is a five-syllable mouthful of a word that, despite a note-worthy four-decade public career, is not a household name. Academics, I've learned the hard way, should use it sparingly in over-the-back-fence conversations with their neighbors. Unless your audience includes parents with ambitions to enroll a child at Cal Tech or the London School of Economics, you will furrow foreheads instantly.

I have even had a professional reference librarian say to me, "I don't know that word." The word causes undergraduates, who are primary players in meritocratic contests, to lower their eyes to their desktops. Perhaps, like me, you've had this response: *"Meri-what-cracy?"*

Even among those proud of their recall of post–World War II cultural terminology often draw a blank at "meritocracy". Ask anyone who has ever had an introductory course in the social sciences about the terms "iron curtain," "McCarthyism," "power elite," "military-industrial complex," or "the other America," and they're likely to take a stab at definition. But "meritocracy" often fails to register.

This small instance of cultural aphasia is unfortunate because "meritocracy" is our most precise single word for educational and occupational selection that presumes to be based, as David Riesman noted, "on judgments as

159

to qualifications." (Riesman, 1975, p. 287) Riesman had reservations about what he called "the spread of meritocratic institutions." But he did think it useful to distinguish the principle of their organization from "earlier modes of selection based on lineage, on patronage, on immediate political pressure, or on personal impressions by the person or group doing the selecting." And he assumed that reasonably objective measures of merit would gain wide public acceptance.

Part of what's interesting about our inability to pull "meritocracy" off the tips of our tongues is that the failure is but one example of our double-mindedness about how young people become eligible for high-paying, interesting, creative employment. In this case, we don't recognize the name, but we are entranced by the heart of the matter: educational access to professional careers. When we're interested in the answer to the questions: "How do you get into a good college?" and "How do you qualify for a good job?" we're interested in the meritocracy.

If the meritocracy is understood as the nation's vast network of educational arrangements for connecting youth to the world of work, it is no longer an academic abstraction. Its inner workings are a staple of popular culture, the subject of frequent portraiture, especially in the print media. Interest in how the meritocracy *really* works is one of the reasons why otherwise dull stories about college admissions, starting salaries, and rising or falling SAT scores are covered so obsessively.

National and international print media are in intense competition to provide their readers with revealing looks behind meritocracy's veil. Stories about the salaries of graduates of Dartmouth's Tuck School of Business, the latest interviewing ploys of McKinsey & Co., the admissions edge that hockey players get at Middlebury, and how to get into Wesleyan after you've been rejected once are now commonplace. Absent a grand narrative describing and explaining the meritocracy, there seems to be a voracious popular appetite for stories that offer digestible bites about particular applicants, schools, and admission and rejection stories.

Then too, there is an unquenchable thirst for the message: The meritocracy doesn't matter. One way of accounting for the ongoing presence of Robert Kiyosaki's *Rich Dad, Poor Dad* on the *New York Times'* bestseller list is that it is designed to be a sharp stick in the meritocracy's eye. This "get rich quick" book is built around the antithetical advice that Kiyosaki's two fathers gave him on how to achieve financial success.

"Rich dad," unimpeded by his eighth-grade education, is cast as the savant, who understands the path to true worldly success. "Poor dad," holder of a Ph.D. and numerous academic honors, plays the role of the bookworm, who made the mistake of taking school and its lessons far too seriously. The book mocks meritocratic faith in education and the good job and champions the entrepreneurial devotion to financial independence. He writes: "One dad taught me how to write an impressive resume so I could find a good job. The other taught me how to write strong business and financial plans so I could create jobs." (Kiyosaki, 1997, p. 16)

The concurrent popularity of these competing images about success would not surprise Riesman. His point was that the meritocracy is *one* institutional mechanism for connecting various kinds of talent and levels of ambition with the world of work. Much of the recent conversation about the meritocracy elaborates this tension. Part of the current discussion is about how often the merit principle is compromised by nonacademic strategies for getting a leg up: wealth, family connections, athletic ability, and political pressure, in particular.

"Meritocracy" and its other grammatical forms are becoming more recognizable in print than in speech. I wouldn't call it a trend, but there has been a slight uptick in the use of the word "meritocrat" among print journalists of late. If you do a quick Minitex search of five national newspapers, New York Times, Wall Street Journal, Los Angeles Times, Washington Post, Minneapolis Star Tribune; you'll find that the word was used only four or five times in the late eighties. But usage steadily climbed through the nineties and peaked at 20 in 2000. Journalists are on pace for another usage record in 2001. It seems fair to ask: How has the transition from academic circles to popular culture changed the way we imagine the meritocracy?

"Meritocracy" at Middle Age

Riesman was one of several prominent American social scientists who found Michael Young's *The Rise of the Meritocracy* (1958) a powerful text for thinking about the role of education in fostering social change. There was, however, an odd slippage in Riesman's account of the term. He claimed to use meritocracy in Young's original sense, but in fact he never did. Young's provocative fantasy described a dystopian England that was governed cradle-to-grave by meritocratic principles. The society was literally ruled by meritocrats, selected rather than elected for the House of Lords, Whitehall, and private industry on the basis of their measured intelligence.

Riesman, Daniel Bell, John W. Gardner, Christopher Jencks, and others did not employ the term in this sweeping, antidemocratic sense. They restricted their gaze to a "small-m" sense of "meritocracy," rather than to the total system of Young's imagination. Young's literary nightmare was a government of, by, and for certified intelligence. Young imagined a totalitarianism of efficiency, but without the terror usually associated with fascist regimes.

Some journalists have tried to expand "meritocracy" to mean government by brain trust, rather than college and job selection based on qualifications.

The result has made for splashy magazine covers and arguments that do not bear much scrutiny. The cover of *The Atlantic Monthly* trumpeted an article about "The Next Ruling Class." (2001) In fact, the article is centered on David Brooks' qualms about the lack of a moral compass among a few Princeton students he happened to meet while visiting the campus.

Jack Hitt, contributing editor at the *New York Times Magazine*, is another journalist attracted to exploring the elasticity of the term.

Hitt attempted one of those "the world is divided into two kinds of people" pieces about presidential candidates Al Gore and George W. Bush and their supporters' differing value systems (Hitt, 2000). He wrote:

> The new divide no longer cuts along liberal and conservative lines or class lines (everyone follows the stock market now) but along the way we see the world, that perspective only the Germans have a word for: *Weltanschauung*. Today there are meritocrats, members of the post G.I.-bill generations whose coming-of-age ritual was taking the SAT. For them, the best individuals are self-made and high achieving. On the other side are those who find meritocracy too tethered to mere ambition. Valucrats, if you will: people who believe that a certain moral framework is a necessary predicate to all good behavior. (p. 6, 13)

It is not hard to see why Hitt's case falls apart. His gloss on the core ideas of meritocrats is simplistic: Gore? Self-made?

And there were problems on the other side of what Hitt calls "the great divide" as well: Bush? A *certain* moral framework? Meaning "unfailing," or "not identified" (and therefore uncertain)? There seems to be an irresistible journalistic temptation to write about a national merit regime, but thus far the results are not persuasive.

Part of the problem is that it is extremely difficult to get an empirical handle on the meritocracy. This was not an issue for Riesman and the social scientists of the mid- and late 1960s. For them the meritocracy was a novel puzzle, a theoretical question that no one presumed to answer with data. For them the concept was a refreshing breeze that helped to organize their thinking about the human capital and national security needs that were triggering educational change. The name of the game was matching wits with Young. The driving question was: How can the United States find and train academic talent in ways that avoid the alarming consequences that Young forecast?

Thinking about meritocracy, even at its inception, was the hopeful project of assessing the potential of instruments for increasing equality of opportunity and social mobility. And it was the unsettling business of appraising the possibility that these same tools for identifying talent would usher in a future with harder and deeper social class cleavages. It was, in other words, the difficult task of assessing two contradictory models of meritocracy.

The first model suggested that merit, measurable, objective, and fair, could be used as a vehicle for the social mobility of the children of low-income families. The second suggested that merit was a tool for legitimating unfair competition between the poor and upper-middle class children, who enjoyed huge unearned educational advantages. No one captured this double-mindedness, this paradox of meritocratic thinking better than Riesman and Christopher Jencks. They wrote:

> Viewed from the top there is always a shortage of talent, and hence an argument for encouraging still more youngsters to compete for elite jobs and life styles, even though no more can make it than in the past. From the bottom, too, there always seems to be a shortage of opportunity, and hence a reason for being even more ruthless in weeding out incompetents who owe their privileges mainly to their ancestry. Both views are correct, and one of the great virtues of meritocratic competition is that it fuses them in such a way as to keep the whole expanding. Nonetheless, there seems to be something basically perverse and sadistic in trying to make society any more competitive and status conscious than it already is. (Jencks and Riesman, 1968, p. 150)

As the concept of meritocracy reaches middle age, the term is becoming more popular, while the underlying social reality defies easy generalizations. The Bureau of Labor Statistics estimates that in each year between 1998 and 2008, 1.31 million college graduates will bring their credentials into the labor market to compete for 1.28 million college-level jobs (Fleetword and Shelley, 2000, p. 9). No one makes serious claims to understand how and why so complicated a piece of the social structure works the way it does. The meritocracy is something we imagine we can get our minds around, but it is, in fact, too sprawling, dynamic, and elusive. And it is not difficult to poke holes in even modest empirical claims about how the meritocracy operates.

Take, for example, the conventional wisdom about the Ivy League's significant contributions to the ranks of corporate leadership in the United States. In Andrew Hacker's view, this common belief is largely myth. He reasons:

> So one part of the story is that most of those supposed to be gifted turn out not to be so, or that the aptitudes they once displayed have not proved germane in later life. Our selection mechanisms have shown to be incapable of identifying individuals with exceptional

abilities. Much more prominent in the CEO roster are graduates of such state universities as Tennessee Tech, Southwestern Missouri, North Carolina State, and San Jose State. Or lower-tier private colleges such as Marquette, Wake Forest, Wabash, and Villanova. Indeed, it is probably not too much to say that the American economy relies on proving grounds such as Purdue and Texas Tech to supply people to make up for the Ivy League's miscalculations. (Hacker, 1997, p. 210)

To Hacker and other skeptics, the meritocracy is as much a phantom at the age of forty-three as it was at its birth. Even the premise that there is a single, national meritocracy is highly debatable. But even Hacker would concede that "meritocracy" continues to be *the* code word for those who think about the identification, recruitment, and grooming of educational elites. What is it that we know, and think we know, about these elites and the college admission processes that govern their passage from high school to college? In what form do we imagine meritocratic college admissions?

Getting In

No aspect of meritocratic life generates as much apprehension, speculation, and debate as college admissions. The transition from high school to college has become an elaborate set of overlapping contests over talent, rankings, and money. Middle-class fretting over admissions has even inspired its own style of humor. Professional cartoonists are keenly aware that the meritocracy provokes powerful emotional conflicts and have made the graphic representation of this angst a widely recognized part of popular culture.

Cartoonists play with middle class anxieties about the life-shaping consequences of success and failure in school. These humorists, particularly those who draw for the *New Yorker*, are attuned to the nervous laughter that surrounds college admissions. Ed Koren's young woman is helping an elderly lady cross the street, while a classmate is observing: "Hey, there's Sara, padding her college-entrance resume."

William Haefeli depicts a school guidance counselor delivering bad news to stressed-out parents: "Unfortunately, all evidence of your son's intelligence is purely anecdotal." And then there is Robert Weber's cartoon about meritocracy's harshest ritual. An elementary-school teacher says to her girls and boys: "Today we're going to learn how to deal with rejection."

Barbara Smaller draws a dad badgering a teacher: "Where do you get off saying my kid is grade level?" Smaller also has a teenage boy comforting his distraught mother with the words: "Don't cry, Mom. Lots of parents have children who didn't get into their first-choice college, and they went on to live happy, fulfilled lives." Perhaps Michael Young had the most useful name for the sort of familial dynamic tapped by these cartoonists. He called it "the principle of compensating aspirations." He explained: ". . . the greater the frustrations parents experience in their own lives, the greater their aspirations for their children." (Young, 1958, p. 110)

The excesses of admission processes are deplored by most of the new meritologists, but they are not of one mind about the significance of these elaborate competitions. Nicholas Lemann sees the system and its failures as deeply injurious to individuals and the nation. Lemann writes: "The culture of frenzy surrounding admissions is destructive and anti-democratic; it warps the sensibilities and distorts the education of the millions of people whose lives it touches." (Lemann, 1999, p. 351) Leon Botstein, president of Bard College, offers a less hyperbolic view: "Given the extent to which most institutions are interchangeable, the obsession with getting into the so-called best college is odd if not irrational." (Botstein, 1997, p. 183)

Can admission to a high-status college significantly alter the course of an individual's life or career? Can one earn credentials of enduring value at any of thousands of colleges or universities? Most commentators would answer "yes" to both of these questions. But which question is the more important one to be asking about admissions depends largely on whether one assumes that "ranking" or "fitting" is the more appropriate mindset to bring to the admissions game.

"Rankers" are primarily concerned with institutional quality, resources, and prestige. They believe that college admissions is primarily a matter of managing the hierarchies of applicants and schools, sorting students into schools by various criteria of merit. "Rankers" tend to think that admissions is critically important to individuals and to society and that colleges should be publicly accountable for the quality of their faculty, programs, and reputations.

"Fitters" focus on personal growth and development and look at admissions from the point of view of students and their parents. They see the process as one of matching individuals and schools that have similar values, aspirations, and educational styles. "Fitters" tend to believe that admissions hype and competition are colossal wastes of energy that serve high-ranking schools and distract attention from core educational concerns, such as teaching and curriculum.

However well this distinction works on the surface, it is extremely difficult to maintain a consistent "ranking" or "fitting" perspective. The new meritologists prefer the liberty that flipflopping affords. Botstein, for example, is close to being a thoroughgoing "fitter." But when it comes to institutional identity, he has no qualms about categorizing only Cal Tech, the University of Chicago, and St. John's Annapolis as "truly distinctive and genuinely unique institutions." (Botstein, 1997, p. 180) In other words, he has no qualms about ranking these schools as head-and-shoulders above their competition.

As early as 1967, Riesman foresaw that an increasingly meritocratic society would be a mixed social blessing: ". . . it becomes more precarious, less relaxed, less arbitrary and corrupt, with fewer respites from competition." (Riesman, 1967, p. 902) Middle-class parents, to offer one site of discontent, would find themselves in a meritocratic knot, loyal to its norms while fearful of the downward social mobility of their children. But unlike contemporary meritologists, Riesman did not assume that these complicated cultural binds could be easily resolved.

Katha Pollitt, Radcliffe class of 1971, did not detect much consternation about downward mobility at her twenty-fifth reunion: ". . . the easy ride for our kids was the happy buzz." (Pollit, 1997) And this bothered her—meritocratic special pleading. She suggests that "white liberals of the professional classes" acknowledge that having their children admitted as legacies to selective colleges is "anti-meritocratic." Pollitt, a "ranker," wants to ensure that the rankings are fair. She challenges liberals to be purer meritocrats:

> Would you renounce alumni privilege for your children? . . . Refuse to donate as long as said school practices this insidious form of racial and economic discrimination, thus perpetuating a heredity-based social elite? (Pollitt, 1997, p. 9)

The new meritologists share a common faith in the reformability of an imperfect but likeable system. Their critical style is to identify an instance of an admissions filter that seems biased or a practice that tilts points toward one group or another. For Pollitt the problem is legacies; for Nicholas Lemann, the SAT; for Ward Connerly, race "preferences"; for Shulman and Bowen, it's jocks. Each imagines workable answers to the question: What policy changes would usher in a "truly meritocratic society?"

Many journalistic accounts attempt to convince readers of meritocratic injustice or unearned privilege at single institutions. Edward Fiske's poster boys for admissions unfairness are a Middlebury hockey player with a paltry 1200 on his SATs, and a Williams College football player who claims that an Ivy League coach gave him false hopes of admission (Fiske, 2001).

Fernanda Moore's model of triumphant persistence is Catesby Holmes, who despite four years on her high school's honor roll and a perfect 800 on her verbal SAT, is rejected by Harvard, Princeton, Yale, Columbia, Brown, and Wesleyan. Moore's story is about how Holmes rebounds from this crushing news by moving to Mexico, taking courses, and reapplying early decision the following year to Wesleyan (Moore, 2001). Alexis Guy, featured by David Marcus and Emily Sohn, has to console herself by choosing among her five backup schools, including Boston University and George Washington (Marcus and Sohn, 2001).

In both the Fiske and the Moore accounts, the driving question is: How does the meritocracy work for upper-middle class kids with high aspirations and strong but not sterling credentials? The answer is: Play by the rules, get good grades and test scores, develop a special talent (preferably athletic), and the meritocracy will have a place for you—though not necessarily the exact place you had your heart set on. The answer is that the elite-identification model of the meritocracy is alive and succeeding too well at eliciting unhealthy levels of competition for scarce spaces.

Two assumptions underlie many of these biographical sketches. The first is that students with impressive credentials are entitled to their first choice of colleges. The implication is that the rejection of any highly qualified student requires an explanation, if not an apology. The logic of this "deserving my first choice" thinking is never explained, but it is likely fashioned from the consumer ethos that one is entitled to purchase the name brand you can afford.

The second assumption is that the meritocracy is defined by the most selective colleges and universities. The new meritologists assume that the act of rejecting highly qualified students—on the basis of qualifications— is the defining meritocratic dynamic. The power and mystique of high rejection rates is a constant refrain in both the journalistic and the scholarly accounts of the meritocracy.

Marcus and Sohn, for example, claimed that some colleges had a tripling of applicants over the past decade, and then observed:

> But it's also true that a slew of selective colleges across the country have fewer spots to fill than they did last year. No, it's not a nefarious plot to drive teenagers (and their parents) to the brink of madness. It is just a matter of numbers (Marcus and Sohn, 2001, p. 49).

The implication of this assumption is that the meritocracy is synonymous with the Ivy League, a small number of highly selective state universities and a few nationally known liberal arts colleges.

Journalistic accounts of the social-mobility model of the meritocracy are harder to find, but the few that exist are detailed and valuable. Ron Suskind's *A Hope in the Unseen* includes an account of MIT's blunt rejection of Cedric Jennings, a star African American student from a dysfunctional Washington, D.C. school, Ballou High. The episode reveals the self-serving sophistication of the meritocracy when the social mobility of low-income kids of color is the issue.

Jennings applied to and was accepted by the highly competitive Minority Introduction to Engineering and Science (MITES), an intensive six-week summer program. MIT covered all expenses for fifty-two promising students for the chance to court and screen students of color for its next entering class. In the seven-year history of the program, eighty-two percent of its participants were admitted to MIT, and nearly all of those graduated. The program acted as an attractive lure and a fine screen—too fine for Jennings.

At the end of the program, the faculty director informed Jennings that the courtship was over: "Well, I don't think you're MIT material, your academic record isn't strong enough." (Suskind, 1998, p. 96) The director cited Jennings's weak SATs (the bottom third of all test takers) and suggested that MIT was simply out of his league. The director bungled an attempt to let Jennings down gently by counseling him to apply to Howard and the University of Maryland. Then the director held out the faint hope that Jennings could reopen negotiations, that he might still drive up his MIT stock: "If you do well at either of those colleges in your first year or two, maybe you can apply to transfer to MIT." (p. 96)

One could argue that MIT did not do Jennings a disservice by discouraging his application. In a recent year, MIT had 300 applications from African American students, accepted 131, and enrolled 71, or 7 percent of the class (Reisberg, 2000, p. 96). Is there a good reason to fault the faculty director for calculating that Jennings would not fare well in the face of such intense competition? One might even make a case that, on balance, Jennings benefited from his MIT experience. He learned he is in the same academic ballpark as the other students in the program, received a realistic taste of college-level work, and did not have to waste time and effort on an MIT application.

On the other hand, the faculty director showed little regard for how Jennings heard the message: "You're marginal. It's too big of a stretch for you. Lower your goals. Narrow your search." Unlike many of the middle-class students of color in his MIT cohort, Jennings did not have anyone at home or school to buffer this message, to put this setback in perspective. Jennings had no one to inform him that even faculty directors at MIT are not omniscient, and that he still had a wide range of options. And he had many peers who were convinced that his devotion to academic achievement was a waste of time.

Jennings was eventually admitted to Brown and received about $80,000 in scholarship money. Still, one of the recurring themes in *A Hope in the Unseen* is the information and know-how gaps that abound: between Jennings and his classmates at Ballou, between Jennings and his peers at Brown, and between all students and the elite institutions themselves.

In the admissions labyrinth, information used quickly and well can mean the difference between application and nonapplication, acceptance and rejection. The institutions know virtually all there is to know about the applicants, while the applicants know only what the schools want them to know—and sometimes not even that much. Suskind documents how elusive and hard-earned helpful information and know-how are for poor kids who need it most.

James Traub provides an account of small groups of high-achieving students in the context of an open-admissions, urban, public college. For the most part, Traub's account is the tale of how open admissions and the decline of the New York public school system has transformed City College into a majority, remedial institution. But his portraits of engineering students and honors history students do suggest that the mobility model of the meritocracy is quietly thriving in hidden programs and for highly dedicated studentsTraub wrote of the chemical engineers that he met: "In the monastic world of engineering students, they were the Trappists." (Traub, 1994, p. 288)

Popular culture currently offers a conflicted double image of the elite-selection model of meritocracy. One side of the portrait is of inspiring Olympics-like competition in which the agony of defeat sometimes dampens the thrill of victory. The other side is of an unnecessarily cruel and narrow passageway that is unfair for hard-working and deserving upper middle class kids. The suggestion is that the meritocracy is unmeritocratic, offering special deals to special people based on family affiliation, race, athletic potential, or other unstated, nonacademic criteria.

Given that the Ivy League's acceptance rates are often below 20 percent, the impression on readers is that the national meritocracy is a hopelessly clogged bottleneck. The image is one of a life-shaping but dysfunctional filter that serves to discourage rather than reward the majority of the nation's high-achieving high school students.

The image is further tarnished by reports on the astounding wealth of many elite institutions, and of their ongoing labor disputes with low-wage workers. Johanna Berkman, for example, tells the story of Harvard's $19 billion endowment, and the protests on behalf of an underclass of workers who are not paid $10.25 an hour (Berkman, 2001). The overall message is that of elitism of the worst sort: an unaccountable country club, stingy with its wealth and hungry for more.

The central image of the mobility model is one of an emergency room, institutional efforts of triage on behalf of a few survivors of failed public school systems. The suggestion is that programs like MITES and City College's Program for the Retention of Engineering Students work, while exacting a terrific personal toll on low-income kids of color. There is the further suggestion that the mobility model itself, once an inspiring image of a strong ladder into middle-class jobs and security, is broken.

Traub quotes a City College remedial-skills instructor accusing the whole system of perpetrating a fraud. The point was that City was no longer a part of a powerful engine for social mobility, a essential up ramp in New York's opportunity structure. Rather, it was involved, so the argument went, in an elaborate public deception by taking tuition for an education it could not deliver.

If there is a tone of grievance in the portraits of the elite-selection model, there is a tone of despair in those of the mobility model. The mobility portraits often raise questions about whether the triage is worth it. Traub editorialized: "But aside from the harm to the institution, it is fair to say that City shouldn't be admitting these [remedial] students because the experience isn't helping *them* enough. Perhaps City hasn't figured out how to help them, or perhaps, as I thought, their problems are too profound to be addressed in a college setting." (Traub, 1994, p. 343)

Traub's skewed views have been countered by Lavin and Hyllegard's history of open admissions throughout CUNY. Using survey information from nearly 5000 respondents, they were able to track the academic and employment careers of students who entered CUNY between 1970 and 1972. Their data and analysis reveal the partiality of Traub's triage imagery.

> By augmenting the pool of minority men and women who received educational credentials, open admissions contributed to the growth of a college-educated class in New York City's minority communities. The policy was a social intervention designed to interrupt the inheritance of socioeconomic disadvantage. In achieving this aim to an important degree, open admissions undoubtedly helped to produce a more promising set of life chances among the children of the students who came to CUNY after open-admissions was initiated. (Lavin and Hyllegard, 1996, p. 198)

Their conclusions suggest how distorted and misleading popular representations of admissions can be.

Markets for Merit

The data on where high-performing students actually attend college reveal much more interesting and dynamic trends than the Ivy League rejection stories would suggest. And these trends raise serious questions about whether the idea of a single national higher-education meritocracy is a concept that has lived a short and happy life but is now on the brink of obsolescence. Even a casual glance at the push and pull of this competition suggests that there is far more to learn about high-performing students from acceptance data than from rejection anecdotes. Here are some of the features of the existing market for high-performing students:

- The eight members of the Ivy League enrolled less than 12 percent (971 of 8170) of all National Merit finalists in 2000. Of the 971, nearly 60 percent became students at just two of the schools (Harvard and Yale). The journalistic impression of an Ivy League stranglehold on the nation's high school academic talent is enormously exaggerated.
- "Merit" is in the eye of the beholder. Admissions strategies exhibit a range of thinking about high school academic merit (Chronicle Jan 19th). Some schools tenaciously recruit National Merit Scholars. Others pursue valedictorians. (The University of Illinois at Urbana-Champaign enrolled 583 in 2000.) Many pursue a talent "density" strategy predicated on class rank. (At Berkeley, for example, 95 percent of incoming frosh were in the top fifth of their high school class in 2000) Others pursue a dual "cream of the crop" *and* open admissions approach. (The University of Oklahoma recruited 142 national merit scholars while admitting 96 percent of its applicants.) There are now thirteen states that offer nonneed tuition to in-state students who maintain a B average (96 percent of the University of Georgia's in-state frosh received HOPE scholarships in 2000).
- States are competing intensely to retain their highest-scoring students. They are financing merit-based aid through a variety of means: general state revenues, state lotteries, the national tobacco settlement, and interest on land leases and sales. Thirteen states planned to spend $709.4 million for merit awards for 320,000 students in 2000. The injection of this state money into the admissions marketplace has touched off bidding wars between nationally-ranked colleges and universities.
- Officials at elite institutions notice they are on the losing end of recruiting competitions with schools short on reputation, conscious of rankings, and eager to boast of high-powered incoming classes. Paul Neely wrote: "As a trustee of Williams College, I am at the tail of a long line of thoughtful, devoted board members. They have had many concerns over the years, but surely none had to worry about competition from the University of Arkansas. We worry about such things now." (Neely, 1999, p. 28)
- There has been a sharpening of institutional and educational styles as schools seek to define and maintain their merit niche. At the large public universities, residential and departmental honors programs for freshmen proliferate. Small liberal arts colleges hone the images of their campuses to reflect their investments in racial diversity,

technological fluency, and faculty mentoring through undergraduate research.

- What might be called regional public merit belts are successfully competing with the Ivies clustered in the northeast. One could, for example, imagine regional merit belts made up of a mixture of eight selective and nonselective state universities, which competed on an equal or better basis with the Ivies for high-performing students in 2000. A Heartland Merit Belt composed of Arkansas, Indiana, Iowa, Minnesota, Missouri, Illinois, Purdue, and Truman State enrolled 1727 valedictorians in 2000. A Sun Merit Belt of comprised of Alabama, Arizona State, Florida, Georgia Tech, North Carolina, Texas, Texas A&M, and Oklahoma enrolled 1102 National Merit finalists.

- This is not to suggest that any of these schools are colluding against the Ivies. The point is that high-performing high school students bring their talents into a market where geographically dispersed and educationally diverse sets of institutions are competing vigorously for their enrollment. The popular image of the meritocracy's rejected Ivy applicant has distracted attention from the emergence of public regional merit belts that are, in some cases, out-recruiting the Ivies for academically talented high-school students.

- The justification for intensifying admissions competition is now frequently made in terms of short- and long-term benefits to the college or university. As Robert Reich has argued, this "betting on the winners" strategy poses a severe threat to the social-mobility model of meritocracy. This investment model favors the high-scoring but low-financial-need students "rather than accommodating more lower-income students whose credentials and test scores do not add to an institution's luster." (Reich, 2000, p. B7) The logic is as follows: Our investment in merit aid will be returned in future alumni donations. There is now a subfield of economics that focuses on alumni giving and asks, among other questions, about how the size of merit awards correlates with the size of future gifts. Underscoring the role of alumni donations in admissions considerations, two economists advised: "Given the importance of graduates' attachment and pride in their alma maters, a comprehensive fund-raising strategy ideally would begin at the time students are recruited." (Baade and Sundberg, 1993)

- And, in fact, there are data to support Reich's foreboding. Tom Mortenson has calculated that the chances for a baccalaureate by age 24 for a student from the bottom income quartile in the U.S. actually dropped from 6.5 percent to 5.4 percent between 1970 and 1996.

Meanwhile the chances for students from the top quarter rose from 39.5 percent to 53 percent. Mortenson also calculated "unmet" and "overmet" financial need for undergraduates in 1995–1996. He found that students from families with incomes less than $10,000 had over $2,500 in unmet need, while students from families earning between $80,000 and $100,000 had $15,000 in overmet need. And both groups of students were attending public, four-year institutions (Mortenson, 1998, p. 3).

It is interesting to speculate about how Riesman would view these emerging features of the meritocratic admissions market. On the one hand, it seems fair to suggest that he would applaud the accelerating "spread of meritocratic institutions." He would take it to be a sign of the overall robustness of public higher education in the United States that as many high-performing students were studying in Kirksville, MO, and Norman, OK, as in Princeton, NJ, and Ithaca, NY.

On the other hand, Riesman would be troubled, I suspect, by the widespread acceptance of the investment model of financial aid distribution. He and Jencks wrote: "If resources are concentrated on those who show promise of joining the future elite while they are still young, the much discussed 'late bloomer' will never bloom at all." (Jencks and Riesman, 1968, p. 152) He would note, in other words, that the tension between social mobility and the elite-training model of the meritocracy is now academic. It is not a subject that finds vivid expression in popular culture. Nor, given the prolific use of merit aid, does the mobility model seem to be a major policy concern in many state capitals.

Why Meritocracies Matter

When President George W. Bush returned to Yale, his alma mater, to deliver the commencement address on May 21, 2001, he did not need to mention the "m" word. He could be confident that his antimeritocratic gibes would be understood and appreciated by at least part of his audience. He said: "To those of you who received honors, awards, and distinctions, I say, well done. And to the C students—(applause)—I say, you, too, can be President of the United States (laughter and applause)." (*Washington Post*, 2001)

Slate editor Michael Kinsley joined the laughter and applause, calling the joke an instance of Bush's "charming self-deprecation." (Kinsley, 2001) Kinsley went on to speculate about Bush's larger message about the meaning of merit, success, and smugness in American culture.

Sure we all know that with gumption and hard work, in this land of opportunity you can overcome a mountain of life's disadvantages to reach the pinnacle of success. That's one option. But as Bush subtly reminded the Yale graduates, there is another option: With a mountain of life's advantages, you can overcome a disposition against working hard and a cultural distaste for vulgar striving and reach the same pinnacles anyway! Our current president opted for the second strategy, and you cannot begrudge him smugness in noting that it worked. (Kinsley, 2001, p. A25).

Kinsley had a point. Who could fault the President for savoring this delicious last laugh? For underscoring the symbolic value of his mediocre academic record and his political success? For implying that studying, grades, and degrees can't compete, in life's long run, with wealth, connections, and charm? For insisting that the meritocracy doesn't matter?

But what about Kinsley's cynicism and that of the other new meritologists? Can they be faulted for not promoting a more searching and mature discussion of whether meritocracies matter? Or is the current level of candor, empirical research, and conceptual sophistication the most that the print media can manage on this complicated and delicate topic? Is there a point to imagining a more interesting and honest conversation about varieties of merit and why we care about them?

An important first step would be to vigorously challenge what I would call "meritocratic denial." This is the convenient and often self-serving position that college (both generally and specifically) adds nothing significant to one's talents, job prospects, and eventual fortunes. There are multiple forms of this popular "the meritocracy doesn't *really* matter" position.

One form, detailed by Benjamin DeMott, is the point that Jack Hitt was trying to make about Al Gore being self-made. DeMott argues that Americans protect themselves with a myth of classlessness by fixating on the meritocracy's tests, hoops, and hurdles. Such a fixation encourages individuals to heroize their own efforts and downplay their privileges. Being self-made, in DeMott's view, is a meritocrat's pet delusion.

Having interviewed Rhodes, Marshall, and Truman fellowship candidates at Amherst College over the years, DeMott was struck by how often the applicants wanted to take full credit for their willingness to explore and take risks. He writes: "Habitually, that capacity [venturesomeness] is seen as a personal trait; habitually, expensive advantages and options are understood to be, at bottom, self-made." (DeMott, 1996, p. 237)

Another form of denial is contained in the idea that meritocratic institutions are *only* about academic achievement, rather than the nurturing of powerful networks for advancement. S. M. Miller's version of his own "meritocratic rise" gives full credit to the "rabbis" in his social network who wrote letters, made phone calls, and opened doors for him. But he never acknowledges that he cultivated the regard of these "rabbis" through the networks of the prestigious colleges and universities that he attended (Miller, 2001).

Alert to the public's fascination with college dropout Bill Gates, some journalists have spotlighted the early careers of young software wizards. Bridget McMenamin, writing in *Forbes*, crafts the impression that the "Education Industry" is a scam to keep teenagers with technical skills from earning $50,000 a year and having their own apartments (McMenamin, 1998).

Jon Katz's *Geeks* (Katz, 2000) takes readers far down this "Who needs college?" road as well. Then Katz, experiencing some mixture of guilt and panic, arrived at the admissions office at the University of Chicago to plead for the acceptance of one of the computer jocks who was the subject of his book. What McMenamin and Katz fail to appreciate is that college is often the place where young people learn how to harness and expand their talents, and where the penalties for risk-taking and failure—poor grades—are lighter than they will be in the dot-com world.

Several self-proclaimed "defenders of meritocratic purity" are in denial about the complicated history and failures of selective admissions. Attacking the "top 4 percent of all high schools" admissions plans of Texas, Califonia, and Florida, Paul Attewell argues that such "percentage rules" victimize professional families who have clustered themselves in excellent school districts. He writes: "Admitting a fixed percentage from every high school into a state university system makes it clear that college admissions has become a political rather than a meritocratic process." (Attewell, 2000)

In advocating for high-scoring kids from the best districts over the high-effort kids from the worst, are we campaigning for an objective and fair meritocracy? Is Attewell really oblivious to the possibility that his own special pleading is also political?

Regents and state legislators continue to play with admissions thresholds for state universities. The University of California recently approved a proposal to guarantee admission to students in the top 12.5 percent of their graduating class, provided they complete two years at a community college and maintain a grade point average of 2.4. The change is expected to raise the number of students of color from 16.6 percent in the incoming class of 2001 to 36 percent in the frosh class of 2003. Ward Connerly voted in favor of the proposal but offered no explanation of the difference between the race preferences he opposed in July 1995 and the race sensitivity he embraced six years later (Selingo, 2001).

The idea that the meritocracy has a political life is not new. As long as there are arguments about what "merit" means, there will be politics in meritocracies. Riesman understood that the politics of merit would not evaporate with the advent of finely tuned tests and the calculation of grade point averages to the third decimal place. He wrote: ". . . the prospect of an administered rather than a politicized society seems remote to me, for people will always use politics to defend themselves against competition."(Riesman, 1967, p. 902)

We should care about academic meritocracies not because we imagine them to be neutral and predictable sieves for prized talents. Meritocracies, whether in the Ivy League, state universities, or public urban colleges, express both our certainty and our confusion about deeply held values. We're certain that we want our children to value—for both intrinsic and extrinsic reasons—the persistence of working hard with the intelligence of working smart. Kinsley is right that there are other options, but are they are options that educational institutions can responsibly endorse?

And it would be helpful to admit that we're confused about how to appraise the wide range of meritorious skills, knowledge, talents, and values that young people possess, and whether we should rank them for admissions or other purposes. Meritocracies presume to operate with a publicly accountable sense of fair play, even as politics corrupt that ideal.

In other words, we should imagine, as Christopher Jencks suggested in 1959, that meritocracies have an ethical as well as a political life. Jencks wrote:

> From the ethical viewpoint, we must ask whether we ought to expect social structure to reward all the virtues which a civilization deems important. Perhaps other institutions (such as the family) can be expected to encourage such things as generosity and sensitivity; these virtues may even become corrupted when they become vehicles to social mobility and status (Jencks, 1959, p. 18).

As "meritocracy" moves through its middle age, it would be useful to revisit this and other difficult questions raised at its birth.

References

"America's Talent Battle: The Real Meaning of Empowerment. *The Economist*, March 25, 2000: 75–77.

Attewell, P. "Mirage of Meritocracy." *The American Prospect* 2 (July 2000): 6.

Baade, R. A., and Sundberg, J. O. "Identifying the Factors That Stimulate Alumni Giving." *The Chronicle of Higher Education*, September 1993.

Barron's Educational Series, Inc. *Profiles of American Colleges* (24th ed.). New York: Hauppauge, 2001.

Berkman, J. "Harvard's Hoard." *New York Times Magazine*, June 24, 2001: 39–41.

Botstein, L. *Jefferson's Children: Education and the Promise of American Culture.* New York: Doubleday, 1997.

Broome, E. C. *A Historical and Critical Discussion of College Admission Requirements.* New York: The Macmillan Co., 1903.

Brooks, D. The Organization Kid. *Atlantic Monthly* (April 2001): 40–54.

"President Bush Speaks at Yale Graduation." *Washington Post*, July 17, 2001.

Connerly, W. *Creating Equal: My Fight against Race Preferences.* San Francisco: Encounter Books, 2000.

DeMott, B. "I Should Never Have Quit School." In DeMott, B. (ed.) *Created Equal: Reading and Writing About Class in America.* New York: HarperCollins, 1996: 227–238.

"Facts and Figures: 2000 Freshman Merit Scholars." *The Chronicle of Higher Education*, July 24, 2001.

Fiske, E. B. "Gaining Admission: Athletes Win Preference." *The New York Times Education Life*, January 7, 2001: 4A, p. 22.

Fleetwood, C., and Shelley, K. "The Outlook for College Graduates, 1998–2008: A Balancing Act." *Occupational Outlook Quarterly*, Fall 2000: 3–9.

Hacker, A. *Money.* New York: Scribner, 1997.

Hitt, J. "The Great Divide." *New York Times Magazine*, December 31, 2000: 6.13.

Jencks, C. "The Cult of Efficiency." *The New Republic*, September 7, 1959: 18.

———., and Riesman, D. *The Academic Revolution.* Garden City, NJ: Doubleday & Company, 1968.

Katz, J. *Geeks: How Two Lost Boys Rode the Internet Out of Idaho*: New York: Villard, 2000.

Kinsley, M. "Bush's Life Suggests the Old Elites Still Have What It Takes." Minneapolis *Star Tribune*, July 22, 2001, p. A25.

Kiyosaki, R. T., and Lechter, S. L. *Rich Dad, Poor Dad: What the Rich Teach Their Kids about Money—That the Poor and Middle Class Do Not!* New York: Warner Books, 1997.

Lavin, D., and Hyllegard, D. *Changing the Odds: Open Admissions and the Life Chances of the Disadvantaged.* New Haven, CT: Yale University Press, 1996.

Lemann, N. *The Big Test.* New York: Farrar Straus & Giroux, 1999.

Lipset, S. M., and Riesman, D. *Education and Politics at Harvard.* New York: McGraw-Hill Book Company, 1975.

Marcus, D. L., and Sohn, E. "Didn't Get In? You're Not Alone." *U.S. News & World Report*, April 30, 2001: 49.

McMenamin, B. "The Tyranny of the Diploma." *Forbes*, December 28, 1998: 104–109.

Miller, S. M. "My Meritocratic Rise." *Tikkun* 16 (2), March/April 2001: 63–64.

Moore, F. "How to Get Into College after Being Rejected." *The New York Times Magazine*, April 8, 2001: 47.

Mortenson, T. G. "Chance for College for Students from Low Income Families by State in 1996–97." *Postsecondary Education Opportunity* 78 (December 1998): 3– 7.

Neely, P. "The Threats to Liberal Arts Colleges." *Daedalus*, Winter 1999: 27–45.

Pollitt, K. "About Race: Can We Talk?" *The Nation*, July 7, 1997: 9.

Reich, R. B. "How Selective Colleges Heighten Inequality." *The Chronicle of Higher Education Review*, September 15, 2000: p. B7.

Reisberg, L. "A Top University Wonders Why It Has No Black Freshmen." *The Chronicle of Higher Education*, April 28, 2000, p. 34.

Riesman, D. "Notes on Meritocracy." *Daedalus*, 96 (Summer 1967): 897–908.

Riesman, D. "Educational Reform at Harvard College: Meritocracy and Its Adversaries." In Lipset, S. M., and Riesman, D. (eds.) *Education and Politics at Harvard.* New York: McGraw-Hill Book Company, 1975, p. 287.

Selingo, J. "Questioning the Merit of Merit Scholarships." *The Chronicle of Higher Education*, January 19, 2001, p. A20.

———. "U. of California Regents Approve Plan to Expand Admissions Opportunities." *The Chronicle of Higher Education*, July 20, 2000.

Shulman, J. L., and Bowen, W. G. *The Game of Life: College Sports and Educational Values.* Princeton, NJ: Princeton University Press, 2000.

Silverman, R. E. "The Jungle: What's News in Recruitment and Pay." *The Wall Street Journal*, December 5, 2000, p. B16.

Suskind, R. A *Hope in the Unseen: An American Odyssey from the Inner City to the Ivy League.* New York: Broadway Books, 1999.

Traub, J. *City on a Hill: Testing the American Dream at City College.* Reading, MA: Addison-Wesley, 1994.

Young, M. *The Rise of the Meritocracy.* Baltimore, MD: Penguin Books, 1958.

9

On Publicity, Poverty, and Transformation: Images and Recruitment in Teacher Education Brochures

GLENN M. HUDAK

From the beginning I conceived of this essay as a prelude to a larger study on the use of publicity images to promote various teacher education programs. Far from making this a "scientific" study of publicity images (see, for example, Williamson, 1981) and their use in teacher education promotional literature, I intend rather to explore in broad strokes the nature of the publicity itself, as a language that proposes we can transform ourselves and our lives by investing into some product, or as in the case at hand, enrolling into some program.

In this essay, the publicity images that I'm referring to are most often found in promotional brochures and informational literature that present, through a sequence of photos and catch-all phrases, the very broad outlines of a program of study. And while commissioned by schools of education, these promotional brochures are often times written and designed by media consultants with an eye towards advertising and hopefully selling a program within a tight market.

In the New York City metropolitan area, for example, there are well over a dozen departments and schools of education competing against each other to attract the prospective applicant to their respective teacher education programs. At issue here is not simply the different tuition costs of these programs—especially the cost difference between public and private institutions—but also the perceived professional status of various programs. Such an "elite" program, for instance, within a private university setting is able to attract students to pay high tuition, in part, by drawing upon its bank of "cultural capital," i.e., the prestige of its programs. The message to the reader is quality costs and you get what you pay for. The point of the brochure then, is not simply to provide information—for many reasons, as we will explore, that would be a boring turn-off to the reader—but rather, to persuade the applicant, the prospective teacher, to apply to "this" specific program. And that "this" specific program is absolutely essential to one's future career as a teacher.

Through the language of publicity and its attendant images the prospective applicant is led to believe that their dreams of a richer, fuller, more creative life as a teacher are close at hand. Indeed, in his book, *Ways of Seeing*, John Berger (1972) develops a brilliant analysis of publicity both as a language and a system of representation that has the power to persuade one to believe that they can be transformed, become glamorous. Berger states:

> Publicity is not merely an assembly of competing messages: it is a language in itself which is always being used to make the same general proposal . . . It proposes to each of us that we transform ourselves, or our lives, by buying something more . . . Publicity persuades us of such a transformation by showing us people who have apparently been transformed and are, as a result, enviable. The state of being envied is what constitutes glamour. And publicity is the process of manufacturing glamour (p. 131).

Notice from this passage that publicity, as a language, proposes that we can transform ourselves, our lives. Central to the persuasive power of publicity is its ability to exploit the rifts, gaps, and contradictions located within our daily lives. Most often these gaps can be located by focusing on our daydreams. Often our daydreams will reveal the gap between the realities of who and what we *are* at the moment as distinct from who and what we *would like* to be in the future; the gap is the distinction between our present reality and our vision of our future life. Strangely though, this transformation comes about not through, say, a critical analysis of one's life, nor is it accomplished by "working through" (in psychoanalytic terms) various issues one faces (or refuses to face). Rather, publicity persuades us to believe that the site of our transformation is not the result of intense inner work, and it attempts to shift our attention to a referent point located somewhere outside ourselves: people who have "apparently been transformed."

The site of transformation, as Berger suggests, is located in the "gap" between who we are and who we would like to be. Here "transformation" itself becomes less a process of intense personal (and social) work and more an act of fantasy, of picturing oneself in terms of future success, as someone who is of value in the social world—as someone of worth. The real trick, of course, is the way in which publicity works to present an image of credibility to the prospective consumer and hence persuade them to "buy into" the publicity message. As Berger writes, what makes publicity credible is:

> The gap between what publicity actually offers and the future it promises, corresponds with the gap between what the spectator-buyer feels himself to be and what he would like to be. The two gaps become one; and instead of a single gap being bridged by action or lived experience it is filled with glamorous day-dreams. (p. 148)

A program brochure, for instance, is able to persuade the prospective applicant that "this" teacher education program can fulfill one's dreams of being a successful teacher by bridging the gap between the present and the future with a glamorous day-dream, a promise of a life to come.

From Berger's analysis, publicity's power to persuade and seduce the potential applicant lies within its ability to tap into our own desires, wishes, and fantasies about who we would like to be in the world. As such, publicity works with us, and not against the grain of our struggle to be a Subject, "a somebody" in the world. Publicity works, in part, through the power of projection; we project an image of ourselves onto the image of the person in the publicity photo, one who has been transformed by the particular teacher program. Here we project an image of ourselves (as we imagine ourselves in the future) into the publicity ad, and as such we make a metonymic switch, a substitution in our mind's eye, between the publicity image (of one who is glamorous) for an image of ourselves. The applicants "picture" themselves in the future as teachers, while their present realities are put on hold, deferred.

More specifically, consider an example taken from a brochure distributed by one teacher program located within the New York City metropolitan area. This brochure presents information pertaining to its "Graduate Teaching Internship Program." The brochure, essentially one page, folded into three flaps, briefly describes the intern program by highlighting admissions requirements, various information about what the intern can expect from enrolling into the program (e.g., tuition credits), and where one can obtain further information. All of this is very straightforward and could have been presented on a single sheet of paper. Instead, the program is "packaged," a common practice today employed by many schools of education. The packaging of the program includes eight photographs of student interns within the school setting. All photos (and attendant information) are formatted upon glossy, sky-blue, high-quality paper, with all information printed in either white or gold letters. The designers of the brochure have also paid careful attention to font and overall placement of images and information.

The brochure is a well designed package. On the cover, under the gold-lettered title of the program, is a photo of an intern with a high school student. The intern is a woman, well dressed, leaning over and writing on some paper. To her left is the high school student looking on with intense interest as the intern writes. The intern is smiling; she looks like she is happy and is obviously enjoying helping/working/instructing the high school student. As one opens the brochure, on the left flap is a photo of an intern doing some paperwork; she is seated and flanked on her right and left by two elementary school students also working diligently. The intern is a woman, and she has a slight smile; she looks intensely interested in her work. She exudes a sense of fulfillment, calm, and being in control of the learning process.

The middle and right flap together merge into one page. This page has five photos: two smaller pictures at the top right and left corners, two smaller pictures at the bottom right and left corners, and one large picture in the center. The large photo is of an intern, a woman, again leaning over and distributing various papers to a group of four elementary students. There is a lively intensity on the intern's face. Her body language suggests that while being an intern is a lot of work, it is nonetheless satisfying and richly rewarding. The four smaller surrounding photos are: a male intern standing behind a high school student (a sense of "guiding" is suggested by this photo); a male intern pointing ahead to two middle school students, giving a sense of "direction" to students (possibly to have them consider some information on the board/viewing screen); a woman intern lecturing to high school students who are taking notes attentively (one gets the sense that this teacher's words "matter"); and a woman intern addressing students, possibly clarifying an assignment to two elementary school girls (here one gets the sense that what the intern says is valuable). On the back flap is one small photo of a male intern and a high school student talking about photography techniques; the student has a smile on his face; he is attentive and seems eager to listen to the intern's advice. The intern looks intense, committed to instruction, and dedicated to teaching this student. Also, adjacent to these photos are bubbles, quotes from the interns themselves that capture, in a short statement, the essential "spirit" of the program. We read about: "the intensity of the learning experience," of how "gratifying" it is to use teaching techniques that work, of how this program experience helps one get started in teaching.

Taken together, this package conveys not just information regarding the intern program, but also the "ambiance" of what it would be like to be an intern within this program. Further in the process of conveying the experience, the brochure argues and persuades through a rhetoric of the obvious. That is, the potential applicant is led to believe that he/she could be the one in the photos. The tacit message is: This could be you! And what we do see of the intern program—at least my reading of it—is that it obviously "looks" pretty good: The classroom environments surrounding the interns are always neat, clean, orderly. Both interns and students are well dressed, eager, attentive, inquisitive, and ready for the challenges ahead. Everything is beautiful; everyone is doing beautiful things. The point to the viewer is obvious. Who, for instance, wouldn't want to intern at a warm, exciting school? Who wouldn't want to feel that they count, that their presence matters to the hearts and minds of children and that the intern's presence is essential to the future success of the children pictured? (In the fifteen years that I've taught in teacher education programs, I've not come across one teacher who wanted to be boring, mean, and alienating to her students.) Indeed, the brochure's message is above all obviously rhetorical. There is no need for the potential applicant to think deeply. The brochure tells you, the applicant, that children are there, now, waiting for your arrival, your input, and your caring leadership. There is a certain air of importance to being an intern as well as an ambiance of glamour that is associated with the interns pictured; they do appear to be in an enviable position.

Brochures, such as the above, are powerfully persuasive, especially if the applicant feels somehow discontent with their current life's circumstances, e.g., their current job. As Berger points out, the location of publicity's persuasive activity is found within the site of our daily daydreams. It is within the context of our daydream we become both the acting Subject of the fantasy and the subject (of the narrative content) of the daydream itself. In our mind's eye, we adopt the narrative initiated by the original publicity image as our own story. On the wings of our desire to be a Subject, we suspend judgment about what we know of our life circumstances for a few moments of what could be in the future: an image of ourselves as liberated from our current circumstance (meaningless work) and transformed into a person of import, a needed helper of children. The concern, as Berger notes, is that the glamorous daydream (its image) is privileged over actual substantial change in our lives. For in the world of publicity, "transformation" can occur only within the context of one's inner fantasy world. It needs to be noted here that there is, however, nothing pathological about having a rich and active fantasy life. It goes without saying that many creative projects begin in one's active imagination—in one's mind's eye.

The concern for Berger is the appropriation of the "gap" (that space of fantasy and imagination between who we are and who we would like to be) by capitalism. Publicity works by taking over a psychological process common to all people. Indeed, Berger begins his book by writing, "Seeing comes before words. The child looks and recognizes before it can speak." (p. 7) That is, there is always a "gap" between what we see and what we can express about the world we see. Our ability to name the world does not exhaust the world we see. There is always "more" to say, and as such there is always that sense of the spiritual, the mystery of living (see Hudak, 2001).

Still further, as psychoanalytic theory tells us, there is a "gap" between what we can think and our capacity to actually experience. We may be able to think more, and imagine more, than we have the emotional capacity to experience. Psychoanalyst Michael Eigen (1998) writes,

> The time lag between and within ourselves also has deep roots. The impact of trauma, and emotional experience in general is often too much for our equipment to process . . . Our equipment produces states it is not able to handle . . . And no amount of growing and learning will supplant or eradicate the permanent embryonic dimension of living . . .
>
> A hallmark of defective hardware, equipment, or mental apparatus is an incapacity to let experiencing build . . . [conversely] the capacity to let experience build begins with the transformation of an impact into dream work, myth, symbolization, affective images and primal narratives . . . [However] we can not keep up with experiential impacts. Production of experience outstrips assimilation. Our experience produces states it can not handle. It is doubtful we can ever catch up with ourselves, or do ourselves justice; we are too much (or too little) for ourselves . . . (p. 100).

At the psychic level, as Eigen notes, there is another gap identified as a time, "a lag," within experience itself This time lag is found in daily living and is located in the temporal space between the impact of emotional experiences we have and our ability to digest or process them. We are not always able to process emotional experiences immediately upon impact to our psyche; there is delay time in the digesting. Indeed in trauma, for example, our psychic equipment is overloaded, and hence we are unable to fully digest this emotional experience into our psychic system.

In health, we transform emotional impacts on our psychic life into dream work, myth, and symbols. However, as Eigen claims, we can never be fully successful in our attempts to transform these experiences into dream or symbols. "It is doubtful we can ever catch up with ourselves." Indeed, he further claims that no amount of growing and learning will eradicate this permanent dimension of living. This is profound, in that Eigen is suggesting that a part of our human condition entails a moment of precocity;

precocious in the sense that we experience and are able to produce more emotional states than we have the capacity to handle. For Eigen, precocity is given an ontological status, a condition that is part of what it means to be human. For the child and the adult there will always be a time lag in the processing of our emotions and in the naming, identifying, or handling them. As adults this sense of precocity is manifested as a feeling that we are unable to catch up with ourselves; emotionally we are always behind ourselves. Daydreams, in turn, are a part of a healthy working through of our precocity in the sense that they provide a site where we can use fantasy and imagination to bring together our desire to transform ourselves, to feel complete.

As a part of this human quest for completion, we search for what psychotherapist Christopher Bollas (1987) refers to as the "transformational object." For Bollas, transformation is a basic human need that is established in early periods of infancy. The infant's first experience of the Other, her mother or the primary caregiver for instance, is identifiable "as a process that is identified with cumulative internal and external transformations." (p. 14) The infant's first experience of the mother, say, is an experience of the mother not as some external object, but rather as a process; a process of "transformation" itself. The mother's care enables the infant to grow and hence transform itself. This "first" experience sets the stage, so to speak, for our search for what Bollas identifies as the transformational object: "the experience of an object that transforms the subject's internal and external world." (p. 28) This early preverbal experience between mother and infant comes to constitute a grid, a template for later experiences associated with the phenomena of transformation.

The search, then, for the transformational object in our adult life is grounded in the early memory of the infant's first object relation: the infant's relationship with the mother/primary caregiver. Bollas writes:

> In adult life, therefore, to seek the transformational object is to recollect an early object experience, to remember not cognitively but existentially—through intense affective experience—a relationship which was identified with cumulative transformational experiences of the self . . . The search for such an experience may generate hope, even a confidence and vision, but although it seems to be grounded in the future tense, in finding something in the future transform the present, it is an object-seeking that recurrently enacts a pre-verbal ego memory (pgs. 16–17).

Our desire to project into the future through daydreaming is in part a reenactment of "a pre-verbal memory," our distant past. It is an existential remembering that generates hope itself; we anticipate the event that promises to transform the present. Our present search to transform ourselves causes us to anticipate a future moment of change; however, this future anticipation is grounded in a preverbal past experience. *We reexperience our past by anticipating our future in our hopes of transforming the present.*

The infant's "first" experience of the transformational object stays with us throughout our lives. As Bollas points out, our search to reexperience this preverbal memory has an aesthetic, cultural, and religious moment. As an aesthetic moment, "when a person engages in deep subjective rapport with an object, the culture embodies in the arts varied symbolic equivalents to the search for transformation. In the quest for a deep subjective experience of an object, the artist both remembers for us and provides us with occasions for the experience of ego memories of transformation." (pp. 28–29) Our search for transformation is then, a kind of "psychic prayer for the arrival of the transformational object: a secular second coming of an object relation experience in the earliest period of life." (p. 17) Certain moments of religiosity are linked to the search for the transformational object, a preverbal ego memory that is never fully articulated. There is always that "gap" in our lives.

But here capitalism enters the picture through the language of publicity. Publicity exploits the gap, the time lag, and our desire to daydream. "We know," writes Bollas, "that the advertising world makes its living on the trace of this object: the advertised product usually promises to alter the subject's external environment and hence change internal mood." (p. 16) Publicity absorbs into its logic our desire for the creative moment, the spiritual moment, the cultural event. Publicity is able to absorb and work with our desire for completion, for transformation, our desire to ease the tension between who we are and who we'd like to be by bridging the gap. However, to be human is to live in the gap, to live in a state of tension between who we are and who we would like to be.

Through therapy we "work through" this tension. "Working through" does not mean that the tension is resolved; transformation does not mean gratification. Rather, we grow, and we expand our capacity to experience more fully the tension that is our life. There is a deep moment of the sacred within this therapeutic encounter. But the sacred moment does not stop here. Indeed, from the more politicized perspective of Paulo Freire (1993/1970), our search for transformation is a part of the "quest for human completion" (p. 29), and our quest, our vocation, is to humanize the world in a way that allows all of us to be more fully human. As such, Freire's quest involves a "conversion . . . [a] conversion to the people [that] requires a profound rebirth. Those who undergo it must take on a new form of existence; they can no longer remain as they are." (pp. 42–43) Our search for transformation is at once spiritual, personal, cultural, aesthetic, and political. Political, in Freire's sense that our individual search for transformation becomes our collective dream for transforming the world. This collective dream is rooted in an ontological moment of "yearning" (p. 26) for freedom and the struggle for human completion. This yearning is powerful and cuts across the grain of capitalism, of the profit motive, and of the rhetoric of publicity. For Freire, the struggle to humanize the world is a collective effort that is accomplished through praxis-action and reflection on our actions as historical beings.

Publicity has us believe there is no history, no becoming; there is instead only acquisition. As Berger (1972) writes:

> Publicity, is situated in a future continually deferred, excluded the present and so eliminates all becoming, all development. Experience is impossible within it . . . Everything publicity shows is there awaiting acquisition. The act of acquiring has taken the place of all other actions, the sense of having has obliterated all other senses (p. 153).

"Becoming" and "development" entail actions and struggle on our part. Indeed, it is one thing to talk idealistically about the quest for human completion, and another to actually experience it, to live it. Understanding is not realization; what sounds right is not the same as the existential moment of experiencing, of developing our capacity to "hold" the tension between who we are and who we want to be, i.e., hold the gap. It is here that publicity plays on the desire to avoid the struggle, the pain. Publicity promises to fill the gap, not with lived action or with real work on self in society, but rather with the promise of being glamorous.

To be sure, Berger is quick to add that the social production of glamour, publicity's own dream of transformation, is located at the heart of capitalism. Berger writes:

> Glamour cannot exist without personal social envy being a common and widespread emotion. The industrial society which has moved towards democracy and then stopped half way is the ideal society for generating such an emotion. The pursuit of individual happiness has been acknowledged as a universal right. Yet the existing social conditions make the individual feel powerless. He (or she) lives the contradiction between what he is and what he would like to be . . . It is this which makes it possible to understand why publicity remains credible (p. 148).

Here Berger is astute in his observation. He observes the immature development of our society—a society that has pushed for democracy but has "stopped half way"—and that this climate is "ideal for generating such an

emotion" as envy and the need to be glamorous. Berger is making a corre-
lation between the political immaturity of democracy and the emotional
immaturity of individuals who live within this society. That is, there is a
correspondence between the arrested development of democracy and the
arrested development of individuals. Both society and individuals look
toward the future to find some external object to transform them; "we"
daydream about transformation collectively rather than looking, so to
speak, within ourselves to work through impasses that block democracy.

We are talking here of breakdowns, both in individuals and in society.
For publicity short-circuits the citizen's ability to "process" their experience
as a social Self. In many ways then the citizen, the sociopolitical Self,
becomes "precocious." Lacking the political equipment to digest the raw
trauma of day-to-day living at work, for example, our imagination produces states of fantasy that it can only partially live. There is a gap between
what we see, imagine, and wish, and our true achievement as citizens.

Publicity tells us we are what we *do*. Transformation, in turn, means picturing oneself acting like a person in a publicity ad, such as the "Graduate
Internship" brochure described earlier. This brochure tells the prospective
applicant that they will do as those seen in the publicity photos. And that,
having acquired certain experiences from the program, they, the applicants,
can look like the interns in the brochure. I find this troubling. For the
interns pictured, while shown posing in action positions, are nonetheless
seen as being complete. There is no sense of becoming for these interns.
They all look as if they have arrived; they appear perfect in a perfect environment. The very desire to project a perfect teaching world in the
brochure serves only to undermine the wonder of being a teacher: that
teaching is about growth; it is about continual learning; it is about process
and struggle. For there is always a gap in teaching between who we are and
what we would like our classes to be. Indeed, the realization of this gap is,
at times, painful for us teachers to contemplate.

Equally important, as theologian Henri Nouwen (1998/1988) elo-
quently writes, when,

> We live in a world where we are made to believe that we are what we
> do. We are important if we do something important; we are intelli-
> gent if we do something intelligent; we are valuable if we do some-
> thing valuable. Therefore, we are very concerned to have something
> to do, to be occupied . . . But, when we live as if we are what we do,
> we have sold our souls to the world. We have allowed the world to
> determine who we are. We have, in fact, become lonely people,
> always anxiously looking around and wondering what other people
> think about us, always needing people to consider us nice, intelli-
> gent, and worthwhile . . . (p. 20).

The publicity image asks us essentially to sell our soul for the approval of others, to be envied, to be glamorous, to be seen as complete. As such, we need to ask: Are the images in teacher education brochures (like the one mentioned) also tempting us to sell our souls to be at the center of the picture? Is this brochure suggesting that by enrolling in a program one will acquire the perfect job? If so, there is a great irony here. For the publicity images in this brochure seem to support a position that many teacher educators are ideologically committed to transforming. That is, in many of our teacher education programs we go to great lengths to stress that teaching is an ongoing project, never fixed or final. And that through teaching, we claim that we would find a part of ourselves, become authenticated in and through our struggles, our joys, our sorrows, our frustrations as we work to bring together our collective hopes to humanize the world with the often times harsh realities we face in educating children in economically poor schools. Indeed, and with regard to the brochure in question, issues (and images) revolving around urban poverty are completely excluded from the presentation. What are we to read from this brochure that omits representations of poverty within the urban school setting? I wonder what would happen if, instead of images of new middle-class schools, the brochure presented photos from actual urban settings, some of which are in economically poor neighborhoods?

I suspect that the designers of the brochure made a conscious decision not to present images from economically poor schools out of fear that such images might scare away prospective applicants from applying and, perhaps, from the profession. This is only a guess on my part. But if there is truth to my claim, then we are doing a disservice not only to the children by not allowing their humanity to shine even in difficult settings, but also to the preparation of future teachers. For the hidden curriculum in this brochure is the haunting specter of the fear of poverty and the struggle of security at all levels of life. This fear is understandable, in part, but if fear is our guide, then how will new teachers develop the intelligence and courage to challenge the injustices facing the children in their classroom?

Indeed, J. Krishnamurti (1953) argues that the purpose of education is,

> To cultivate right relationship, not only between individuals, but also between the individual and society; Intelligence lies in understanding oneself and going above and beyond oneself; but also there cannot be intelligence as long there is fear. Fear perverts intelligence and is one of the causes of self-centered action. Discipline may suppress fear but does not eradicate it, and the superficial knowledge, which we receive in modern education, only further conceals it. . . . The right kind of education must take into consideration this question of fear, because fear warps our whole outlook on life. To be

without fear is the beginning of wisdom, and only the right kind of education can bring about the freedom from fear in which alone there is deep and creative intelligence (p. 34).

Krishnamurti's observations must be taken to heart if we are to help our students develop the "right kind of education." For at issue is this: by not allowing student teachers to work through their fears—especially the fear of poverty that they have internalized from proliferation of publicity images we breathe daily—we collude by denying them the opportunity to develop the intelligence needed to do what theologian Aloysius Pieris refers to as confronting "mammon."

Liberation theologian Aloysius Pieris (1988) speaks to many of the issues revolving around poverty and wealth. For Pieris, poverty takes two forms. There are those who live in poverty, and there are those who opt to be poor to follow the model of a Christian as seen in the life and actions of Jesus. Indeed, from a theological perspective, Pieris defines two biblical axioms: "the irreconcilable antagonism between God and wealth, and the irrevocable covenant between God and the poor, Jesus himself being the covenant." (p. 15) The enemy, then, for Pieris is "mammon." Mammon is more than money in the traditional sense; rather it is a particular way of being and acting in the world. Mammon creates the sinful condition of imposed poverty.

In an important passage, Pieris links the concepts of poverty and mammon:

> Poverty, however, is not merely a material rejection of wealth, because mammon is more than just money. It is a subtle force oper- ating within me, an acquisitive driving me to be the rich fool . . . Or again, mammon is what I do with money and what it does to me; what it both promises and brings when I come to terms with it: security, success, power, and prestige—acquisitions that make me appear privileged. It makes me seem to possess a special gift of lead- ership (p. 16).

Notice, then, how mammon is what we do with money; it is a disposition that brings with it the "promise" of success, power, and prestige. Mammon makes one feel special, superior, and a leader—privileged. Extending the logic of this quote, we begin to notice that when ideas become cultural cap- ital, they operate as that subtle force that has the potential to make us feel superior by virtue of the status we receive. Here, ideas as cultural capital become mammon, as they are exchanged for success, power, and privilege within the hierarchy of the academy.

Pieris continues his discussion of poverty by pushing us to consider that the only way in which we are likely to transcend and move beyond the influence of mammon is to follow the path taken by Jesus. He suggests that, "the new humanity will not be achieved by power and prestige, but by weakness, failure, and humiliation." (p. 17) What does it mean to be weak, to fail, and to experience humiliation? My sense is that the new humanity referred to implies that we must die, so to speak, from this life built upon the false premises of the importance of prestige and status. If we are truly motivated to help humanize the world, we need to become one with the poor and the suffering and experience weakness, failure, and humiliation. For without this experience and realization, it is still possible to act in ways such that we (un)intentionally profit at the expense of those whom we are attempting to help, the poor. Indeed, "Let's purge our minds," writes Pieris,

> Of the exhibitionist model of social messianism whereby we become heroes of altruism at the expense of the poor. Far from being subjects of their own emancipation, they remain perpetual objects of our compassion thanks to our organized charity, or instruments of self-aggrandizement thanks to our "organized struggles." . . . An introspective analysis should make us question the honesty of our involvement in light of social analysis of structures that so easily allow us to exploit the poor for our personal fulfillment. The source of this exploitation once again could be the monies that flow in for the poor. Whoever dares to be with God on the side of the poor must renounce all hope of being a hero. It is a criminal's fate— the cross—that Jesus holds out as the banner under which victory is assured (p. 23).

This is a powerful passage. It drives home the necessity of deep introspection in our attempts to aid the poor. Further, it warns us against becoming a "hero of altruism at the expense of the poor." Here we must be on guard against a false sense of generosity, a deceptive mode of generosity that aids the poor with the hope of self-aggrandizement (gain in cultural capital) in the background.

Finally, Pieris reminds us that the goal is not necessarily to eradicate poverty. For poverty has two dimensions: The first, opting for poverty, is where we opt to follow the life of Jesus. The second sense of poverty refers to imposed poverty, the condition faced by those forced to exist in conditions of extreme economic and psychological hardship. Our struggle is to work with the poor to alleviate the sinful conditions that perpetuate suffering. Wealth, then, is not evil in itself for,

> Wealth is at the service of poverty, and poverty is the condition for liberation from acquisitiveness and greed . . . Hence . . . the antonym of wealth is not poverty but acquisitiveness or avarice . . . The primary struggle, therefore, is not eradication of poverty, but the struggle against mammon—that undefinable force that organizes itself within every person and among persons to make wealth antihuman, antireligious, and oppressive (p. 75).

Again, our struggle is with mammon, not wealth *per se*. Indeed, within the current play of capitalist power relations, wealth is needed to aid the poor in a material ways (e.g., to provide food, shelter, and medical care) as well as dismantle oppressive structures.

Adding to the discussion, Gustavo Gutierrez (1979) discusses poverty as a sort of Christian version of private property, a sort of spiritual form of cultural capital. Traditionally the vow of poverty was perceived as a particular kind of lifestyle available only to a privileged elite within the church hierarchy. And where "above and beyond the realm of pure and noble intentions, poverty seemed to be the private property of a certain group of Christians who often seemed to flaunt it as if it were their particular form of wealth." (p. 12) Notice here how Gutierrez fleshes out the essential issue: the egoism and pride connected with the vow of poverty and how egoism works in subtle ways to transform a liberating moment (opting to be poor) into a commodity for exchange—prestige. For Gutierrez, and Pieris, poverty is viewed as embodying two forms: Christian poverty and the sinful state of material poverty that is the result of social injustice. Christian poverty means that those who fight against poverty are asked to bear a radical witnessing of this injustice and the evil it embodies. As such for the Christian, poverty is "not taken on insofar as it represents some ideal lifestyle." Rather, we are asked to fight injustice, as Jesus did, out of a spirit "of love and fellowship in order to redeem human beings from their sins; in order to combat human egotism and abolish the injustice and divisiveness existing between human beings." (p. 14)

And finally, like Pieris, Gutierrez (1996) discusses the multidimensional aspects of poverty. For Gutierrez,

> Poverty can be an act of love and liberation. It has redemptive value. If the ultimate cause of human exploitation and alienation is selfishness, the deepest reason for voluntary poverty is love of neighbor. Christian poverty has meaning only as a commitment of solidarity with the poor, with those who suffer misery and injustice. [As such] you cannot really be with the poor unless you are struggling against poverty . . . Christian poverty, as an expression of love, is solidarity with the poor and is a protest against poverty (p. 172).

Notice that, for the Christian, poverty has a redemptive value; it is the desert wherein we struggle to overcome mammon, or egoism. To be poor, as an option for Christian living, means to let go of selfishness so that we may truly love our neighbor. The conceptual issue for Gutierrez is to make the analytic distinction between material poverty and Christian poverty.

In sum, the question of poverty revolves around two poles: the first being the undeniable realities of imposed, material poverty, a result of the sinfulness of capitalism. The other pole is opting to be poor, where the Christian follows the path of Jesus, by struggling against mammon. Indeed, the focus of the discussion revolves around mammon, that force that seduces us to accumulate wealth at the expense of others. The result of mammon is greater disconnection, rather than connection, between people. And as distance between people grows it becomes hard to empathize, harder to care about our neighbors' suffering, and most important, harder to maintain our connections with our neighbors' suffering. Martin Luther King, Jr. spoke to this issue when he said:

> What affects one directly, affects all indirectly. As long as there is poverty in this world, [no one] can be totally healthy . . . Strangely enough, I can never be what I ought to be until you are what you ought to be. You can never be what you ought to be until I am what I ought to be (quoted in Cone, 1996, p. xvii).

And here we come to the crux of the matter: For me to be me, you have to be you; for you to be you, I have to be me. So simple to understand, and yet so hard to realize and to live, given the current hierarchical structure of institutions, especially the university.

Now while I do not have a complete answer to the set of questions I posed at the beginning of this essay, I feel at least I have a better sense of direction, albeit a vague one. Namely, this issue at hand is not poverty per se, but rather the subtle and not so subtle ways in which we exploit ourselves, each other, and our planet for profit. This is John Berger's point in his discussion of publicity. And as long as we, the academics, allow our teacher education programs to be guided by a "for-profit" logic, a logic that allows for glossy recruitment brochures, then we, too, are part of the problem.

References

Berger, J. *Ways of Seeing*. New York: Penguin Books, 1972.
Bollas, C. The *Shadow of the Object*. New York: Columbia University Press, 1987.
Cone, J. *A Black Theology of Liberation*. Maryknoll, NY: Orbis Books, 1996.
Eigen, M. *The Psychoanlytic Mystic*. Binghamton, NY: ESF Publishers, 1998.
Freire, P. *Pedagogy of the Oppressed*. Boston: Continuum, 1993. (Original work published 1970.)
Gutierrez, G. *A Theology of Liberation*. Maryknoll, NY: Orbis Books, 1996.

194 • Glenn M. Hudak

———. "Liberation Praxis and Christian Faith." In *Frontiers of Theology in Latin America*, edited by R. Girellii. Maryknoll, NY: Orbis Books, 1979.
Hudak, G. "Addicting Epistemologies?" In *Labeling: Pedagogy & Politics*, edited by G. Hudak and P. Kihn. London: Routledge/Falmer Books, 2001.
Krishnamurti, J. *Education and the Significance of Life.* New York: Harper, 1953.
Nouwen, H. *Henri Nouwen: Selected Writings.* Maryknoll, NY: Orbis Books, 1988.
Pieris, A. *An Asian Theology of Liberation.* Edinburgh: T & T Clark, 1988.
Williamson, J. *Decoding Advertisements.* London: Marion Boyars, 1981.

3

Exploring Identity and Difference in the Context of Higher Education

10
"Should I Stay or Should I Go?" Lesbian Professors in Popular Culture

ALLISON J. KELAHER YOUNG

The Dis-closing of that Original Integrity *is* actively participating in the Unfolding of Be-ing as Good. It is following one's Final Cause. The Final Cause, then, is the beginning, not merely the end of the becoming. It is the First Cause and the Cause of causes, which gives an agent the motivation to Act. (Daly, 1992, p. 329)

Should I stay or should I go now? If I go there will be trouble and if I stay it will be double. So come on and let me know—Should I stay or should I go? (The Clash, 1981)

Historically, the popular perception of professors involves the older, distinguished, white gentleman-scholar, the liberal intellectual who sits in the Ivory Tower, contemplating questions about which the majority of people could not care less. Clearly, the conventional image conveys both hierarchy and separateness to higher education, an aura of exclusive elitism that keeps out the intellectually unwashed. And this particular reputation may be well deserved. Some of us choose lives in academia because we enjoy the fact that intellectual work *separates* us from others in different kinds of careers. Some of us choose academia because we *enjoy* intellectual work, and that alone may separate us from others who see us as heady and overly analytical. Either way, being a professor holds some social clout, traditionally putting us in positions of authority whether we want or deserve it.

This clout may lead others to perceive us as a threat, in the sense that our work is to question commonly held assumptions, values, and beliefs and to ask questions about the world around us.

This assumption that higher education is based on radically liberal frameworks leads us to think of academia as a haven for gay, lesbian, bisexual, or transgender (GLBT) people. Indeed, many GLBT people have placed faith in this assumption and have entered into various levels of academia, hoping to find a working environment where they have an opportunity to be themselves. However, it turns out that "higher education, like its K–12 counterpart, all too often preserves and even endorses the prejudice of its surrounding culture. Simultaneously, colleges and universities are seen as guardians of truth and sources of new knowledge." (McNaron, 1997, p. 7) In particular, lesbians pose a threat to the natural order of things both inside and outside of academia because our lives serve to question the assumptions about the intersection of gender roles and female sexuality in society. Describing this questioning of assumptions, Rycenga (1999) writes that "being a lesbian is never stable, solid, or grounded; its status quo is status-less: a free-floating agent of disruptive change and momentous insight." (p. 171) This kind of experience is a particular challenge in academia because these dynamic characteristics are considered oppositional to the dominant curricular paradigms in higher education, which often seek to codify and essentialize knowledge and learning in ways that are consistent with the market consciousness required of contemporary universities.

Thus, those of us who wear the auspicious title "lesbian professor" may experience a margin unto ourselves. Lesbian sexuality in itself interrogates the dominant discourse in academia, so that the lesbian professors are border crossing by definition. Traditionally, professors have held positions of authority. As lesbian professors, we work from within a position that doubly de-legitimizes our authority. Not only are we women, but we are women who have little need of men in terms of interpersonal validation and relationship. Thus, we bring to higher education one of the most unauthorized discourses. Our presence questions one of the central purposes of higher education, to reproduce and uphold cultural norms. This heightens the tension around border crossing with integrity, around being "ourselves" in the context of academe. This leaves us with central questions that echo those raised by Talburt and Salvio (this volume) in their discussion of the phenomenon of academic stars in the post-historical university, the overarching one being "Is the academy open enough to individuals' authentic identities?" It can be argued that this issue of authenticity is one that a great many of us in academia experience. Can any of us have integrity in the context of the institution of higher education? The multiple border crossing (heightened when we add social class, ethnicity, and ableness into the equation) negotiated by lesbian professors creates a point of greater articulation around issues of integrity and authenticity, which invites us to explore these questions using their narratives.

When I first began this project, I asked several of my lesbian friends if they could think of any films with lesbian professors. It took almost twenty minutes for us to recall that *Lianna* (Sayles, 1982), *Desert Hearts* (Deitch, 1985), and *When Night is Falling* (Rozema, 1995) are all films which feature a lesbian professor. Remarkably, this initial inquiry demonstrated that these depictions were not particularly memorable to us, which serves to highlight the invisibility of academic lesbians even within the lesbian community. We are more likely to recognize Ginger and Sydney, who are lesbian professor–cartoon characters who appear with their entire lesbian community in a series entitled *Dykes to Watch Out For* (Bechdel, 1996). This comic strip is popular in the lesbian community, and I have a few heterosexual friends who read it as well. Regardless, I find it questionable that portrayals of lesbian professors are more frequently found in a comic strip than they are in popular film or television.

There seems to be a general absence of lesbians everywhere in popular film. We are more likely to be represented in the art film genre. Referring to the release of *Desert Hearts* in 1985, Schulman (1994) notes, "the lesbian feature boom that seemed imminent in 1986 still feels a long way off, lagging behind gay film progress in financing and in the discarding of stigma." (p. 156) Stacey (1995) expresses the same lament, noting that the mainstream Hollywood depictions of lesbians in the 1990s have either rendered us in a pathological light (*Single White Female*, 1992; *Basic Instinct*, 1992) or the producers and directors have dimmed down the lesbian relationships (*The Color Purple*, 1985; *Fried Green Tomatoes*, 1991) to a point "in which female admiration and solidarity becomes the acceptable face of lesbianism on the Hollywood screen." (p. 93) Even *The Incredibly True Adventures of Two Girls in Love*, the one major mid-1990s feature film focused on lesbian content, exposes a variety of problems. It could be argued that the girl who identifies as a lesbian "seduces" the straight girl away from her boyfriend, and the ending, while humorous, leaves the viewer conflicted.

Given these conditions, I set about investigating the images of lesbians in higher education in popular film. Ultimately, though, this analysis offers one particular perspective on these films (Weaver and Daspit, 1998). I am framing this from my space as an untenured, assistant professor who happens to be white, middle-class, and lesbian. To me, the border crossings portrayed in these films serve to expose the silencing conservatism of institutions of higher education, which exist in stark contrast to the popular perception of academia as liberal.

I have chosen to focus my analysis on *Desert Hearts* and *When Night is Falling*, both of which hold to the conventions of a Hollywood-style romance, where the lesbian couple "rides off together into the sunset." (Stacey, 1995) In addition, in these films the protagonists are the professors themselves, while the professor in *Lianna* plays a catalyst. *Desert Hearts* and *When Night is Falling* depict the evolution of relationships between the protagonists and the wild, artistic women who lure them out of their stiff, academic shells. These films depict the lesbian professor as initially rigid and focused almost solely on her career as well as her increasing disenchantment with her relationships with men. These professors seem to be searching for something that they cannot yet name.

At the time it was released, Donna Deitch's 1986 film *Desert Hearts* was touted in the *Community News* (April 1986) as an important film, particularly within the gay/lesbian community (Schulman, 1994). Based on the novel *Desert of the Heart*, by Jane Rule (1964) this film is recognized as one of the few popular films in which the lesbian romance ends happily (Merck, 1993; Stacey, 1995). *Desert Hearts* left audiences with two conflicting reactions: relief and disappointment. While there is a happy ending, many viewers felt that it lacked the emotional intensity of typical romance films (Stacey, 1995). The film is set on a ranch outside of Reno, Nevada, in 1959. The ranch and its wide-open spaces provide a place of respite for divorcées awaiting the finalization of divorce proceedings. It is owned and operated by Frances Parker, whose stepdaughter, Cay, is the lesbian-artist. The film traces the story of thirty-five year old Vivian Bell, a professor of English literature at Columbia University in New York City. Vivian is looking for something she cannot name, and as she interacts with Cay more and more in the context of the Nevada desert, she develops a fondness for the wild artist. In time, Cay seduces Vivian, and they begin to negotiate their relationship. Eventually, Vivian's divorce becomes final, and as she is preparing to leave, she asks Cay to go with her to New York. In the final scene of the film, Cay gets on the train with Vivian as it is pulling out of the station. While this ending was significantly more positive than previous films, there was little in the way of character development as well as minimal chemistry between the characters, leaving the viewer ambivalent about the film as a whole.

Released ten years after *Desert Hearts*, *When Night is Falling* was hailed as "a romantic fairy tale, really, about confronting our fears, seen and unseen, and making that journey, over enormous barriers and unseen terrain, to our essential selves." (Guthman, 1995) Perhaps more appropriately framed as an "art" cinema narrative, this film, by Canadian director Patricia Rozema, was acclaimed at the Los Angeles Gay and Lesbian Film Festival and Berlin Film Festival (Shulgasser, 1995). Regardless, this film frames its subject matter in terms of the convention of the Hollywood romance (Stacey, 1995). *When Night is Falling* leaves the viewer with all of the relief and little of the disappointment of *Desert Hearts* because there is an emotional intensity between the main characters that is lacking in *Desert Hearts*. The film is set at a Christian college in Toronto, where Camille teaches mythology. Her lover of three years, Martin, teaches theology there also, and the two are being considered as a team for the chaplainship of the college. After the death of her beloved dog, Bob, Camille meets the beautiful and exotic Petra, who is a magician in the circus that is passing through town. Petra makes the initial move, which Camille rejects, though this clearly exposes her to important life questions. The circus must leave town quickly. Camille, apparently despondent over her conflicting feelings, both personal and professional, makes an attempt to end her life. This attempt is foiled by Petra and her friends, and the final scene of the film shows Petra and Camille studying a map in Petra's circus trailer as the circus convoy drives away from the city.

These awakenings are not without a price, since in each film the professor must eventually consider the impact of her newly realized sexual identity on her career. The professor may resist at first, but eventually she realizes her desire for the other woman and confronts this in a way which leads to a positive outcome for the couple. In *Desert Hearts*, Vivian begs Cay to get on the train to New York with her, while in *When Night is Falling*, Camille and Petra ride off into the sunrise. This is where every lesbian in the theatre breathes a sigh of relief, and perhaps of enchantment as well, because the onscreen lesbians have not turned psychotic or suicidal, nor have they died, nor conformed to the heterosexual norms (Stacey, 1995), as has been the case in typical film depictions of lesbians. Indeed, the professors in these films must face what many lesbians, professors or not, face in our daily lives—the potential loss of friends or the loss of a job.

But these depictions of lesbian professors leave us with many questions involving issues of identity, visibility, fear, and freedom within and without the academy. One such question comes from feminist philosopher Mary Daly (1992), who asks ". . . How to Move in the Direction of breaking the brokenness of women's bodies, spirits, memories, minds by patriarchal institutions of education, most specifically, of 'higher' education, while at the same time Righteously using these institutions?" (Daly, p. 120) Implicit in this question, I believe, is the question of what it means for openly lesbian women to be in academia, and at what cost? Perhaps more apropos of the subject of this particular volume, can the academy be open enough to individuals' authentic identities more generally?

Rigidity and Fear

The first glimpses of the professors in these films are striking. Both are appropriately well ordered and stately. We first see Vivian Bell of *Desert Hearts* getting off of a train in a professional gray suit, her hair pulled back severely under her hat. Our first glimpse of Camille in *When Night is Falling* is in her classroom, where she is lecturing students on "transformation in mythology," a foreshadowing of the transformation of her own personal mythology. She, like Vivian, is wearing conservative clothing, an ankle-length skirt, a long-sleeved, button-down blouse, and a vest. Her hair is also pulled away from her face, though not as severely as Vivian's is. Both Vivian and Camille carry themselves in a reserved manner, as we would expect if we draw on the professorial stereotype we hold in Western culture. The professors themselves symbolize the kind of orderly, objective thinking demanded by the academy (Astin, Astin, Antonio, Astin, and Cress, 1999; Martin, 1981). As the films progress, we see the professors recognize the restrictions ensuing from such submission to that degree of objectivity, recoil in fear, and then finally face the possibilities of a life outside of the constraints of heterosexual normativity and of academia.

For instance, as *Desert Hearts* begins there is a sense that Vivian is uncomfortable with herself. The sharp contrast is immediately drawn in the film between Vivian Bell and Frances Parker, the owner of the ranch, who meets Vivian at the train station. Frances wears jeans and a flannel shirt, her hair loose around her head. On the way to the car, Vivian complains that her feet are uncomfortable in her shoes. This is our first suggestion that Vivian is less than comfortable in her orderly, rigid self.

Throughout the film, Vivian makes a number of comments about her sense of self that are consistent with her outward appearance. In a scene at the lawyer's office, the lawyer, Mr. Warner, begins the conversation by saying, "From the looks of the agreement, it looks like Dr. Bell's walking off with the whole store." Vivian's eventual response is

> "I haven't practiced this—Mr. Warner, I am 35 years old. I want an honest life. I'm leaving a decent marriage to see if I can find one. Not having children helps, although our careers serve much the same purpose binding us together for all those years. We were very big on form, right friends, right prints on the wall—I yearn for something we couldn't analyze or reason away. I want to be free of who I've been."

This sense of the "professional couple" is raised a few times in the film and is indicative of Vivian's self-awareness concerning how she presents herself and that she is aware there is something missing. In a later scene, Cay asks her if she has realized all her ambitions, to which Vivian replies, "No, just my plans." Vivian knows that her neatly planned life has not fulfilled her in some way.

For Camille, in *When Night is Falling*, this level of self-awareness is never verbalized as much as it is acted out. In the course of the film, the men in her life are heard defining who she is, both personally and professionally. For example, the Reverend DeBoer comments, "And Camille, your book on Christian ethics, your student counseling last year, and your general behavior as a fine Christian woman make you a credit to the college and to the faith." Later, Martin, sensing impending change, says to her, "You've been saying it a hundred different ways—this pressure for us to get married for the sake of the job feels like a sham. You don't want to be this career Christian who does what she's told . . ." Camille herself never explicitly states that she is looking for something different until late in the film, when she is driving back to her apartment after spending the night with Petra. She says, "She answers a wordless question in me. That's good—wordless question." Camille is talking to herself, in preparation for a conversation with Martin.

Obviously, physical intimacy with another woman presents a challenge to this rigid orderliness. In the climactic scene, in an attempt to explain away their first kiss together, Vivian says to Cay, "I enjoy order. What happened between us was innocent—I'm a respected scholar. I've been married for many years to a respected scholar. And for a moment's indiscretion, a fleeting lapse in judgment, I stood in the rain and let Frances Parker, a figure bearing not the slightest resemblance to anyone in my entire life's experience, to humiliate us as if we were a pair of delinquents." Vivian's indignant self-awareness threatens to move her away from the very place she needs to go, toward the messy subjectiveness of intimacy.

This backpedaling occurs for Camille in *When Night is Falling*, though less overtly. She meets with the prospect of physical intimacy when Petra says to her "You moved me—I can't explain—I'd love to see you in the moonlight with your head thrown back and your body on fire." Camille coolly replies, "That was uncalled for—I must be fun to shock." The next day, as Petra tries to apologize for "being so aggressive," Camille invites her into the foyer of her apartment building, and they kiss. Later, she tries to convince Petra that they can simply be friends: "We are not animals and we don't always have to act on our attractions" (The twin towers of Christianity and academia hold Camille tight, away from involvement with anyone outside.

All this academic rigidity appears to breed a sense of frigidity and fear. This may be both a function of academia's staunch frame of objectivity impinging upon the lesbian professors as well as the professors' use of order as a coping strategy against the fear of intimacy. Holding objectivity as a central tenet leaves little room for things irrational, such as non-linear styles of communication, emotions, caring, relationships, and sexuality (Boler, 1999; Clinchy, 1990; Daly, 1992; Edgerton, 1996; Holland and Eisenhart, 1988; Martin, 1981; Noddings, 1981;Tannen, 1993). It is an imperative that we only deal with things that do not affect us personally. There is a certainty about goals and plans that does not exist in relationships, especially lesbian relationships, which lack the social sanctions that are generally granted to heterosexual relationships. It is easier to do as Vivian does after arriving at the ranch; she holes up in her room, so that when she comes down to "stretch her legs," a fellow guest at the ranch asks her, "What have you been doing in that room for the last five days?" The work itself can be made to be more important than any relationship that might come along. In either case, the orderliness is juxtaposed with the exoticism of lesbianism in an effort to draw a sharper contrast.

Clothes Make the Woman
One of the first signs of impending identity transformation in these films is a change of clothing. Since Vivian arrives at the ranch in *Desert Hearts* without any riding clothes, Cay responds by taking Vivian shopping for new clothes: a Western shirt and more casual pants. And though her hair is still up, it is the first time in the film that we see Vivian smile. Her rigid presentation of self is beginning to respond to the less formal desert environment. Vivian acknowledges this shift in the next scene, in the casino where Cay works, telling her "I think I'm going to try my luck." Later in the film, a fellow guest encourages her, though metaphorically, saying, "C'mon, let your hair down for once." He, like the others, senses Vivian's need to let go of her all-too-rigid self.

The most obvious example of this transformation occurs just prior to the climax of the film. Cay arrives at the hotel where Vivian is staying after she was kicked off the ranch for spending all night out with Cay. They talk through the door for a while, and finally, Vivian lets Cay in. Vivian is wearing a pink bathrobe, and her hair is down and in a disheveled state. Cay smiles and tells her, "You look wonderful," and Vivian says, in an unbelieving tone, "Are you kidding?" This is the first scene where we see Vivian with her hair completely down and virtually naked.

In *When Night is Falling*, Camille returns to her apartment after meeting Petra in the laundromat with Petra's laundry in her bag. Petra has purposely done a "switcheroo" with the laundry. Camille tries on one of Petra's blouses, which is more form-fitting than Camille's typical button-down style. Martin comments on how he likes the blouse, saying, "It's wild." She replies, "I think it has a certain reckless charm." Martin's response is, "You can't wear that to a meeting with the Reverend," and he grabs a sweater that hangs over a chair on their way out. This is Camille's first step out of her "button-down" self, and from her refusal to take off Petra's blouse, it is clear that she is interested in where this may take her.

As a caterpillar weaves its chrysalis, Vivian and Camille gradually shed their former conservative clothing and selves to "try on" and experiment with new selves. They let their hair down, they put on a new blouse, and they eventually let it all hang out. This might be an example of what Daly (1992) refers to as "Shape-shifting . . . defined as: transcendent transforma-tion of symbol-shapes, idea-shapes, relation-shapes, emotion-shapes, word-shapes, action-shapes; Moon-Wise Metamorphosis (Wickedary)." (p. 212) The fact that this Shape-shifting/Metamorphosis is symbolized through clothing is not coincidental. As Daly describes in exploring the ety-mology of the words *fascinate* and *fascist*:

> Both are from the same Indo-European root. Contemplating the fact that phallic fascist fashion designers force women to appear "fascinating," we thought about how they do this by imposing fashions, making women *fashionable* for their purposes. (Daly, 1992, p. 216)

The professors in these films are able to shed the fashions that have defined them as orderly and uptight for clothes that allow them to define their own purposes more clearly.

Wet and Wild: Watery Images and Female Sexuality
Another symbolic aspect is the use of water—rain, ice, or snow—to fore-shadow the elemental female sexuality. The first sense of this in *Desert Hearts* comes in a scene where Vivian and Cay are horseback riding in the desert. As they walk along with their horses, Cay asks, "What do you tell folks when they ask what went wrong in your marriage?" Vivian replies, "I'll tell *you* that I drowned in still waters." Later in the film, Vivian and Cay take a drive to a lake in the wee hours of the morning. After a discussion where Cay reveals her lesbianism and Vivian refuses to acknowledge her attraction to Cay, a rainstorm hits, and we see Vivian get into the passenger side of the car. Cay asks her to roll down the window and Vivian complies. Cay then leans in and kisses Vivian, who doesn't really protest, though she does stop it after a minute. Later, we find Vivian in the shower, just prior to her first full sexual encounter with Cay. All this water presages "diving into" greater intimacy, or "flowing" towards more openness with her sexuality.

When Night is Falling begins with a dream sequence where two women are underwater, moving together and touching. This sequence ends with one of the women finding herself trapped under ice. This sequence is later repeated during the climax of the film, where Camille attempts to bury the body of her dead dog, Bob, in the snow. She lies down in the snow on the ground and falls asleep, just as it begins to snow. She becomes buried and, in her sleep, dreams of being trapped under the ice, as in the opening sequences of the film. Here, the water both frees her to be who she is and traps her.

Aside from the obvious connection between moisture and women's sexual response, water is representative of the female or feminine forces or energies that imply attributes such as emotionality, changeability, fluidity, creativity, and reproductivity. This connection between water and feminine energy can be found in a wide variety of philosophical and spiritual texts and paths, from Aristotle and St. Thomas Aquinas (Daly, 1992) to Yin-Yang theory (Kaptchuk, 1983) to Wiccan spirituality (Starhawk, 1989). For instance, in the traditions most closely associated with Western thought, this "moisture" is seen as detrimental or deviant (Daly, 1992). In contrast, Yin-Yang theory depicts the Yin element as ocean or river and considers Yin to be yielding, dynamic, and nourishing (Kaptchuk, 1983). Regardless, the characteristics represented by water are inherently threatening to the "objectivity" upon which academia is predicated.

"Free to Be You and Me"

Desert vistas replete with mountains and mesas, cacti and color set the scene for possibilities in *Desert Hearts*. A car-ride away, the casino lights flicker, inviting drinking and gambling. In *When Night is Falling*, the circus lights and colorful activities (i.e., juggling, trapeze, dancing, magic acts, card playing, etc.) become the natural metaphor for freedom of expression. These are far from the typical staid images of academia in film—lecture halls in buildings with gothic-style architecture set on well-manicured lawns. This visual comparison is reminiscent of feminist criticism in education, which posits that there are ways of knowing that challenge those perpetuated within the orderly, disciplined environment of academia (Belenky, Clinchy, Goldberger, and Tarule, 1986; Martin, 1981). The vivid and vibrant contexts in which we first meet the lesbian artists suggest alternative paradigms for thinking about the world, as Martin (1981) describes "ones which would join thought to action, and reason to feeling and emotion." (p. 78) This world of subjective expression is in stark contrast to the academy and appears to intrigue our professorial heroines, as each seeks entrée into the world of the lesbian artist.

For example, the initial meeting between Vivian and Cay occurs during the drive back to the ranch. Vivian and Frances meet Cay, who puts her own car in reverse and drives alongside Frances's car, hair flying in the wind, eyes covered by Ray-Bans, with the desert vista behind her. This is our first glimpse of the wild, reckless, vibrant lesbian protagonist, and she is set against the backdrop of the desert's endless potential. This seems to intrigue Vivian, who later offers to bring Cay's mail over to her cottage on the ranch. In a subsequent scene, Cay invites Vivian to go horseback riding. During the ride, Cay and Vivian walk their horses and talk, getting to know each other better, the beautiful desert vista in the background. All of these desert vistas occur prior to Cay and Vivian's first kiss, allowing the desert to symbolize freedom and possibility (Merck, 1993).

When Night is Falling uses the traveling circus as the setting. Though Camille and Petra first meet in a well-lit laundromat in the middle of the afternoon, there are hints of what is to come. Petra's world is as exotic as she is. While everyone else in the film is pale and Caucasian, Petra is a beautiful woman of color. Camille's first foray into Petra's world finds Camille intently watching a magic act of which Petra is the main attraction; Petra's shadow juggles balls of light. Everything about the circus is exotic—the people, the activities, the part of town where the trailers are parked. Camille is drawn to Petra. She is the one who instigates their first kiss and their first tryst at the circus, which occurs on a large bed with deep red sheets. These scenes of their tryst are juxtaposed with scenes of two women performing a trapeze act together.

The natural beauty of the desert and the strange beauty of the circus set an exotic/erotic backdrop for the transformation we see in Vivian and Camille in these films. This transformation would never have occurred in the conservative context of academia. Using the context as a catalyst, Vivian and Camille allow themselves the courage to risk losing themselves, and potentially their livelihoods, to try something new.

Images of Risk-Taking

> " . . .at its core, Courage is ontological, that it is the Courage to Be through and beyond the patriarchal State of Negation, participating in the Unfolding of Be-ing, continuing on in the Journey always."
> (*Daly, 1992, p. 198*)

Both films employ an overt metaphor for risk-taking. In *Desert Hearts*, it is gambling. Gambling is antithetical to the self-described orderly existence that Vivian Bell leads. However, she has already invested in one gamble—a divorce. The next gamble will be on Cay. In one scene in the casino, Vivian is walking around observing the clientele. A Hungarian woman (cameo appearance by Donna Deitch) playing the slots says to her, "If you don't play, you can't win." Vivian walks to the dice table, where a man invites her to throw for him, hoping she'll be luckier than he is. He convinces her, and she gets lucky, winning him some money, so he offers her some of the winnings. Apparently, it does pay to play, metaphorically speaking.

In *When Night is Falling*, the central metaphor for risk-taking is hang gliding. In one scene as Camille tries to convince Petra that they can be friends instead of lovers, Petra takes her to go hang gliding in the snow with some of her friends. Camille asks, "Why?" and Petra replies, "Because fear is what you pay for eventually, Camille." After Petra and Camille take off together, Petra tells her, "You have to ride with the wind, not against it. Can you feel it?" Camille passes out, which disturbs the balance of the glider and upon landing, she injures her knee. When Petra apologizes for pushing her, Camille smiles and replies, "But I did it, didn't I?" These scenes are pivotal in the films because they show the uptight, rigid professors actively breaking away from their safe societal constraints and reinventing themselves. In earlier scenes, Vivian and Camille appear to be "trying on" new selves in a relatively risk-free manner. They can always put back on their conservative, uptight clothing. In these scenes, though, they acknowledge the risk and take the plunge. In doing so, they face some fundamental fears—fear of losing the known and familiar, fear of committing, fear of losing others, and fear of losing themselves. This constellation of fears play a significant role for gay, lesbian, bisexual, and transgender people because of the bigotry and prejudice that we face. We can lose our jobs if we choose to live in a way that we believe is living with integrity. In some respects, though, these are fears we all must face, whatever our sexual identity, in the development of our sense of authenticity.

Desperately Seeking Authenticity

A compelling analysis of these films recognizes the lesbian relationship as a metaphor for personal authenticity in the profession of academia. In the course of these films, it appears that Vivian and Camille have been liberated by their sexual relations with women, that this act has allowed them to find and name what they have searched for all this time. Neither woman comes to the situation deliberately questioning her sexual identity. For instance, Vivian is not a lesbian until she has sex with Cay. Camille, as well, uses sex to define herself. As she becomes increasingly attracted to Petra, she becomes more sexually assertive with Martin. At one point, Camille seduces Martin, though she can only think about Petra while she is with him. Later, she has sex with Petra, and it becomes more obvious that she is more connected with Petra. Vivian and Camille each are left with an altered identity, one that appears more authentic. Authenticity implies some internal compass by which an individual navigates with minimal regard for contextual features.

This sense of authenticity is noted by the women within the text of these films. For instance, as Cay and Vivian leave the courthouse, Mr. Warner, the lawyer, says to Vivian, "You look different. I see you have yourself a new pen pal." She replies, "I have much more than that, Mr. Warner." Likewise, Camille says about Petra, "She answers a kind of wordless question in me." Camille's actions are juxtaposed with those of Martin, her male lover. He is willing to play the game of academia; he's ambitious and willing to silence himself and her. Camille will not allow her career to silence her true feelings, her Self.

Feelings of authenticity are contrasted with the ordered, rigid environment of academia, which creates an atmosphere where authenticity and integrity are difficult to attain and retain. This oppression is particularly evident in Camille's eventual choice to leave her position in academia. Taylor (1991) defines authenticity as "the idea that I am free when I decide for myself what concerns me, rather than being shaped by external influences." (p. 27) Through the course of these films, Camille and Vivian have decided for themselves, rather than allowing the institutions of higher education to continue to control them.

However, it is also important to problematize this modernist notion of authenticity with its desire to define and categorize. Such definitions and categories are often useful in an anthro-political context, allowing people to have an immediate frame of understanding the individual as well as allowing the individual to take a politically distinct position. But these definitions and categories also serve to codify and reify positions of power and privilege, thus reproducing current sociocultural inequities. In questioning the ways in which power and privilege are expressed and navigated, postmodernist frameworks strive to blur these same definitions and categories.

For instance, a postmodern analysis of the concept of authenticity is that a number of problems in our society are created by reifying the various socially constructed divisions and hierarchies (Gergen, 1992). What is more important is understanding the constructions within their sociohistoric frameworks than categorizing people using the constructions. Gergen admits "Even if there is no inner self to which our actions should be true, life goes on; we continue to act." (p. 188) Thus, postmodern analyses would argue that authenticity/integrity are more a function of "understanding how lesbian and gay identities are articulated within and in relation to their cultural and historical contexts." (Katz, 1990, p. 15) The postmodern construal of identity is one that assigns more explanatory focus to the embedded contexts in which we find ourselves. Gergen (1992) states:

Concepts of truth, honesty, and authenticity now turn strange. Not only do attempts at characterizing the actual person—the workings

of the mind, the human spirit, or the biological individual—
become suspect. The very concept of an internal core—an intentional, rational agent—also begins to fray (pp. 111–112).

Thus, while we desire to define ourselves, this definition leads to essentialism and subsequent marginalization of particular groups and individuals.
In contrast, blurred definitions and categories leave us with nothing on
which to hang our figurative hats. Given this dilemma, how do we make
sense of the actions in the films?

One way to reconcile this space is to reframe the notion of authenticity
using Daly's idea of Realizing. The word "Realizing" is a verbal noun, a part
of speech that indicates continued action and implies a dynamic aspect of
the word. Through their interaction with the lesbian-artists, the professors
are *realizing* themselves. Daly uses *Webster's Dictionary* to show "the verb realize means: to make real . . . bring into concrete existence: ACCOMPLISH . . .
to bring from potentiality to actuality: ACTUALIZE . . . to conceive vividly
as real: be fully aware of." (Daly, 1992, p. 274) Thinking in terms of a
verbal noun, rather than the noun *authenticity,* makes it possible to envision an ongoing process rather than a static entity. Realizing is socially
mediated; it happens in the context of relationships, both interpersonal
and institutional. This may be a more accurate way of characterizing the
characters' understanding of their lesbian sexuality as well as their role in
the academy.

Queer Among Queers

While in the process of realizing authenticity, one area of conflict is that the
professors themselves are "othered" in the context of the film. They do not
fit in as lesbians, and they do not fit in academia. This may be self developed
or other imposed, and the professors in these films show how the mystique
(or mistake) of professorhood keeps people at a distance. This may be, in
part, due to the way some lesbians understand and explain their sexual
identity development. For instance, on the first page of her comic *Coming
Out Story,* Bechdel's autobiographical character says "Since earliest childhood, I knew I was different from other girls . . . for a long time, I thought
it was just because I was *smarter.*" (Bechdel, 1993) Another example is
given by McNaron (1997), who points out that "[o]verachievement has
long been a coping strategy for some members of oppressed groups within
our society." (p. 127) How we see ourselves shades the way we interact with
others.

In *Desert Hearts,* Vivian is perceived in a certain way (educated) and portrayed as sterile. Nobody has a problem with her while she is isolated in her
room with her books, but as soon as she begins to interact with others there

is trouble. Early in the film, one morning Vivian emerges, entering the screened porch where Frances and two other divorcees are sitting on the porch, talking. One of the women addresses Vivian by stating, "We're discussing sex versus marriage—want to join us?" and Vivian responds, "I'm not an expert in either one." The woman responds with, "I hear you cultured types go at it like banshees," clearly disdainful of Vivian's status as a professor. Later in the film, Frances kicks Vivian off the ranch, saying, "To think I let you come here with your books and your influence over my family." A few moments later Frances says to Cay, "It'll be a cold day in August before I take in another educated type." Even Cay questions her own ability to fit with the professorial lifestyle to which Vivian is inviting her. As Vivian's train is about to pull out of the station, Cay says, "Can you imagine me with your set?"

These types of responses may also be in part due to Vivian and Camille's social standing. Stacey (1995) writes:

> Even Vivian, who clearly comes from an environment where reputation matters very much, academia, is not intimidated by gossip and other people's disapproval. In the 'riding scene', for example, Lucille (Kati Labourdette), fellow divorcee at the ranch, declares herself 'out to lunch when it comes to queers', to which Vivian replies that she doubts either of them will be sorely missed'. Her confident refusal to condone such homophobia, however, may have as much to do with her class superiority as with her apparently liberal attitudes towards homosexuality." (p. 100)

For Camille, the issue of social status is a little less developed in *When Night is Falling*, although it is still evident in the visual images: the tidy, gothic college buildings in a downtown area versus the dilapidated, industrial section of town that temporarily houses the circus. Camille tells the Reverend DeBoer at one point, "She [Petra] is just a street kid. I flatter myself thinking that I might teach her something." There is a terrible irony here, in that it is Petra who teaches Camille about herself. Late in the film, Camille arrives at the circus to find a party in progress. Tim, one of the circus directors, tells her, "We've been invited to Circusdance. It's a very prestigious event in San Francisco." It seems as though he wants her to know that the circus's work is as important as hers is. Camille then finds Petra, who wants to dance with her. Camille is obviously uptight as Petra tries to dip her and exclaims, "That was vulgar!" Petra then asks, "Are you ashamed of me? Am I your dirty little secret?"

Another possible reason for this othering comes from deeply rooted suspicions that the "lesbian-in-progress" may be acting from a position of experimentation. The impostor syndrome is always suspected in the lesbian community, though rarely does it stop many of us from getting involved with someone who at first glance seems heterosexual. Both Cay and Petra observe that their respective professorial love interests may be acting out of a position of experimentation. In a later scene in *Desert Hearts*, Vivian and Cay are having a fight in the parking lot of a restaurant after the first time they have sex. Vivian is upset about being with Cay in public, who says, "Listen, you're just visiting the way I live. It suits you fine to hide away in that hotel room until your train leaves." Likewise, in *When Night is Falling*, after Camille and Petra have sex for the first time, Camille leaves, and Tim, one of the circus directors, tells Petra that the circus will be leaving town soon. He asks Petra about Camille. "You're not thinking of jumping ship are you? Are you very serious about this girl?" Petra replies, "I think she might just be experimenting. All good things go eventually."

In both cases, it is a case of role reversal where the lesbian-artist must educate the professor. For Vivian, there's a mystique around Cay, so she seeks her out—brings her the mail, goes horseback riding with her, goes shopping with her, hangs out with her at the casino. Similarly, Camille is drawn in by Petra's mystique at the same time as she struggles with her career at a Christian college. She continues to seek Petra out even after a conversation with Reverend DeBoer, and when Petra asks her to leave with her when the circus leaves, Camille says "I love your openness, I love what you do—I love—love you." The professors must open themselves up to seeing the world as more subjective, more unpredictable, and more rich, and they do this through their artistic guides.

Implications for Lesbian Professors

These films portray several fragile moments in the lives of the two professors. Vivian finally relinquishes her books in order to let Cay into her life. Camille takes the leap by leaving her career to join Petra in the circus. It is clear that the directors are interested in establishing a conventional romance with a small twist. Neither plot is particularly compelling, though the visual symbolism is, especially in *When Night is Falling*. And while these romances would appeal most directly to lesbian audiences, the narrative would hold interest for wider, albeit liberal, audiences. Most viewers, however, would be likely to miss the subtle commentary on academia presented in these films.

For instance, my first viewing of *Desert Hearts* was in the late 1980s. I remember when it came out because I was walking across campus at my undergraduate college when a friend came up to excitedly tell me about the film and that I should go and see it. My read at the time was of a conventional Hollywood romance: girl meets girl, girl almost loses girl, girl rides off with girl into the sunrise. Set against other 1980s films like *Personal Best*, *Desert Hearts* was uplifting. A decade and graduate school experience later, I have turned a more critical gaze toward the professor and her representation of academia.

Both Vivian's and Camille's portrayals of higher education resonated deeply with me in my most recent viewings of these films. Though I was "out" long before I came into academia, I found compelling the tension between their process of self-actualization in the context of the professorship. Talburt and Salvio (this volume) assert that "Who one is and who one can be is a function of where one is and how one experiences the place of the academy" (chapter 1). To some extent, these films represent the struggles many gay, lesbian, bisexual, and transgender people face in trying to be themselves in the context of higher education.

My sense is that many of my faculty colleagues similarly experience the Scylla and Charybis of the post-historical university. On the one hand, we spend our time in graduate school learning that we are called to produce new knowledge, new ways of framing the disciplines that we study. Then we come to our first year in the professorship all fired up, just to find that the goal is really to maintain the status quo. However, I fear overgeneralizing this point because I believe that the experiences of gay and lesbian professors, in particular, clearly articulate the dilemmas of border crossing with integrity.

Given the dual role posited by McNaron (1997) and the criticism of academia leveled by Daly (1992) and Stuck (1999), it would appear that the academy is not a place flexible enough to support the transformational processes that border crossing implies. Even the title of Mintz and Rothblum's (1999) recent volume, *Lesbians in Academia: Degrees of Freedom*, indicates the inconsistency that lesbian women find in their interactions with academia. The range of narratives presented in their edited volume indicates that lesbian professors are faced with the same conflicts as Vivian and Camille are, as well as the major dilemma, "Risk the rewards of academia or risk loss of identity?." (Stuck, 1999, p. 215) These kinds of dilemmas are sure to eventually raise questions about any lesbian professor's sanity. In fact, a number of the narratives discuss the uses of or the need for therapy. This may be more indicative of a sane person's response to the pathology of the multiple contradictory demands of academia. In fact, Daly (1992) refers to academia by using the split term "academia/academentia" to represent the pathology of higher educational institutions. And as Talburt and Salvio (this volume) highlight in their discussion, academementia is emotionally costly.

The implications of these films are incendiary for lesbian professors, raising more questions than have been answered. Should we stay, or should we go? Assuming we choose to stay, what will it take to be allowed to, in a way that supports our personal and professional integrity? What will we have to give up? Should we just pack up and join the circus? Or should we stick around with our unauthorized discourses and continue to mess with higher education? As far as I am concerned, I still believe in the notion that higher education is here to incite critical discourses, which requires as many *unauthorized* discourses as possible. But at what cost? So come on and let me know—should I stay or should I go?

References

Astin, A.W., Astin, H.S., Antonio, A.L., Astin, J., and Cress, C.M. *Meaning and Spirituality in the Lives of College Faculty*. A Report from the Higher Education Research Institute, Los Angeles, University of California, 1999.

Bechdel, A. "Coming Out Story." In *Gay Comics #19*, edited by A. Mangels. San Francisco: Bob Ross, 1993.

———. *The Indelible Alison Bechdel: Confessions, Comix, and Miscellaneous Dykes to Watch Out For*. Ithaca, NY: Firebrand Books, 1998.

Belenky, M. F., Clinchy, B. M., Goldberger, N. R., and Tarule, J. M. *Women's Ways of Knowing: The Development of Self, Voice, and Mind*. New York: Basic Books, Inc. 1986.

Berardinelli, J. review of *When Night Is Falling*, directed by P. Rozema, 1995. http://movie-reviews.colossus.net/movies/w/when_night.html

Boler, M. *Feeling Power: Emotion and Education*. New York: Routledge, 1999.

Clash, The. "Should I Stay or Should I Go?" *Combat Rock*, Epic Records, 1982.

Clinchy, B. M. "Issues of Gender in Teaching and Learning." *Journal on Excellence in College Teaching* 1, 1990: 52–67.

Daly, M. *Outercourse: The Be-dazzling Voyage*. San Francisco: Harper Collins, 1992.

Deitch, D. (Producer/Director). *Desert Hearts* [Motion Picture]. United States: Samuel Goldwyn Company, 1985.

Edgerton, S. H. *Translating the Curriculum: Multiculturalism into Cultural Studies*. New York: Routledge, 1996.

Gergen, K. J. *The Saturated Self: Dilemmas of Identity in Contemporary Life*. NY: Basic Books, 1992.

Guthmann, E. "A Fabulist Tale of Desire: Sexual Awakenings in *Night Is Falling*." *San Francisco Chronicle*, November 24, 1995: p. c –5. http://www.sfgate.com/cgi-bin/article.cgi?file=chronicle/archive/1995/11/24/DD72454.DTL

Holland, D. C., and Eisehhart, M. "Moments of Discontent: University Women and the Gender Status Quo." *Anthropology and Education auartedy* 19(2), 1988: 115–138.

Kaptchuk, T. J. *The Web That Has No Weaver: Understanding Chinese Medicine*. Chicago: Congdon & Weed, 1983.

Katz, L. "Strategies for Lesbian Representation: Kaucylia Brooke's Photography." *SF Camerawork Quarterly* 17, no. 2 (1990): 15–18.

Martin, J. R. "The Ideal of the Educated Person." *Educational Theory* 31 (1981): 97–109.

McNaron, T. A. H. *Poisoned Ivy: Lesbian and Gay Academics Confronting Homophobia*. Philadelphia: Temple University Press, 1997.

Merck, M. "Dessert Hearts." In *Queer Looks: Perspectives on Lesbian and Gay Film and Video*, edited by M. Gever, P. Parmar, and J. Greyson. New York: Routledge, 1993: 377–382.

Mintz, B. and Rothblum, E. D. *Lesbians in Academia: Degrees of Freedom*. New York: Routledge, 1999.

Noddings, N. *Caning a Feminine Approach to Ethics and Moral Education*. Los Angeles: University of California Press, 1981.

Renzi, M. (Producer), and Sayles, J. (Director). *Lianna* [Motion Picture]. United States: United Artists, 1982.

Rule, J. and Rozema, P. (Director). *When Night is Falling* [Motion Picture]. Canada. October Films. 1995.

Rycenga, J. "The Perils and Pleasures of Being an Out Lesbian Academic; or Speech from the Scaffold." In *Lesbians in Academia: Degrees of Freedom*, edited by B. Mintz and E. D. Rothblum. New York: Routledge, 1999: 171–179.

Shulgasser, B. "Search for Passion in *Night.*" *San Francisco Examiner*, November 24, 1995. http://www.sfgate.com/cgi-bin/article.cgi?file=/examiner/archive/1995/11/24/WEEK-END8595.dtl, p. 8.

Schulman, S. *My American History: Lesbian and Gay Life During the Reagan/Bush Years*. New York: Routledge, 1994.

Stacey, J. "'If You Don't Play, You Can't Win': *Desert Hearts* and the Lesbian Romance Film." In *Immortal, Invisible: Lesbians and the Moving Image*, edited by T. Wilton. New York: Routledge, 1995: 92–114.

Starhawk. *The Spiral Dance: A Rebirth of the Ancient Religion of the Great Goddess*. San Francisco: Harper Collins, 1989.

Stuck, M. F. "The Lesbian Experience: An Analysis." In *Lesbians in Academia: Degrees of Freedom*, edited by B. Mintz and E. D. Rothblum. New York: Routledge, 1999.

Talburt, S., and Salvio, P. M. (2005). "The Personal Professor and the Excellent University." In *Imagining the Academy: Higher Education and Popular Culture*, edited by S. Edgerton, G. Holm, T. Daspit, and P. Farber. New York: Routledge, 2005.

Tannen, D. *Gender and Conversational Interaction*. New York: Oxford University Press, 1993.

Taylor, C. *The Ethics of Authenticity*. Cambridge, MA: Harvard University Press, 1991.

Weaver, J. A., and Daspit, T. "Critical Pedagogy, Popular Culture and the Creation of Meaning." In *Popular Culture and Critical Pedagogy: Reading, Constructing, Connecting*, edited by T. Daspit and J. A. Weaver. New York: Garland Publishing, 1999.

11
Mamet's *Oleanna* in Context: Performance, Personal, Pedagogy

LEE PAPA

I. Situating Myself/Situating the Play

I am sitting in my office, writing this article. It is a small office for a tenure-track professor, may be ten feet by six feet. The walls are painted a bright blue—within a certain spectrum, we are allowed to choose what color we want our walls. My walls are filled with shelves filled with books, many books, like most of the offices here. In fact, when students enter my office, the first thing many of them do is ask, "Have you read all these books?" My books are broken into sections: theory, world literature, American drama, anthologies. It's not a consistent system, but for the most part I know where everything is. I keep pictures of my wife and four-year-old daughter around my desk. A photo of my daughter is the wallpaper on my computer screen. Surrounding me, with the books and a very large, imposing file cabinet are bits of detritus from various places—kitsch, tchotchkes that are calculated to make the office seem less than academic—Tom Waits poster, Mighty Mouse action figures, a boomerang actually from Australia, a rubber monk holding a cup of coffee. I keep several dozen compact discs in my office, and when students meet with me, I ask them, "What kind of music do you like to listen to?" Inevitably, from punk to rap to classical, I have something. I also have piles of papers on my desk, papers graded, to be graded, copies of sources for this and other articles, memos—Christ, so many memos. There's a couch against the wall behind me, and a coat rack on which I keep a spare tweed sports jacket in case I can't get home to change for an event. I am exceedingly comfortable in my office, even now, when it's a mess. I am constructed by the space I have constructed, somewhat knowingly, somewhat subconsciously or unconsciously.

Foucault speaks of space as a means to discipline: "Each individual has his own place; and each place its individual." (Foucault, 1977, p. 143) Spaces, for Foucault, "provide fixed positions and permit circulation; they carve out individual segments and establish operational links; they mark places and indicate values; they guarantee the obedience of individuals." (p. 148) My office creates me for my students; when they enter, they accede to and acknowledge power through their knowledge of a hierarchy at the moment they come into this space. They willingly empower me, even when they are here to argue, here to question a grade or an idea. They come to my space to do so. They're on my turf, surrounded by my books, listening to my music (no matter what they choose, it's mine), sitting on a couch or chair that is framed by all of which is about me. And I am framed, too, by the computer I type this on, which is owned by the university and can at any time be taken away by that university, with all my files and sometimes incredibly personal correspondences. The writing of this article is contextualized by my own tenure pursuit; do I write out of some need to say something meaningful, or for another line on the tenure document I must submit each year to the tenure committee? The space in this room, on this campus, creates that meaning. I do not. For the most part, people outside the walls of the academy do not understand these particulars. They understand space, they understand power, but they do not understand this right here. Right now. As I write this.

So what is this? It is a discussion of an intersection between performance, culture (pop and otherwise), and academia. It is about how teaching a play about power issues in the classroom both deconstructs and reifies that power. In the end, it is an essay about how David Mamet's *Oleanna* creates a discursive paradox for teachers like me, teachers of drama at the university.

Oleanna is a rarity in nonmusical theater: a work that moves beyond a traditional theater audience and becomes debated in the culture outside the stage. Mamet traces the disintegration of the relationship between a professor, John, and his student, Carol. John, a young about-to-be-tenured husband and father, meets with Carol in his office as she grapples with ideas from his class that she cannot understand. While constantly interrupted with calls from his wife about a house he is trying to buy, John proposes that Carol meet with him alone in his office so he can teach her there. He attempts to console her when she nearly breaks down, and he receives a call just as she is about to reveal a secret about herself. In the next two acts,

Carol accuses John of sexual harassment and, later, rape (for "pressing [his] body" into hers when he attempts to block her from leaving); she claims her "Group" has helped her go about the pursuit of John. John loses his tenure, his position, and his house; when she gives him a list of books her Group wants banned, a list that includes the book that John authored, he defies her. At the indefinite ending, Carol overhears John on the phone with his wife and exclaims, "Don't call your wife 'baby'." (Mamet, 1993, p. 79) John physically beats Carol until she cowers below him, and the two of them are left on stage, staring at each other.

II. In Which the Literature Is Reviewed

The first New York production in 1992 was framed by the Anita Hill–Clarence Thomas hearings, which had occurred the previous year, and audiences and critics responded irresistably to comparisons. *Newsweek*'s Jack Kroll simply called the characters "Mamet's 'Hill' and 'Thomas,'" and compared the play to watching the hearings (Kroll, 1992, p. 65). *The New York Times* devoted a full page to the responses from writers, activists, and others. In the article, titled "He Said . . . She Said . . . Who Did What?," Susan Brownmiller tells about a friend who wanted to picket *Oleanna* because "the play is a wicked denial of real rape and harassment," while Brownmiller herself called it "a welcome jolt of nervy political theater." (Brownmiller et al., 1992, p. 6) Deborah Tannen comments on the beating, "The evening I saw the play, the audience cheered and urged him on . . . Right now, we don't need a play that helps anyone feel good about a man beating a woman." (p. 6) For most of its initial run, these protests and comparisons charged the production with a certain ideological weight. And certainly the production was burdened with a concentration on what is admittedly a single element of a complex linguistic and ideological exploration: As Susan Bennett points out in *Theater Audiences*, protest refocuses the intent or "potency" of a script (Bennett, 1997, p. 105–6). One cannot deny the effort of the play to address, or even attack, issues of gender and political correctness, but this focus denies other aspects of the script.

More recent criticism has moved the argument squarely to within the academy. Christine MacLeod (1995) writes of her uncomfortable reaction to *Oleanna*:

> [T]he fact is that my discomfort in the theater did not arise solely from my identification with Carol's gendered vulnerability. Rather, it arose from the sharp and embarrassing recognition that *as a teacher* [emphasis hers]—by virtue of academic status and a competence in certain privileged forms of discourse—I too could be and perhaps have been guilty of the same insensitivity towards

students, the same arrogance and verbal aggression, that is so patently deplorable in John. In other words, what compelled me most in such tutorial scenes was not so much the sexual clash as such, but questions about hierarchical power and the linguistic practices which both constitute and reflect it (p. 203)

MacLeod's feelings reflect an attempt to tie the play to personal and pedagogical concerns: to what extent is she participating in what Donaldo Macedo calls (1994) "the pedagogy of big lies" (p. 9), that is, a pedagogy that reifies hegemonic power structures through academic discourse. She acknowledges a keen awareness of the power dynamic of her position; she acknowledges that she may have become John.

Going even further, Richard Badenhausen (1998) says that the play "ultimately explores the perils of inferior teaching . . . this is more a play about teaching, reading, and understanding . . . Oleanna offers an ominous commentary on education in America and more particularly functions as a dire warning both to and about those doing the educating." (p. 2) Most recently, Stanton Garner, Jr. (2000) writes about Oleanna performed within the academy; in "Framing the Classroom: Pedagogy, Power, Oleanna," Garner discusses teaching the play as it is being performed on his campus, an experience he calls "unusually rich in institutional awareness." (p. 42) By including student reactions, as well as his own ambivalence about the play and his position as a professor teaching the play, Garner successfully recasts discussion of the play as a product of and from the classroom: "Oleanna defamiliarized our relationship and its institutional parameters, disclosing the contradictions and ambiguities underlying the classroom and its modes of interaction and performance." (p. 42) Garner uses the play as an opportunity for decoding the space of the university:

> We spent some time on the question of space and the often unclear boundaries that characterize settings within the university as an institutional context: the fact that university offices, for instance, are at once ambiguously offstage and onstage, public and personal. We suggested how this particular boundary is negotiated and the risks it presents (p. 43).

In some ways, discussion of the play must always come back to those questions of space: the office, the classroom, the stage. I think about how shocked my students are when they see me at a local bar or supermarket. I am decontextualized; I do not have the same level of power in those other spaces.

I have been teaching David Mamet's Oleanna since 1994 in a variety of graduate and undergraduate classes, including drama surveys and a course in gender and identity in world drama. Some of my colleagues question my dedication to the play, not only as an example of contemporary American drama, but as a representation of the power of performance. It is invariably provocative; students squarely defend one character or the other, more often John, seeing Carol as a manipulator. In many ways teaching the play carries with it the burden of self-reflexivity: like Garner, I am a professor teaching about a professor who talks about university teaching. The play can frame office and classroom discussions with students in the period during and after the reading of the play. In this way, Mamet has created a subtly subversive text, a dog-bites-man play in that to teach it at the university is to acknowledge its power and its potential insight into the university system. As Garner points out, since its 1992 premiere, *Oleanna* has become a quickly canonized play, appearing in anthologies and regularly as a part of syllabi for drama and American literature courses (2000, p. 41), indicating the enduring power of a text that intersected with history and culture and, as we shall see, continues to intersect with the classroom.

III. On Space

We enter the space of a performance bearing our own interpretive constructs: "The spectator comes to the theater as a member of an already constituted interpretive community and also brings a horizon of expectations shaped by the pre-production elements." (Bennett, 1997, p. 139) Within the space, a performance interpretation may be a production of the contextuality of space as much as it is a production of the elements staged. According to Kershaw, "the context of performance directly affects its perceived ideological meaning." (1992, p. 33) To attend or take part in a theatrical production is to accede to certain contextual and ideological frameworks: "A performance text gains meaning for an audience through its relationships to other texts." (p. 33) Obviously the audience attending a Broadway performance must confront and accept or deny the power of the image of the space and its environment. "The milieu which surrounds a theater is always ideologically encoded and the presence of a theater can be measured as typical or incongruous within it," says Kershaw (p. 126), and the performance of a play on Broadway begins before the curtain rises with the area around the theater, even in Times Square's new Disney-clean form, being part of that performance. Indeed, it could be said that the cultural weight of attendance at a Broadway theater is mimetically reified in theaters around the country. However, an audience attending a performance at an off-off Broadway house in Tribeca bears another cultural weight in viewing experimental or radical theater. Though both experiences contain the self-consciousness of expectation, the space itself imposes a structure on the performance and experience. For instance, the Tramway Theater in Glasgow, Scotland, is housed in an old trolley garage. When one attends the theater, upon entrance one sees that the lobby still has the tracks in the floor. The cavernous space of the theater and the bleacher seats remind one constantly of the history of the transformed space. This effect forces a paradigmatic shift in how one approaches the theatrical experience: This is distinctly not a traditional theater, and the performances in that space often bear that out. Contextuality of space, then, both restricts and enhances potential interpretations in that the exigencies of space force performative aspects to be achieved in a certain way.[1]

Space does not create meaning in and of itself; in addition to the play text, it is always already created in relationship to its audience and historical circumstance. Such a context can prevent or even pervert meaning: "The specific location of a [performance] is especially significant to its wider influence. The ideological identity of a community may reflect to a greater or lesser degree the chief socio-political concerns of a particular historical period." (Kershaw, 1992, p. 250) For instance the critical emphasis on *Oleanna* as reflective of Hill–Thomas could arise from the performance of the play in an off-Broadway theater, reviewed by nonacademic critics in the year after the hearings. However, when the play's performance space is shifted to the university with an audience of students and teachers, and distanced from the hearings, the text is less an allegory of contemporary American gender wars than a direct reflection of the lived experiences of the viewers. As Bennet points out, "we should not talk of theater as an art form in isolation from cultural practice." (Bennet, 1997, p. 93)

IV. Performance

Oleanna is a problematic text: In addition to the extremes to which it pushes its dialectic on political correctness and the university, Carol is surprisingly inconsistent as a character. She cannot understand the word "transpire," yet a moment later talks about a "capricious" answer to a professor's question (Mamet, 1993, p. 70). And the increasing violation of Carol's personal space by John—the comforting arm, the blocked exit, the beating—perhaps makes the play turn all-too-possibly into a phallocentric revenge fantasy by the end: The male defends wife, home, and life against the forces mounted against him. However, many of the play's problems can be seen as performative challenges for theaters or groups producing the play. My own interactions with the play have come both inside and outside the classroom. In each case, the play's performative and textual meanings have been a circumstance of its context. Using these ideas, I want to look at three performances of all or parts of the text of *Oleanna* within the college campus.

Performance Number One
At Tennessee Technological University in Cookeville, Tennessee, the theater program staged the play in the winter of 1996. During the time the production was staged, two separate sexual harassment lawsuits were being handled by the university, one filed by a student and one filed by a female faculty member. In one case, a professor felt she had been unfairly singled out as the sole junior female faculty member in a department and given a heavier teaching load than her colleagues for less pay. The student case involved a nonnative English-speaking male professor accused of harassing female students in his office. According to the director and associate professor of theater, Mark H. Creter, an atmosphere of paranoia, especially among faculty, existed on campus, heightening the play's innate tension. The use of the performance space itself also heightened the taut dialogue. The audience was seated on the stage in bleachers on all four sides of the set so that audience members were forced to watch each other in addition to the play. Hanging in front of two sides of the audience was a window, which implied that we were eavesdropping, as if we were seeing a process that we are not supposed to witness. John, played by Frank Kutzler, a chemistry professor at Tennessee Tech, was physically slight, as was Carol, played by student Anna Gorish. Kutzler was a reticent John, pausing to consider Carol's remarks, constantly, before dismissing what she had to say. John not only had no ready answers, he simply had no answers at all, so the production allowed us to dismantle John's actions more readily, but each action carried a greater semiotic weight, especially in light of the defense of the actual professor being charged with harassment on campus, who defended his actions by pleading cultural misunderstanding of his gestures. In fact, male faculty members who attended the play reacted strongly to Carol, according to Creter, with one senior colleague telling him, "I wanted to get up on stage and kill the bitch myself." [2]

Performance Number Two
Two students from Iowa State University performed the play at the 1996 Pedagogy and Theater of the Oppressed Conference at the University of Nebraska–Omaha. The conference is obviously devoted to Paolo Freire, Augusto Boal, and their adherents, and it usually climaxes with some confrontation among the participants about issues related to the politics of pedagogical theory versus practice. The performance occurred just after Paolo Freire had spoken, on a panel with Augusto Boal and pedagogical theorist Peter McLaren. The panel discussion itself had broken down into a near shouting match between the audience and the panelists. At one point, a young African American woman asked the white male McLaren if he could give concrete examples of how his theory on multicultural education was

applicable to an urban teacher. In the view of the woman, McLaren offered more pedagogy without practicality, and this response caused an uproar in the theater where the discussion occurred.

The Omaha Children's Theater is not on the university campus and is a traditional space with a balcony and box seats, as well as a painted ceiling with the night sky and statues around the eaves. The panelists sat at a table on the stage, and when Freire entered he walked down the aisle in the theater seats. People were literally reaching out and touching this frail, elderly man with long white hair and a white beard. The religious connotations were hard to ignore, and the presentation on the stage, on a space that privileged the speakers, even elevating them physically, distanced the three keynoters from the audience. However, once the call for questions began, and the confrontational tone increased, the distance and privilege evaporated as the audience commandeered the theater, forcing the speakers to extend their time on the stage by more than an hour. The performative aspects of this event deserve a longer discussion, but I describe this in a bit of detail as a means of comparison to the performance of the play: here before us was the theatrical setting, alive with the conflict between academic discourse's exclusionary power and those without whom that discourse would not exist.

Under this cloud, the students performed *Oleanna* in a small auditorium in the university's conference center, with entrances and exits in the aisles next to the audience. This blocking created an especially strong effect at the end of Act 2, when John pursues Carol and attempts to physically block her from leaving so he can finish his point. Carol's cries for help were played out in the audience. The Carol of this production was a far more wounded person than in any other I have seen. Every first act movement indicated she was falling apart, so that by the second and third acts her reversal seemed measured, not instinctual. Carol was physically larger than John, so the use of force took on greater significance.

Within the context of the performance space and time, at each mention of issues of power, especially those regarding disempowering John, the audience reacted with audible murmurs of agreement. The actors said that the audience in Omaha was far more sympathetic to Carol; they felt the audience noted in advance every gesture, every movement Carol made. In Iowa, as in many of its performances, *Oleanna* was met with cries of outrage for what the audience believed Carol was doing to John. How much of the frame of the conference, and our own predispositions formed by the conference's events, led those of us in the audience toward sympathy with Carol? Our awareness of the privilege of power had been heightened by the earlier confrontation in the theater and the fact that we had been part of that audience that protested the answers being given to the questioners.

If we didn't completely understand Carol's motivations, we at least understood the roots of her discontent.

Performance Number Three

At the beginning of the fall semester at the University of Tennessee–Knoxville, where I was teaching as an instructor, the chair of the department opened the first faculty meeting with these words from Carol in *Oleanna*:

> What gives you the *right*. Yes. To speak to a *woman* in your private ... Yes. Yes. I'm sorry. I'm sorry. You feel yourself empowered ... you say so yourself. To *strut*. To *posture*. To "perform." To "Call me in here ..." Eh? You say that higher education is a joke. And treat it as such, you *treat* it as such. And *confess* to a taste to play the *Patriarch* in your class. To grant *this*. To deny *that*. To embrace your students ... How can you *deny* it. You did it to me. *Here*. You *did* ... You *confess*. You love the Power. To *deviate*. To *invent*, to transgress ... to *transgress* whatever norms have been established for us. And you think it's charming to "question" in yourself this taste to mock and destroy. But you should question it. Professor. And you pick those things which you feel *advance* you: publication, *tenure*, and the steps to get them you call "harmless rituals." And you perform those steps. Although you say it is hypocrisy. But to the aspirations of your students. Of *hardworking students*, who come here, who *slave* to come here—you have no idea what it cost me to come to this school—you *mock* us. You call education "hazing," and from your so-protected, so-elitist seat you hold our confusion as a *joke*, and our hopes and efforts with it. Then you sit there and say "what have I done?" And ask me to understand that *you* have aspirations too. But I tell you. I tell you. That you are vile. And that you are exploitative. And if you possess one ounce of that inner honesty you describe in your book, you can look in yourself and see those things that I see. And you can find revulsion equal to my own (Mamet, 1993, pp. 51–52).

To many of us in that large classroom where the chair read this, the circumstances behind this seeming tirade were confusing at best. Was he giving us a warning about sexual harassment of students? Was there an actual case? Was he simply admonishing us to use our superpowers for good and not for evil? Or was he telling us to be careful about confrontations with students and to abide by university policy? Besides some vague words about "too much political correctness" on campuses, the chair simply left his meaning uninterpreted, allowing us to head into the semester with this strange knowledge. Indeed, we were the students at that moment, taking the position of our pupils in the impersonal lecture room.

V. Pedagogy

I acknowledge my own shifting predispositions toward the characters in *Oleanna* as a viewer, reader, and teacher of the play. In each of these cases, my reaction as an audience member, and the audible reactions of those around me, as well as later discussion with them, was contextualized by circumstance and space. While all plays have a varying degree of interpretive tension that performance dissipates to an extent, when played on the college campus, Mamet's play naturally intersects with its milieu in a way that reflects an ever-shifting geography of gender, power, and politics. For Garner's students, the performance confirmed their own anger against Carol, to which Garner responds that this is a "discouraging response: a dialectic of sympathy and responsibility is abandoned in favor of *Oleanna's* cathartic demonization." (2000, p. 49)

In teaching the play, I decided I wanted to take the play one step further into the lives of the students, much like my former chair had taken the play into our lives: by moving the play into the classroom. For a course on twentieth-century American drama, I decided to arrange a performance of long excerpts of the play where I acted with a female student from the class.[3] In an admittedly showy exercise, I wanted to use *Oleanna* as a way of demonstrating the meaning of performance in a personal context. I set up the exercise by selecting the student in front of the class and asking her if she would talk to me after the class period ended. The first rehearsal was held in my office and the difficulties of the exercise became clear very quickly. Like John, I am in tenure pursuit here at my university. Like John, my wife called during my discussions with the student. Like John, I regularly flout the conventions of the classroom in a kind of performance of teaching. Jenn, a theater major, claimed she was at ease with the entire process, but the dynamics of the power relationships evident in the play were laid bare in the director/teacher/actor relationship established during our rehearsals. Simply put, we walked a very fine line. Jenn was a student whom her peers had already called "teacher's pet." Was I using the play as a means to harassment? Did I have motivations beyond pedagogical? These questions were imbued in the text of our performance.

In a preperformance discussion with students, the class almost as a whole sided with John and some even expressed outrage that he had not beaten Carol sooner. Students discussed Carol as misrepresenting feminist causes and demonizing and belittling those who are actually raped by her charges against John. Many questioned me about the path to tenure: Was this something I was pursuing? What does "tenure" mean to them as students? This latter question is interesting in relation to the play: John's power would have been completely different had he already been a tenured professor.

Several students thought, as many critics have, that Carol was setting up John in order to make a case against him.

Jenn and I performed sections of all three acts, excluding the beating and the exit-blocking incident because of the brief rehearsal period. I did not introduce the performance with anything more than saying that I would be reading John, with Jenn as Carol. This activity fit right in with the rest of the semester, when students would regularly read scenes in the class. During the performance, I did put my arm around Jenn to comfort her in the first act, when Carol nearly breaks down from her nervousness over her lack of understanding. In the ensuing scene, when John tries to calm down Carol with repeated "Sshhh" and "It's all right," coaxing her to tell him a secret (Mamet, 1993, p. 36–7), I slowly approached Jenn until I was right in front of her and we were staring at each other. Our movements were basic and simple, with one or the other of us standing to indicate a power position.

Student reactions ranged from the usual nonplussed, apathetic reactions to the many students who said the performance changed their minds about the play and about the act of performing:

> "Power is a perception. No one is powerful alone. We create power in others, and you have the power here."

> "When you read the speech about performing as a teacher, I cringed. That's you, isn't it?"

> "It made me feel strange about every time I've spoken to a male professor."

> "The performance made me tense for Jenn. I know she's not Carol, but I couldn't help seeing a friend get harassed."

> "The teacher-student relationship is all about power. This power drives a student to extreme measures and the teacher to insanity."

> "I am the same age as the character, so I put myself in her shoes. I could not separate myself from her in the performance."

> "Carol seems to desire power and she strives to get it however she can."

Most jarring was Jenn's written reaction:

> This has to be the strangest, most intense personal experience I've ever had performing. Having the sense that I, as a student, am in the exact same position as Carol was a frightening, provoking one. What was truly testing was rehearsing this in your office in the evening alone behind a closed door. To know that someone of a higher stature has the power over me to manipulate is very creepy.

Because of this statement, I question the motivations behind my exercise. I believe I am cognizant of the exploitative and exhibitionist qualities of the performance—exploiting Jenn by asking her to rehearse this, exploiting the students by forcing them to view it—but that question of space never recedes. I violated some parameter in my office and in my classroom (even the possessive "my" forces me to acknowledge a belief in the power of the space), but as a means of personalizing a text through performance by invading the classroom space with that performance, the exercise achieved a breakthrough for the students: One of them was up there, and in her they could see themselves.

VI. Conclusion

An essay such as this is filled with self-reflexivity. I am writing about myself. The text of the play is a reflection of my daily life. The discussion of *Oleanna* in the classroom is naturally self-referential for the students and the teacher. I use scholarly discourse in this. (I quote Foucault, for God's sake.) This continuous cycle of text responds to life responds to life responds to text/article responds to text and on and on cannot be ignored. Other recent plays about academia locate their battles as functions of characters in the plays. In Rebecca Gilman's *Spinning Into Butter* (1999), the accusations of racism are played out in a realistic, linear fashion. Margaret Edson's *Wit* uses the professor character to comment on the disempowerment of the patient in a medical situation. But *Oleanna* doesn't provide anything quite so comforting. It instead creates a world, a space within a space, the office on the stage, which jars our notions of space. It deconstructs itself and its context even as we who teach it try to grapple with those things that the play draws upon in its attack on academia. Bennett claims that "academic attention [to a work] does something to reinscribe the work into mainstream discourse" (1997, p. 98), but Mamet's play resists such inscription by anticipating its audience inside and outside the academy. In this way, *Oleanna* becomes an evolving product of circumstance, a pop culture surfacing of the processes of academia and their connections to the outside world, a glimpse through a window, into those spaces.

Notes

1. I am reminded of a small, storefront theater in Lafayette, Louisiana, that had a support pole in the middle of its stage area: Every set on the stage, from *Othello* to *Cat on a Hot Tin Roof*, had to take into account how to incorporate or work around the pole. Mostly, it was done ingeniously, and an audience unaware of this limitation would have interpreted this arrangement much differently than someone who was cognizant of the need to use the pole.

A side note to this side note: Every year this theater would give an award to the set designer who best used the pole.

2. Information on this production comes from my own viewing, as well as interviews with the director.

3. In a graduate gender studies course I taught, students performed parts of the play in various configurations: male/female, female/male, male/male, and female/female. This method was used to discuss how the power was reified and whether or not it was a circumstance of phallic prerogative. Interestingly, the power issues shifted in each permutation; the play seemed successful only in its male teacher/female student arrangement.

References

Badenhausen, R. "The Modern Academy Raging in the Dark: Misreading Mamet's Political Incorrectness in *Oleanna*." *College Literature* 25 (Fall 1998): 1–19.

Bennett, S. *Theater Audiences: A Theory of Production and Reception.* 2nd ed. London: Routledge, 1997.

Brownmiller, S., et al. "He Said . . . She Said . . . Who Did What?" *New York Times*, November 15, 1992: 2–6.

Foucault, M. *Discipline and Punish: The Birth of the Prison.* Translated by A. Sheridan. New York: Pantheon Books, 1977.

Garner, S. B., Jr. "Framing the Classroom: Pedagogy, Power, *Oleanna*." *Theater Topics* 10 (March 2000): 39–49.

Kershaw, B. *The Politics of Performance: Radical Theater as Cultural Intervention.* London: Routledge, 1992.

Kroll, J. "A Tough Lesson in Sexual Harassment." *Newsweek*, November 9, 1992, 65.

Macedo, D. *Literacies of Power: What Americans Are Not Allowed to Know.* Boulder: Westview Press, 1994.

MacLeod, C. "The Politics of Gender, Language and Hierarchy in Mamet's *Oleanna*." *Journal of American Studies* 29 (1995): 199–213.

Mamet, D. *Oleanna*. New York: Vintage, 1993.

12

Vampires on Campus: Reflections on (Un)Death, Transformation, and Blood Knowledges in *The Addiction*

MORNA McDERMOTT AND TOBY DASPIT

Looking Back Without a Reflection

From: Morna McDermott <morna.mcdermott@wmich.edu>
To: Toby Daspit <toby.daspit@wmich.edu>
Sent: Thursday, October 19, 2000 2:19 PM

Metaphorically . . . as a student I feel DRAINED! Maybe being the vampire is "empowering" to the extent that i get to drain others! Ha ha ha . . . can I eat my committee too?

We begin by considering the irony that we finally finish this piece after Morna completes her Ph.D. We say this because the idea for this chapter started over three years ago in the fall of 1999 while Morna was beginning her doctoral program, when we realized our shared "blood lust" might prove for some interesting academic theory. Toby suggested that Morna watch Abel Ferrara's 1995 film *The Addiction*, a movie based on the premise of a young woman, Kathleen, who is transformed into a vampire during the completion of her philosophy dissertation at New York University. At the time Morna wondered if she would find parallels between Kathleen's life and her own as a doctoral student, as Toby had several years before. What *does* it mean to compare oneself to a vampire in the academy?

Scholarly associations between the academy and vampires, at the offset, might appear strange at best. However, using *The Addiction* as a bridge between vampires and "the Ivory Tower," we propose that the world of academe parallels the netherworld of the undead in several ways. We track Kathleen's journey through her various stages as both a doctoral student and a newly transformed vampire, to explore what it means to "imagine the academy," and to investigate our own intentions as academics interested in knowledge construction and meaning-making. Kathleen, as both a vampire and an academic, makes the parallel tangible. Further, we wonder whether vampires and academics are more than mere parallels to one another, more than simply metaphorical connections. Perhaps being a vampire and an academic are one and the same.

Drawing from Suzi Gablik's work on post avant-garde art (1984, 1991, 1995) we pull together Gablik's thoughts on post avant-garde art and our experiences as academics/vampires, creating possible relationships to life and work in the academy. However, through the process of writing this piece, and watching and dialoguing about the film, our theories kept shifting and changing. What began with one theory, based on the premise that vampires are appropriately suited to represent the postmodern academic, eventually took us somewhere altogether different from where we had intended to go. This journey doesn't reach an ending point with answers neatly sewn up at the seams. Instead, we find ourselves standing at the periphery of unknown space, where words and answers fall away into hitherto unimagined possibilities.

In essence, in the process of exploring relationships between post avant-garde art theory, vampires, and imagining the academy, we "murder" our initial theory in favor of yet another theory, a still emerging notion—that perhaps something exists even beyond the undead state of the vampire. Can we possibly imagine altered states of becoming for which we still lack the language to articulate? Using Gablik's definition of post avant-garde art as a foundation, we find the role(s) of the contemporary artist to be similar to those of contemporary academics and vampires in the twenty-first century. In the end, we propose a venture into previously inexpressible states, suggesting that although a transformation from human to vampire might help us imagine the academy in contemporary culture, we crave more. Our quest stems from wondering if being an academic vampire is, in fact, enough to reimagine the academy, if it is to provoke sustainable social changes? To consider this question, using *The Addiction* as our medium for discussion, we deliberate over what perhaps lies beyond being undead.

By providing examples from the film itself and including excerpts from e-mails in which we create "bloody" exchanges of ideas regarding the film and vampirism, we trace Kathleen's journey through her bloodsucking creative processes, one which suggests that knowledge can be "addicting." Furthermore, as any addict knows, one will "kill" for the next fix. Finally, we struggle with meanings around Kathleen's demise at the end of the film. Although at first we found ourselves smiling and rooting for Kathleen as a scholastic vampire who assaults unsuspecting victims, especially her professors (a form of anger-release therapy as the stress of academic dead-lines leads us to find heroes in the strangest of places), by the end of the film we were both troubled by its "inconclusiveness" (a trait developed from years of being forced into thinking in terms of "absolute" conclusions, proofs, and concepts such as reliability and validity). Ultimately, we wonder if it is "better" to be a vampire in postmodern times? Was becoming a vampire necessary for Kathleen's survival as a doctoral student?

Vampires in Postmodernity

From: Nancy C. H. <@cms.mail.virginia.edu>
To: Morna McDermott <morna.mcdermott@wmich.edu>
Sent: Tuesday, October 17, 2000 2:19 PM
Subject: Re: careful of new virus

So sweetie, this vampire must go feed, on what I'm not sure, but I must tell you that the idea of a never-ending life as a Doc student scares the hell out of me. So, I hope our vampirism: not seeing the light of day, developing pale and pasty skin, being feared as a freak, etc., doesn't last forever. I for one want out of here.

The doctoral student as vampire creates many layers of possible meanings. The first and most obvious to us is the idea that doctoral students, like vampires, represent the undead. Kathleen's fellow vampire and mentor, Peina, says, reflecting on her current condition: "You can't eat. You can't sleep. You can't even go out to satisfy the urge during the day. You are a slave to what you are and you're nothing." As any doctoral student knows, to become part of the academy is, so to speak, to lose oneself. Through a series of ritual-like and often self-destructive behaviors, we witness our former lives waning like a candle flame denied adequate oxygen. Then, with our previous identities drained from us, we emerge as "doctor," our identity transformed.

The issues of identity and meaning construction, between self and other, between survival and death as presented within the walls of the academy, suggest why, as Hollinger (1997) explains, "some vampire texts 'mirror' aspects of that peculiar human condition which has come to be termed 'postmodern.'" (p. 199) Postmodernism, she argues, "is one of the more productive" and challenging "paradigms through which contemporary Western reality is currently being conceptualized." (p. 199)

This identity transformation is embodied by the vampire, who represents an older version, perhaps, of our new world of hyperrealities, where place becomes dislocated, where the body ceases to be a reference point, and where acts of desire and self-transformation are exhumed from darker regions of the human psyche or soul. Somewhere after image and before reflection, in the world of the in-between, live vampires as "postmodern creatures, as desiring un/dead, and the complexity of vampires is such that, unable to be seen in mirrors, they are yet dispersed throughout the world." (Brown, 1998, p. 126)

Similarly, Hollinger (1997) note that "certain previously sacrosanct boundaries—political, philosophical, conceptual, ethical, aesthetic—have tended to become problematized" (p. 201), blurring the traditionally held Eurocentric (Enlightenment-era) definitions of self and identity. She explains that:

> (T)his deconstruction of boundaries helps to explain why the vampire is a monster-of-choice these days, since it is itself an inherently deconstructive figure: it is the monster that used to be human; it is the undead that used to be alive; it is the monster that *looks like us*. For this reason, the figure of the vampire always has the potential to jeopardize conventional distinctions between human and monster, between life and death, between others and ourselves. We look into the mirror it provides and we see a version of ourselves. Or, more accurately, keeping in mind the orthodoxy that vampires cast no mirror reflections, we look into the mirror and see nothing *but* ourselves. (p. 201, emphases in original)

The feeling of "nothingness" was one that we, and essentially everyone we knew who had undergone the rituals of doctoral work, understood well. Although we may appear in the guise of our former selves, we are in fact drained, sucked dry by the invisible forces of the university and the doctoral process. In essence, we "kill" ourselves for the sake of our work, dying in order to live.

In the beginning of *The Addiction*, Kathleen is confronted in a dark alley by a vampire named Casanova, who says, "Tell me to go away." Kathleen does not respond, and she is bitten. This exchange becomes one of blood for transformation: The vampire drinks Kathleen's blood, and Kathleen is bestowed with the gift of eternal "life." Similarly, no one "forces" us to become doctoral students. We choose to stay and be "bitten" in exchange for what feels like an eternity of sleepless nights, food deprivation, and isolation from "the world of the living"—an annihilation of self.

In her vampiric form, Kathleen's disgust for food symbolizes her disgust for intellectual pursuits. Meeting with a non-vampire friend Jean over lunch one day, she asks, "How can you eat and read that stuff at the same time?" Kathleen's distaste stems from her realization that she and Jean have been asked to "swallow" information, which in her postmortem state, Kathleen finds contemptible and meaningless. Once the vampiric transformation of the doctoral student begins, we start hunting for knowledge, drinking the lifeblood out of texts, lectures, ideas, dreams—anything that might sustain our existence. Knowledge becomes a need, a craving—an addiction.

In a similar vein (pun intended) the vampire's "condition" is also a struggle against modernistic and fixed concepts of meaning. The vampire metaphor, Allucquere Rosanne Stone (1997) argues, illuminates the necessity of altering postmodern modes of perception in a shifting world. She writes:

If we are going to survive into the next century, we need to learn how to see properly—how to make meaning, in all senses—in a world that has already changed beyond recognition, and that we still think we recognize only because nostalgia is such a terrifically powerful force. (p. 61)

Survival, Stone contends, this need for a new vision, can be achieved in two ways: "One is by becoming aware that the control of the apparatus of meaning has slipped out from under us." The other means to survival, Stone writes, is "to accept the vampire's kiss." (p. 61) What might happen, Golding (1997) asks, if we accept the vampire's kiss, the multiple identities and subjectivities of postmodernity, and see where they might lead us—"if we stop 'sterilizing' the wounds" (p. xii) of epistemological and metaphysical fractures and ruptures:

What if it were to be admitted that the usual, empty phrases like the so-called deep and violent cut of meaning, truth, death, indeed identity itself: the who are we and what are we to become of science and of life have collapsed under their own bloodless, sexless weight of self-reflexive reason? For though the very cunning of dialectical logic (historical, metaphysical, or otherwise) has already produced many interesting political dalliances with empowerment, necessity and change, it has, more often than not, simply recast, or (worse) simply reproduced, the very practices it is seeking to overcome . . . (Golding, 1997, p. xii).

Munro (1998) offers possible "answers" to Stone and Golding, noting that rejecting "the unitary subject for a more complex, multiple, and contradictory notion of subjectivity results not in a lack of agency but in forms of agency not solely dependent on a universal subject" (p. 35)—a vampire of agency, or an agent of change touched by the complex identities of vampirism.

As a postmodern character, Kathleen's existence stands somewhere between "terrorism and nihilism." (Pinar et al., 1995, p. 481) She is a liminal creature, beyond Western notions of either/or. Acknowledging our own agency and shifting identities, like Kathleen's in her vampiric state, often leaves us in perpetual states of "in-betweenness." In her newly transformed state, Kathleen revels in the powers bestowed upon her. Her words and actions suggest that she believes she has found a "transcendent" state of being, one of power and total free will. She scoffs at her fellow students, as they pathetically try to drain knowledge from the carcasses of dusty books and dead theories, and drain each other of words or ideas. In one scene at the library, Kathleen thinks, "Oh, the stench here is worse than a charnel house. This is a graveyard. Rows of crumbling tombstones. Vicious libelous epitaphs. And we're all drawn here like flies."

With the (in)"sight" of a vampire, she begins to realize that living knowledge is more useful than dead and lifeless theories. In response to her dissertation chair's advice that they "get to work," she retorts, "Some things are more important than others. Besides, aren't you the one who eschews speculative philosophy? I'm coming to terms with my own existence, applying what I've learned to my own being. We'll get to the thesis in good time." As a vampire she represents Nietzsche's (1891/1999) *Übermensch* (superman), whose agency in the world is built on free will and self-creation. By "coming to terms with [her] own existence," Kathleen is playing on the existentialist notion that meaning and being are created rather than revealed, that we are what or whom we choose to become. However, as the e-mail from our friend Nancy suggests, being a vampire has its downsides as well. What appears to be a total embrace of free will, a Nietzschean "will to power" as perpetual agent of self-creation, when held in the light of day reveals a fight for survival, a space precariously balanced between murder and suicide.

Between Suicide and Murder: Annihilation of Self

And it's like a 'trap'—hence the addiction—the craving of an addiction is to get something out of a source from which it cannot be gotten—that's why its never enough—you always need "more" We seek knowledge in this dry vacuum of a knowledge production system that produces addictions to making more of the same—so do we have free will? Even as a vampire she has the addiction . . . (Daspit and McDermott, 2000, p. 3)

Jacques Daignault, citing Michel Serres, argues that "to know is to kill" (in Pinar et al., 1995, p. 199) and "that running after rigorous demonstrations and after confirmations is a hunt: literally." (p. 198) He quotes Serres: "From Plato and a tradition which lasted throughout the classical age, knowledge is a hunt. To know is to put to death . . . To know is to kill, to rely on death." (p. 199) Pinar et al. (1995) note that:

> Daignault calls for us to live in the middle, in spaces that are neither terroristic or nihilistic . . . For Daignault "thinking happens only between suicide and murder . . . between nihilism and terrorism" . . . Thinking is a passage, but this passage is always in danger of being defined and known . . . The only way to avoid this fate is to allow thought to think itself, to go beyond or to disrupt dualism, and to think the difference between them. It is to introduce paradox. It is not to stop defining, but to multiply the definitions. It is to invite a plural spelling, to experiment, to problematize (p. 480–81).

Shaun McNiff (1992), quoting William Wordsworth, similarly suggests that following traditional and scientific paradigms of thinking, we "murder to dissect" (p. 194), we kill in order to know things.

Strangely, it is living that Kathleen finds murderous, rather than vampirism. She prefers "living" knowledge, in the form of bloody exchanges, a commingling of fluids that represent things that cannot be fixed but remain fluid and in flux. These "blood knowledges," both relational and transitory, are qualitatively different from the dead, static forms of knowledge typically espoused as legitimate forms of "data" used in most textbooks and across many, if not all, blackboard "lectures."

Subject: banwv
Date: Thu, 29 Jul 1999 17:33:16 -0400 (EDT)
From: "Morna M. McDermott" <mmh3x@unix.mail.virginia.edu>
To: Toby Daspit <toby.daspit@wmich.edu>

Here's my two cents in print regarding Kathleen in *The Addiction*. She IS the "embodiment" of the new doctoral student—the postmodern figure—in contrast to her old "charnel house" committee— and their addiction to "old" forms of knowledge—i.e., reference to the library—she is going to show them what SHE has learned—notice it has NOTHING to do with what THEY have taught her—maybe I identify with her in this way because I am a doctoral student—the point is that our identity DOES change as the result of doing this work— she IS her study—not that cold objective stance that her friend takes—as an observer—the point of becoming the vampire

> is (to) become the thing that is studied—changed—the thing we really come to understand—is ourselves and Christopher Walken says she/"we" are nothing—hmmm . . . nothing IS something but more elusive. Ok—that's it. We have WAY too much—overdosing on our own blood?

The lack of a vampire's reflection leads us to wonder how "self" can be represented, if not reflected, in our work? It leads to postmodern questions about the existence, or the lack thereof, of an "essential" self. The catch-phrase throughout *The Addiction* is "tell me to go away." We contend that this phrase represents the desire for the annihilation of self (suicide?) in favor of some altered condition, which hinges upon our relationships with others. Kathleen's very being is one of perpetual "becoming" or, rather, an identity that has no original self at all. In order to survive, she must con-tinuously feed off others (murder). She says to her dissertation chair, who is also her drug-addicted lover, "Dependency is a marvelous thing. It does more for the soul than any formulation of doctoral material."

We now struggle with our initial theory, that it is the vampire who embodies the future academic in the Ivory Tower. Although we agree with Gordon and Hollinger (1997) that vampires are "one of the most powerful archetypes bequeathed to us from the imagination of the nineteenth cen-tury" and that they are "a late twentieth-century cultural necessity" (p. 1), we still wondered whether it was possible to be transformed into yet an even more transient and liminal creature than the vampire. Is it this "unknown" creature that truly represents the future of the academy, extending beyond the realm of postmodernism?

We hear the words in our own heads (echoing Kathleen's words at the height of her own addiction): "I will not submit!" To what? To the craving to prove some theory? To espouse some answer? We struggle against our own positivistic addictions to create "meaning." Is this academic suicide . . . to murder our own theory? Perhaps. But in viewing the film we cannot evade the obvious fact that in order to survive, to avoid suicide, Kathleen must commit murder. As we watch the movie repeatedly we begin to take yet another perspective on Kathleen. As former doctoral students, of course we find ourselves "naturally" siding with her, especially at that sub-lime moment where, following her successful defense of her dissertation, she "eats" her committee. But we realize that despite her "superhuman" and unfixed state, she is as addicted to something as the professors and students she so scorns.

This posed a dilemma for us. If Kathleen, too, is addicted to the patterns, the behaviors, and the system reproduced by the university, is she really any "better" than the humans she scorns? In other words, in considering the dilemma of addiction, Kathleen acknowledges later in the film, "We drink to escape the fact we're alcoholics. Existence is the search for relief from our habit, and our habit is the only relief we can find." So we ventured into another theory, one that coincides with Kathleen's final transformation, beyond her vampire state, beyond "death."

The Post-Vampire in the Ivory Tower

> Philosophy is propaganda. There is always an attempt to influence the object. The real question is 'what is the philosopher's impact on other egos?' If we eliminate the verb we eliminate the meaning. The predicate defines the noun's role in being . . . Essence is revealed through praxis. The philosopher's words, his ideas, his actions, cannot be separated from his value, his meaning. That's what it's all about, isn't it? Our impact on other egos.
>
> (Kathleen Conklin, *The Addiction*, 1995)

Our initial ideas, based on "the vampire of agency," begin to change as we rethink the end of the film. Kathleen realizes that she, too, is addicted. We debated whether she is really better than the humans around her. After all, she too, as a vampire, is a slave to her own addiction for blood. Before she eats her committee, she is seen fighting against herself in the coatroom, screaming "I will not submit," but ultimately she does. Gallagher (2000) refers to this scene as a "vampiric orgy accurately dramatizing the life of academics on the prowl." (p. 38) This binge leads to an "overdose" of sorts, and she collapses in the street and awakens to find herself in a Christian-run hospital. Realizing she cannot go on, she attempts her own self-destruction ("suicide" seems like the wrong word for the undead) by pulling up the blinds to face the sunlight, but her attempt is thwarted by the presence of Casanova, the vampire who first bit her. Casanova represents the nihilistic fear that perhaps there is "no way out" from the addiction. However, after Casanova leaves the hospital, Kathleen requests "last rites" at the hands of a priest and then passes into another state. In the final scene, which leaves us a bit perplexed to this day, Kathleen is seen standing in the sunlight beside a gravestone with her name inscribed in the heading. As she walks away from the graveside with her face pointed towards the sun, she reflects, "Revelation comes though annihilation of self."

Although at first glance this final scene appears to be one of classical redemption, when seen through the metaphorical lens that we have been using throughout this chapter, that of vampire as postmodern academic/ doctoral student, the question becomes, "What does this act mean for those languishing within the walls of the Ivory Tower?" If our initial idea is that the vampire represents a change to alternative ways of thinking and being in academia, then what of Kathleen's addiction and her ultimate desire to escape her eternal condition? Perhaps this annihilation is some other "death." Or perhaps the annihilation of "self" transforms Kathleen into what we call a "post-vampire." We construct our meanings of "post-vampire" largely from Gablik's (1991; 1995) ideas on post avant-garde art and its role in society.

Post avant-garde, as an art genre, is a loosely knit set of sociopolitical and ecological ideals. Generally speaking, post avant-garde emerged as a response to the perceived "failure" of the avant-garde movement to change the status quo as the artists had intended. "The popular modernist term 'avant garde,'" according to Milbrandt, "implied a duality of aesthetic innovation and social revolt." (1998, p. 47) In essence, faced with the shattered idealism of post-war America, avant-garde artists found themselves caught in a contradiction between "myth and transcendence, the roots of art in the unconscious, and of art itself as a solitary act" and "the hostility of the age, and the traps of any sense of community and security." (Harrison and Wood, 1992, p. 497) In avant-garde art's attempt to remove itself from the daily concerns of the bourgeois middle-class culture during the early- to mid-twentieth century, it produced a genre of "art for art's sake." Although the intent was to produce a cultural "cutting-edge" as an attempt to produce "revolutionary change," avant-garde artists instead found their ideals "defeated and rendered impotent by . . . absorption into the mainstream." (Gablik, 1991, p. 14)

We contend that ideals of post avant-garde art theory directly correlate Kathleen's final transformation. Turning Kathleen's final words over and over in our heads, we began to focus less on the term "annihilation" and began to focus on the term "self" and what that word suggests in traditional Western thought. If she has annihilated her "self," then into what state of being has she (walking off the screen as the credits roll) emerged? This question drew us to Gablik, who contests the Western notions of self identified with contemporary art movements and argues for a rethinking of self through aesthetic and social transformation. She writes:

> Although it may seem as if the individual in today's world has little power, the truth is that only we have the power to transform our situation: there is no one else. The source of creativity in society is the person. Where individuals and social transformation converge is the in this personal breakthrough to a new way of seeing (1991, p. 23).

Under the guise of Western modernist epistemologies, art, according to Gablik, was perceived through a "disinterested, distanced, formal contemplation of the world." (1995, p. 246) She further contests that such views of art reveal a "hidden elitism" in which "only certain people can take (such a view) . . . they are people whose practical world is already taken care of."

(p. 248) This is what she calls the "museum conception of art." (p. 248) Museum conceptions of art reinforce the view of "the observer (as) a passive receiver, essentially Locke's blank slate, rather than as an active agent with a role to play in the construction of aesthetic experience." (Carey, 1998, p. 291)

Post avant-garde art redefines this concept into one that considers art "in the practice of living, in how we organize our lives and how we improve them, that the idea of confining art to what we hang on walls is a pathetic failure of theoretical as well as artistic imagination." (Gablik, 1991, p. 265) Post avant-garde style embraces spontaneous creation and synchronous engagement between the self, art, and the context in which both are embedded. Gablik contends that rather than viewing the post avant-garde as a fully realized framework, we might consider it more as a way to "think about new connections, participatory aesthetics, and to speak for a value-based art that is able to transcend the modernist opposition between the aesthetic and the social." (p. 9)

Another key feature of the post avant-garde is that, as opposed to the modernist perception of the individual artistic genius working alone, art is a socially constructed act. In reflecting on her work with the post avant-garde, Gablik explains:

> As my sense of art slowly transformed from a visual language of forms into something more interactive and dialectical in nature, I began to se how the model of the lone genius struggling against society, which has been the philosophical basis for Western culture, has deprived art of its astonishing potential to build community through empathetic social interaction (1995, p. 17).

Post avant-garde art also contests the notion that any form of art can be considered "new" or "ahead of its time" in favor of the idea that "art constructs the reality that is perceived . . . and offers multiple interpretations . . . each imbued with politics and ethics." (jagodinski, 1997, p. 143) As an art form it does not attempt to "transcend" society but rather reimmerses the individual self into a mode that is interactive and relational to the concerns and problems of society. Rather than searching for new "discoveries" (Gablik, 1995) out there, the post avant-garde seeks out previously unacknowledged relationships. Richard Shusterman, in his interview with Gablik, explains, "We are all recycling, quoting and appropriating," despite the strong emphasis we still place on the ideal of "pure innovation." (in Gablik, 1995, p. 255) Art becomes a vehicle for social awareness and collaborative action that lives in and through us.

If nothing can be "new," can transformation be possible? jagodinski (1992) grapples with the social role of art in the postmodern world where two approaches, "one nihilistic and the other critical" (p. 171), stand in direct contradiction to each other. Gablik supports jagodinski's idea of the artistic "split" in her definitions of postmodern art, one "a deconstructive version" and the other a "reconstructive version." The former, like jagodinski's nihilistic version, suggests "that change is no longer possible," while the latter suggests that "change is inevitable." (Gablik, 1991, p. 157) Rather than becoming nihilistic (as represented by Casanova standing at Kathleen's bedside), post avant-garde art reconstructs sites for being and living aesthetically, using art to reconstruct our worlds.

Looking back over Kathleen's journey, we realized that as a vampire she was never able to break away from traditional academic constraints, which she rejected in favor of blood knowledges. Her addiction suggests a loss of will, or freedom of choice, a condemnation to reproduce the same cycles, like avant-garde artists reproducing the same standards to which they were opposed, becoming replicas of the things they opposed. Despite her initial claims to "self-overcoming" and claims to "thus I willed it," Kathleen discovers "the impulse . . . is not wonder but terror . . . [Harold] Bloom's 'horror of finding oneself to be only a copy or a replica.'" (Rorty, 1989, p. 29)

Kathleen perhaps stood at the crossroads of the dilemma: whether change was impossible or inevitable. Her change from human to vampire ultimately led to a viewpoint of nihilism and eventually her own "suicide." Jardine (2000) reminds us, "the nausea of narration sickness comes from having heard enough, from hearing many variations on a theme, but no new theme." (p. 164) Kathleen in fact becomes more nihilistic and fatalistic as a vampire. She considers the proposition that "We are not evil because we do evil . . . we do evil because we are evil." Her cynicism suggests that we are addicted to who we are because of a need we cannot escape. In academia, the question is, "Can we really know anything beyond the paradigms out of which we can know anything in the first place?" Or are we doomed, as Casanova suggests, to "feed off" the paradigms of thought that, even as postmodern vampires/academics, we struggle to break free of? In relation to aesthetic ways of thinking, "it is precisely at this crossover between the reactive mode of deconstruction and the more active mode of reconstruction," Gablik argues, "that a change from old-paradigm dynamics into new is likely to occur." (1991, p. 26)

Kathleen manifests the idea that self-revelation occurs through annihilation of self. Perhaps this idea suggests a rejection of our old notions of identity in the academic community in favor of a post-vampiric state. Here, what exists is the annihilation of notions of a unitary or individual "self" as separate from our relationships to others, to community. Like a post avant-garde artist, the doctoral student/academic might adopt an artistic relational mode of perpetual "becoming" that does not feed off others but instead constructs a dialogue of the imaginations, "changing forever the way we see ourselves and the way we see our societies." (Highwater, 1994, p. 4) Kathleen perhaps was aware of this well before her actual "change." During her oral defense she explains:

> If we eliminate the verb, we eliminate the meaning. The predicate defines the noun's role in being . . . Essence is revealed through praxis. The philosopher's words, his ideas, his actions, cannot be separated from his value, his meaning.

We begin change by restating the problem in terms of "becoming" rather than of being. Whether it be for the creation of art, or for the creation of an academic identity, becoming allows work or knowledge creation to be evaluated by criteria that are not finite or absolute in relation to some knowledge out "there" in the form of observational, objective gazes that "kill to know." From this perspective, we might see why the vampire itself, with all its liminal powers of postmodernity, perhaps could only go so far and inevitably never break out of the addictive knowledge production cycle. Becoming arrives in the form of revelation rather than observation (Highwater, 1994). Kathleen reminds us that "Revelation comes through annihilation of self." Here the connections between the post-vampire and the artist continues to. "And it is in that unique role," Highwater concludes, "that the artist finds it necessary to create metaphoric forms of expression that are capable of dealing with the ineffable—the revelation." (p. 15) Our task as post-vampires within the Ivory Tower is to redefine our work and ourselves in aesthetic terms of becoming and in terms of creative knowledges that might help us reimagine our world by articulating "the unutterable." (Rimbaud, 1975, p. 65)

The post-vampire is an emerging identity in a transformed world of academia, where the annihilation of self is not destructive, nor does it represent the "removal" or absence of self in more traditional or objective senses. Instead, it shatters the notion of an "authentic" self and replaces it with elements or fragments of self that are continuously reshaped into shifting mosaics of multiple selves in the context of community. Similarly, Mullen suggests, "Identity is like a collage, variously arranged and glued together." (1998, p. 150) Rather than forming "new" identities, we see instead a collaged design, the form of becoming that changes what can be seen or known in the first place.

Kathleen is not a "non"-vampire. We presume she never returns to a human state. We are left only with the unknown, and infinite, possibilities. She has changed in form, but we're never sure of the substance. The post-vampire gestures to the idea that our identities are collaged, glued together, by context (socio-cultural-political) and that these fragments in turn correlate to the types of knowledge we reveal or construct. These shifting images counter more modernist notions, which in art create images of static boundaries. The self as unitary object in singular operation is replaced with a more community-based, socially oriented construction of academic ideals and practices. Although as vampire, there exists an exchange, Kathleen still operates on finite ideals of will of self to control and addiction grounded in the illusion of choice. Using the model of post avant-garde art:

> [T]he meaning is no longer in the observer or the observed but in the relationship between the two. Interaction is the key that moves art beyond the aesthetic mode: letting the audience intersect with, and even form part of, the process, recognizing that when observer and observed merge, the vision of static autonomy is undermined (Gablik, 1995, p. 151).

The image of the lone academic, whether vampire or human, like the avant-garde image of lone artists producing art for art's sake (for academics it might be "knowledge for knowledge's sake"), is transformed into the image of the post avant-garde artist, the post-vampire, or perhaps the post-academic. The term "post-doc" unfortunately already functions in another context. Thinking back again to the key phrase of the film, "tell me to go away," we consider that here lies its deeper meaning. Perhaps we are everything *but* ourselves, where the "me" might "go away" and be replaced with some alternative form of identity.

The avant-garde artist, like the vampire, "scorns notions of responsibility toward the audience." (Gablik, 1995, p. 61) In terms of our work as academics, especially in our transitions from doctoral student to "doctor," we might imagine ourselves like Kathleen, walking off screen to create knowledges previously unimagined. Our work takes on the responsibility, like post avant-garde artists, to "see our interdependence and interconnectedness." (p. 178) The world of academia, where objectivity was once prized, serves "as a distancing device, offering illusions of impregnable strength, certainty and control." (p. 178) Knowledge in this sense, Gablik contends, "can be used as an instrument of power and domination." (p. 178) But as post-vampires, knowledge and identity are no longer sites of violence, where as human we "kill to know," or where as vampires we feed nihilistic addictions. Drawing parallels between the Ivory Tower, knowledge, self, and art through post avant-garde lens leads us to a particular charge:

> When we see cynicism even in our art, it reinforces our belief in a negative, cynical reality. We've come to appreciate and expect cynicism in art as an intellectual game about the definition of reality . . . we've seen that art has the power to form negative visions of the

world through magnifying the undercurrents of cynicism, so it must be possible to create a positive vision of the world through focusing aspirations of hope (Gablik, 1995, p. 28).

So what began for us as a theory of the vampire as "poster-monster" for the postmodern academic arena ultimately gave way to something we had not anticipated—a revelation, if you will. If Kathleen, as vampire, were in fact the desired creature of choice in today's Ivory Tower, she would have remained that way, leaving us with the happy ending we often "crave" in Western narratives. Through the first half of the film, we cheer her on with delight, supporting her carnivore-like resistance of the status quo. But being a vampire, too, becomes trap, much like avant-garde artists struggling to break free from the traditional sociopolitical games of modernist art find themselves re-creating the same ideals they seek to dissolve. Vampires, although different from humans, ultimately are addicted, and hence, not truly different from the humans they scorn. If this were the film's ending, we might be left with feelings, as Gablik writes, "of cynicism" and hopelessness. Is it possible to break free from *The Addiction*? Is it possible to reimagine an academy without nihilistic and fatalistic fears that we are simply chasing our highly-educated tails?

As post-vampire (representing possibilities in the academy), Kathleen leaves us with "aspirations of hope" for something else. However, this is where we, the authors, walk off screen with the imaginary credits rolling, leaving the reader, like the viewers of the film, to imagine what might happen next. Our conclusion (or lack thereof) we hope incites readers toward an infinite number of possibilities, to imagine the ineffable and "experience the astonishment of the unknown." (Highwater, 1994, p. 10) Perhaps to concertely define more than we already have here what an "annihilation of self" could mean in a not yet re-imagined academy might be to force answers where we should be embracing and be empowered by the unknown. So we prefer to "finish" with such possibilities running "free" rather than to pursue with a blood lust, a hunt for language to say what has no language yet to be spoken. And we have somewhat kicked our craving to kill in order to know, although we are wearing the "patch"—the willingness to change an addiction is never easy.

References

Brown, C. (1997). Figuring the vampire: Death, desire and the image. In S. Golding (Ed.) *The eight techonologies of otherness* (pp. 117–133). London: Routledge.

Carey, R. (1998). *Critical Art Pedagogy: Foundations for a Postmodern Art Education*. New York: Garland.

Daspit, T., and McDermott, M. "Blood Knowledges: Reflections on (Un)Death, Transformation and Addiction in the Academy." Exhibit and paper presented at the JCT Conference on Curriculum Theory and Classroom Practice, Dayton, OH, October 2000.

Ferrara, A. (Director). *The Addiction*. United States: October Films, 1995.

Gablik, S. *The Reenchantment of Art*. London: Thames & Hudson, 1991.

————. *Conversations Before the End of Time*. London: Thames & Hudson, 1995.

Gallagher, T. "Geometry of Force: Abel Ferrara and Simone Weil." *Screening the Past* 10, 2000. Available at http://www.latrobe.edu.au/screeningthepast/firstrelease/fr0600/tgfr10d.html (accessed October 8, 2003).

Golding, S. (Ed). (1997). *The Eight Technologies of Otherness*. London: Routledge.

Gordon, J. and V. Hollinger (1997). Introduction: The shape of vampires. In Gordon J. and V. Hollinger (Eds.) *Blood read: The vampire as mataphor in modern culture* (pp. 1–11). PA: University of Pennsylvania Press.

Gordon, J. (1997). Fantasies of absence: The postmodern vampire. In J. Gordon and V. Hollinger (Eds.) *Blood read: The vampire as mataphor in modern culture* (pp. 199–212). PA: University of Pennsylvania Press.

Harrison, C., and Wood, P. "The Individual and the Social." In *Art in Theory*, edited by C. Harrison and P. Woods. Oxford: Blackwell Publishers, 1992.

Highwater, J. *The Language of Vision: Meditations on Myth and Metaphor*. New York: Grove Press, 1994.

jagodinski (1997). *Postmodern dilemmas: Outrageous Essays in Art and Art Education*. Mahwah, N. J.: Lawrence Erlbaum.

Jardine, D. W. *"Under the Tough Old Stars": Ecopedagogical Essays*. Brandon, VT: Psychology Press/Holistic Education Press, 2000.

McNiff, S. *Art as Medicine: Creating a Therapy of the Imagination*. Boston: Shambhala, 1992.

Milbrant, M. "Postmodernism in Art Education: Content for Life." *Art Education* 51 (6), 1998: 47–53.

Mullen, C. (1998). Whiteness, cracks, and inkstains: Making cultural identity with Euramerican teachers. In C.T.P. Diamond and C. A. Mullen (Eds.) *The postmodern educator: Arts-based inquiries and teacher development.* (pp. 147–190). New York: Peter Lang.

Munro, P. (1998). *Subject of Fiction: Women Teacher Life History Narratives and the Cultural Politics of Resistance*. Buckingham, UK: Open University Press.

Nietzsche, F. W. *Thus Spake Zarathustra*. Translated by T. Common. Mineola, NY: Dover Publications, 1999. (Original work published in 1891.)

Pinar, W., Reynolds, W., Slattery, P., and Taubman, P. (1995). *Understanding Curriculum*. New York: Peter Land.

Rimbaud, A. (1975). *Arthur Rimbaud: Complete works*. Translated by P. Schmidt. New York: Harper and Row.

Rorty, R. *Contingency, Irony, and Solidarity*. Cambridge, U.K.: Cambridge University Press, 1989.

Stone, A. (1997). In the language of vampire speak: Overhearing our own voices. In S. Golding (Ed.) *The eight technologies of otherness* (pp. 58–76). London: Routledge.

13

Black Higher Learnin':
Black Popular Culture and The
Politics of Higher Education

LINWOOD H. COUSINS

In the backdrop of the recent "culture wars" and anti-affirmative action debates (Appiah and Gutmann, 1996; Graff, 1992; Kelley, 1997; Loury, 2002; McWhorter, 2001; Steele, 2002) black[1] popular culture discourses in two films about blacks in higher education—*School Daze* (Lee, 1988) and *Higher Learning* (Singleton, 1995)—offer instructive insight about race and class relations that are embedded in these debates. In addition, these films document the significance African Americans have given education as a means of upward mobility and assimilation from slavery forward (Morgan, 1995; Perry, Steele, and Hilliard, 2003). Taken in this light, these films tell more about sociocultural relations than meets the eye.

The endeavors of blacks toward education have been obscured in America's public knowledge through the misconstrual, if not outright distortion, of non-white people's participation in education (Graff, 1992; Jacob and Jordan, 1993; Ravitch, 2000; Said, 1993). Indeed, black culture in general has been publicly rendered largely in terms of an ethos of apathy, self-destruction, and non-aspiration, alongside a fun-centered and happy-go-lucky ethic (Cose, 2002; Kelley, 1997; Jewel, 1993; Levine, 1977; McWhorter, 2001). And it seems to have escaped the discerning eye of many social critics of late that such distortions, and the processes maintaining them, are part and parcel of sociocultural representations in various black popular culture genres. Such omissions make for an incomplete portrait of the internal and external struggles of blacks in the American contest for equality and upward mobility (Allen and Chung, 2000; Jewel 1993; Lipsitz, 1990; Ramsey, 2003). Hence, both the meaning and import of education among blacks, as well as the significance popular culture has held for illustrating important facets of black life in general, stand to be righted in both the American conscience and the contemporary debates.

In particular, contemporary black popular culture highlights the solidarity and strain among African Americans regarding higher education (Cose, 2002; McWhorter, 2001; Spears, 1999). It awakens historical discourses that document the importance of education within black people's general aspirations for economic, political, and social equality. Black films about higher education in contemporary America add to this by exposing an ongoing battle among and between blacks and whites over what blacks are really about, and challenges two perceptions within the culture and anti-affirmative action wars.

On the one hand is a mainstream perception of the near-impotence of black culture in producing agents who embrace, respect, and contribute to a Western tradition of educational participation and aspiration. This perception is driven by the historically continuous omission of African American contributions and participation in mainstream American schooling, mythology, and folklore, in particular, and in Western education and its traditions, in general (Hallinan, 2001; Shapiro and Purple, 1999; Stam and Shohat, 1994; Tyack and Cuban, 1995). This amounts to nothing short of mainstream denial and negligence of the traditions of black participation and leadership in building segregated and integrated institutions of primary, secondary, and higher education on this side of the Atlantic Ocean (Bullock, 1967; Franklin, 1988; Litwack, 1961; Morgan, 1995; Perry, Steele and Hilliard, 2003).

The above circumstances, on the other hand, reinforce and are reinforced by the perception among some opponents of affirmative action, who say African Americans' current negative plight in educational performance is largely a thing of their own making (McWhorter, 2001; Steele, 2002). Proponents of this claim stand on black students' lower academic and intellectual performance, as measured by IQ and SAT scores (Jencks and Phillips, 1998; Lemann, 1995; Ogbu, 2003), the reams of low performance data published by school districts and states across the nation, and the association of these measures with chronic poverty and its concomitants among blacks (Bennett, Dilulio, and Walters, 1996; Gamoran, 2001; Hallinan, 2001; Herrnstein and Murray, 1994; Jencks and Phillips, 1998; Murray, 1984; Ogbu, 2003).

Another element of the above perceptions is that this malaise among black people can be ameliorated only if blacks do as follows: assert greater effort toward and assign greater importance to education; improve their moral character; and/or accept a lower, more fitting, station that fits their performance and skills in the world of occupations and jobs (Herrnstein and Murray, 1994; McWhorter, 2001; Steele, 2002; W. J. Wilson, 1996; J. Q. Wilson, 1995). Notwithstanding a host of scholars challenging such a narrow view of the problem (Allen and Chung, 2000; Fordham, 1996; Loury, 2002; Pattillo-McCoy, 1999; McCarthy and Crichlow, 1993; MacLeod, 1995; Weis and Fine, 1993), the films that will be the focus of discussion give samples of these views and others as expressed by blacks and non-blacks, both in a predominantly black and an integrated institution of higher education.

Of course, class relations are as much an issue as race in the above discussion. And in as much as higher education is assumed to place one on an upward class trajectory, thereby making class relations part and parcel of education, racial equality, and the plight of blacks in the United States, class simply cannot be excluded (Allen and Chung, 2000; Loury, 2002; Pattillo-McCoy, 1999; Trow, 1992; Weis and Fine, 1993). Thus, class relations are an indispensable, key element in the films to be discussed. To clarify what I mean by "class," as well as "race" and "popular culture," a brief discussion of these concepts follows. Afterward are a discussion and an explication of the themes of race and class in the two films within the context of the other themes I have introduced.

Race, Class, and Popular Culture

Race is a fluid symbol, taking on different meanings in different places and historical moments. As a folk concept, race signifies social, cultural, and biological differences, both real and imagined, and raises them to the level of immutable differences between people who differ by skin color, ethnicity, or nationality (Harrison, 1995; Loury, 2002; Omi and Winant, 1994; Shanklin, 1994). Conceptions of race have changed over the centuries and decades. Such conceptions have accommodated just about every realm of life, from the scientific hierarchies of eugenics in the halls of higher education, to the sublime images of stupidity, ignorance, and super sexual power and drive in contemporary TV and film (Cose, 2002; Jewel, 1993; Correspondents of the *New York Times*, 2001; Spears, 1999).

The economics and politics of upward mobility and higher education have their own relationship with race (Gamoran, 2001; Hallinan, 2001; Harrison, 1995; Jencks and Phillips, 1998; Loury, 2002; Trow, 1992). But perhaps most important to this discussion is race's central role in defining black people in such a way as to diminish, if not obliterate, facts about their educational aspirations and contributions in the United States. A key element in this is the overrepresentation of blacks in popular culture. But perhaps more important is the distortion of black popular culture as a "sideshow." (Lipsitz, 1990) Both elements service images and meanings that support white superiority and overall class subordination and hegemony (Lipsitz, 1998). Such processes have weakened, but not eliminated, chances for some aspects of black culture to gain salience as cultural capital (Cose, 2002; Kitwana, 2002; Lyne, 2000). Left in place, however, is that the most significant amounts of economic capital and the surplus needed for economic development and expansion flow largely away from black communities and their productions (Browne, 2000; Danziger and Lin, 2000; Malveaux, 1992; Patterson, 1995; Pattillo-McCoy, 1999; Wilson, 1996).

My view of class, and its links with race and popular culture, is likewise fraught with complexities. The complexities are based on the shifting relationships between economic, social, and political forces that serve as structural constraints, on the one hand (Allen and Chung, 2000; Browne, 2000; Pattillo-McCoy, 1999). And on the other hand is the fact that these constraints reveal, if not force, the creative hands of blacks as individual and collective agents (Danziger and Lin, 2000; Patterson, 1995; Wilson, 1996). In these roles, blacks have to improvise in order to garner as much control over their lives and productions as possible. Black people's participation in higher education serves both sides of this equation. Thus, educational processes reflect a many-sided paradox of race and class processes for black people, at the very least acting as both bane and blessing, bridge and gatekeeper (Hallinan, 2001; Loury, 2002; Morgan, 1995; Ogbu, 2003; Trow, 1992).

Notwithstanding the long history of class as a concept, however, I have chosen to interpret class as relational and cultural (Ortner, 1991, 1996). The more familiar and common use of the concept has been to capture one's objective social station in life and the life chances these stations often circumscribe (Herrnstein and Murray, 1994; Lubrano, 2004; Wilson, 1996; Wright, 1991). This is common in research and related discussions that correlate education, income, and occupation with positions of upper-, middle-, working-, and under-class status (Darity and Myers, 1998; Pattillo-McCoy, 1999).

In another sense, class is "experience near" (Geertz, 1983, pp. 57–59), as well as an historical category (Thompson, 1966). It "describ[es] people in relationships over time, and the ways in which they become conscious of their relationships, separate, unite and enter into struggle, form institutions and transmit values in class ways . . . through a process of self-making, although under conditions which are given." (Katznelson, 1981, pp. 204–205) In other words, class, as I understand it, entails paying attention to the ideologies and frames of reference, which are sources of meanings and maps for people's actions. I examine how these are expressed through racial relations around the meanings of education in discourses among black people, and between black people and mainstream (i.e., white, black, etc.)[2] Americans. Because these elements will be discussed in the context of popular culture, we now turn to its definition.

In asserting that popular culture "ain't no side show"—metaphorically, not something subordinate in status and meaning to a main show—George Lipsitz (1990) affirms the importance of Stuart Hall's assertion that popular culture is "the arena that is profoundly mythic . . . where we discover and play with identification of ourselves, where we are imagined, where we are represented, not only to audiences out there who do not get the message, but to ourselves for the first time." (quoted by Dent, 1992, pp. 2–3) Hall goes on to say that

> In one sense popular culture always has its base in the experiences, the pleasures, the memories, the traditions of the people. It has connections with local hopes and local aspirations, local tragedies and local scenarios that are the everyday practices and the everyday experiences of ordinary folks . . . at the same time it is the scene, par excellence, of commodification . . . where control over narrative and representations passes into the hands of the established cultural bureaucracies sometimes without a murmur . . . Black popular culture, like all popular cultures in the modern world, is bound to be contradictory (quoted by Dent, 1992, pp. 25–26).

Accordingly, popular culture can easily complicate the dynamics of race and class exposed in the films to be discussed. Popular artifacts, such as music, language, and ways of dressing and acting, are all aspects of black popular culture spinning around the axis of black life and black people's experiences of race and class. But if such artifacts are allowed to roam outside an awareness of their sociocultural and political-economic import, we will sorely miss their contribution to the discourses of blacks in higher education in the films we will discuss. For example, what Samuel Floyd says about music more or less applies to the other popular artifacts as well. He says music is about

> men, women, and children at leisure, at play, and at work—striving, achieving, thinking, longing, desiring, and creating. In these activities, we experience the ebb and flow of life in complex manifestations of tensions and repose, such as imbalance and adjustment, opposition and accommodation, aspiration and hope, failure and

achievement . . . [M]usic communicates values associated with remembrances, anticipations, and interpretations of ordinary living [and] can take on qualities of the comic, the sublime, the grotesque, the poetic . . . African American musics . . . are such expressions (1995, pp. 226–227).

In short, the two films under review—*School Daze* and *Higher Learning*—present the importance and urgency of the historical and contemporary educational aspirations of black people. Yet, as suggested above, this analysis must interrogate dominant popular cultural symbols (images, language, music, etc.) within these films and expose their meanings and implications for race and class distinctions and processes in higher educational pursuits in contemporary U.S. society.

Struggles Within: *School Daze*

Can higher education be a meaningful site for simultaneously exposing conflict among black people and uplifting their race (Early, 1993)? Can black higher education present different worlds within one world, yet arrive at a multifaceted explication of how to "make it" or move up in the world according to those different worldviews? Aside from homophobia and rampant sexism, among other attributes of Spike Lee's film *School Daze* (Lubiano, 1991; Wallace, 1988), these questions occupy our interests here.

School Daze is set in the late 1980s against the backdrop of an historical black college. Based loosely on Spike Lee's four years at the renowned Morehouse College in Atlanta, Georgia, this film highlights what some black students might recall as the most memorable aspects of their education, even though classroom scenes are absent. I refer to fraternity life, parties, and dorm-room interludes between young men and women who have heightened sexual longings and opportunities galore to satisfy them, and to the politics of what a college education is "supposed" to be about for black people.

Many of the film's scenes center on the genuine "jiggaboos" (blacks representing white caricatures of black traits) and the fake "wannabees" (blacks who value white social traits). They battle over the social values black people assign to skin color, hair texture, ways of speaking and acting, or, in two words, "racial authenticity." (Appiah, 1994) This implies that black people have a responsibility to uplift themselves and the collective group of black people by embracing social values that are compatible with educational success, but without casting aside the soul of "black-ness," whatever that may mean at any given moment. As a historical discourse on education, this relates to similar debates of "identity loyalty" among and between slave owners, abolitionists, and free black people from the time they first set foot in what is now the United States (Franklin, 1988; Gutman,

1976; Litwack, 1961, 1979; Morgan, 1995). It additionally relates to debates from the first half of the twentieth century to the present among the likes of Booker T. Washington, W. E. B. DuBois, and many others (Appiah and Gutmann, 1996; Early, 1993; Loury, 2002; McWhorter, 2001, 2003; Morgan, 1995).

As a contemporary discourse, racial "authenticity" and "loyalty" relate crudely to issues such as "acting white," "racelessness," "resistance," "assimilation and accommodation," and other characteristics and processes associated with black educational success and failure (Cook and Ludwig, 1998; Cousins, in press; Fordham, 1988; Fordham & Ogbu, 1986; Gibson & Ogbu, 1991; Harpalani, 2002; Ogbu, 2003). Themes of black ethnic/racial authenticity easily resonate with social class even outside of a discourse on higher education. But they are much more pronounced in a society where upward mobility through education has been, and remains, one of the most powerful myths for individual and collective rise, contradictions notwithstanding (Trow, 1992). Let us examine of few of these themes.

Different Worlds Within One

It is Friday morning at Mission College. It is also the eve of Homecoming weekend. Setting out to keep black students focused on the "real deal," the real purpose of higher education, Dap, a black pro-nationalist student leader, cries out, "Yo. This is it! Once again we as a people are late." After comparing Mission College's nonexistent divestiture efforts (from apartheid-riven South Africa) to the successful efforts of colleges such as Dartmouth and Harvard, he says "We backwards Negroes here at the so-called finest black college in the land, Mission College, we are holding on to ours. Like a wino clutching his last bottle!" His audience of peers responds in an affirming call-and-response mode.

In a later scene, Dap takes a similar path to reducing blacks to a homogeneous people who all have common relations and common worlds. Initially, he did this by invoking the "wino" metaphor and characterizing black people as either enlightened or unenlightened. But while in his dorm room trying to educate his homies (friends), he goes further. Dap says, "All they gotta do is get a bus and put a sign on it saying 'All the fried chicken you want!' And you know black folks will be on the bus in a hurry"; or (if the sign says), "All the drugs you want, or All the alcohol you want . . ." Taken together, the images and language in this interaction reduce (or essentialize) the black experience to a set of common transactions in a common black community, where the wino and chicken are omnipresent. Added to this is the earlier blatant trope on "Negro" as old school and unenlightened, which contrasts with being black or African American and enlightened, forward-thinking, and "awake!" "Negro" is often invoked among contemporary black people as a way of keeping continuity with past struggles, as well as making distinctions about one's current place in that struggle. This shows up repeatedly in the film.

Themes such as these and others are shared in relations between participants in fraternity and sorority life. Consider Mission College's signal fraternity, Gamma Phi Gamma (also called the Gammites), led by Big Brother Almighty, Julian. Their sister sorority is the Gamma Rays. Both groups are marked by members who largely make the point of speaking mainstream or "good" English, women with light skin and long—sometimes even blond—hair, and by a sense of haughtiness that comes from assimilation into the mainstream and being adept at accommodating certain realisms of making it in the white world. For example, after making the above speech, Dap and his peers are interrupted by the Gamma men, led by Julian. Dap says, "Why don't you take your Gamma boys and get the fuck outta here." Julian responds with "We of Gamma Phi Gamma do not agree with this African mumbo jumbo, and I am here to let you know that your revolutionary activities here at Mission College are detrimental not only to the student body and the administrators, but to our brothers and sisters in South Africa as well."

Later in the film, Dap and Julian encounter one another without a crowd present. Julian takes this opportunity to reiterate the personal side of the public statement he made earlier. He makes clear that his nationalism and racial identity is tied to the United States, not to Africa. As Julian and Jane, Julian's girlfriend, are walking down the street, Dap gets out of his friend's car and approaches Julian. Face to face and eye to eye, he says to Julian, "Look, I gotta talk to you about somin." Julian says, "You talk more shit than a little bit. Back to mother Africa. That's bullshit! Without question, we are all Black Americans. You do not know a goddamn thing about Africa. I am from Detroit. Motown! So you can Watusi your monkey ass back to Africa if you want to." As Julian walks away, Dap says softly, "Boy you need to check that alarm clock and wake up, my brother."

The counterpart to this scene and its significations of internal racial and class division are exposed in a chance encounter between the Gamma Rays and Rachel in a narrow dorm corridor. Rachel dates Dap and hangs out with a crew of dark-skinned women who wear their hair short and natural: Rachel looks at Jane's blond hair and says, "It ain't even real." Jane says, "You wish you had hair like this." Rachel responds with, "Girl, you know you weren't even born with blue eyes." One of Rachel's friends says, "Blue contact lenses!" Jane says, "You just jealous." Rachel says "Jealous?" Jane brings in mating competition by saying "Rachel, I've been watching you look at Julian . . ." Things escalate. Another Gamma Ray says to Rachel's crew,

"Piccaninny Barbie doll." Someone from Rachel's crew says, "High yellow heifer. Wannabe white." Building to a climax of emotions, a Gamma Ray says, "Jiggaboo!" Later in the film, skin color and hair texture differences among blacks are the theme of a song and dance routine about good and bad hair set in a beauty salon.

Remember, the backdrop for all of this is college and what a college education confers on a black person. Thus, the above scene, like others, does not leave one who is familiar with such a discourse guessing about the message Spike Lee is trying to deliver regarding historical black identities, or, in a contemporary sense, who one is or should be as a black person in the context of higher or a "real" education. Yet the overtness of Lee's message does not always do justice to the complexity of these issues. Some of the material for getting at the complexity of race and class relations among blacks is in the film, but it is scattered in different places, leaving one to make assumptions about Lee's intentions and how these issues fit and resonate with each other.

Women's simultaneous complicity with and resistance to submission to black men in the name of lifting up the race is one example. Consider a scene in which the Gamma Rays are discussing preparations for a party for the Gamma men. One Gamma Ray comments about music. She says, "We are having none of that hip-hop, B-Boy nonsense." But blurring the seemingly straightforward class demarcation indicated by the student's taste in music, and bringing in gender and power relations, are comments made by another Gamma Ray. In a discussion about preparing the room in which the party would be held, she says, "We have been cleaning up after those sorry, tired, trifling, shiftless Negroes from day one, and I am not cleaning up!" Her friends dismiss this attitude.

Similarly, in confronting Dap and his racial/ethnic righteousness, Rachel says "You color struck. You definitely have a thang against light-skinned blacks." Dap says, "It's them, it's not me . . . those mulattos. They're so unpure." Rachel responds with, "And you're 100 percent pure? Massa was in your ancestors' slave quarters just like everyone else." After a love scene, Rachel tells Dap she's pledging Delta next semester. They debate the value of sororities. Dap confesses his concerns about losing Rachel and says, "People change." Rachel says, "I'll be the same Rachel. And I'll still love you. You know, Vaughan [Dap's real name], I've always wondered if you were with me because I'm one of the darkest sisters on campus; good for your all-the-way-down, pro-black nationalist image." One could call this Dap's personalized wake-up call!

These and other encounters between these parties mark the contentious space regarding both the appropriate impact higher education should have on blacks, as well as how blacks should participate in schooling. In fact,

Mission College's administration, though decidedly divided, reinforces Julian's ethic and ideology—a resounding accommodationist and assimilationist one—rather than Dap's. The administration's comments on two separate occasions highlight the role of economics and politics in relationship to Historical Black Colleges and Universities (HBCU).

Before Dap is called in for a meeting with both the president and the chairman of the board of the college, the following dialogue takes place among administrators as a signal of race/ethnicity and class relations and the "melting pot" or assimilative role of higher education beyond the black world of Mission College. The president says Mission College's aim is to educate the sons and daughters of former slaves. By contrast, the chairman suggests that perhaps HBCUs have outlived their usefulness. He says the need no longer exists in an integrated society. The president says, "That's absurd. Notre Dame, Yeshiva, Brandeis, Brigham Young, are all constituent-based colleges and universities. What's the difference?" The chairman responds, "No support for black colleges beyond the federal government and a few philanthropists." He suggests snipping Dap's divestiture talk in the bud or else. He says, "People like them—college investors—don't like to be told what to do with their money. Old, old, money." Later in the film, the president and chairman hold a private meeting with Dap where they confront or try to "educate" him regarding divestiture from South Africa and black higher education. In sum, they threaten to expel him if he continues his protest. The chairman in particular, a man who marched with Martin Luther King, Jr. in the 1960s, tells Dap to go along or he will become like some of the chairman's former classmates at Mission College who are now "old and bitter." Dap remains defiant.

Perhaps the most salient and well-known scene marking race and class relations takes place between Dap's crew and a group of local men in an encounter at a Kentucky Fried Chicken restaurant off campus. This scene marks economic and social distinctions associated with higher education. These distinctions are expressed in racial and class terms between black college students who are aspirants to the middle class, albeit with a spurious racial identity, and locals who are "genuine," everyday working-class people with an "authentic" black racial identity.

While riding to the restaurant, Dap and five of his homies tease one another about "knowing how to articulate" or talk properly, rather than in Black English. They also discuss how to bed a woman. After they arrive and go inside to order, four black men, who are sitting in a corner eating, look up at them and then mumble some words before returning to their conversation and meal. Three of the men in the corner have Jeri Curl hairstyles, one has on a red jogging suit, and one of them has on a plastic shower cap (to keep his hair moisturized and to catch the dripping chemicals of the Jeri Curl product).

The initial encounters between the Mission College men, the cashier, and the townsmen are contentious, signaling the association between masculinity and education, among other elements of working-and middle-class identity. For example, a confrontation in which the Mission College men ask the town men for salt leads to the first encounter. Dap and his friends get up to leave because they sense the tension. One of the townsmen says in a mocking, high-pitched, feminine tone, "Do you boys go to Mission? Dap says, "Let's go." The townsman says, "Yo, missionaries?" One of Dap's homies turns to face the local man while walking out of the restaurant. He says, in a confronting tone, and with what one can presume to be masculine fervor, "What's up with that!" Dap says, "Yeah, brother. What do you want? One of the townsmen says, "You ain't no kin to me!" Another says, "That's right. And we ain't your brother! How come you college motherfuckers think y'all run everything? You come to our town year after year and take over. We was born here, gon be here, gon die here, and can't find a job 'cause of you! We may not have your ed-u-ca-tion. But we ain't dirt." Slipping into black, presumably working-class vernacular, Dap says, "Look. Ain't no body said all that, ar'ight." The townsman says, "You Mission punks always talkin' down to us." Dap says, "Look brother, I'm real sorry that you feel that way. I'm real sorry about that." The townsman asks Dap, "Are you black?" Another townsman says, "Take a look in the mirror, man!" Dap says, "Look, man. You got a legitimate beef, ar'ight. But it ain't with us, OK!" A townsman raises his voice and asks again, "Are you black?" Dap responds with his voice raised, "Look man, don't ever question the fact of whether I'm black." Dap slips into his black, working-class vernacular again and says, "In fact, I was gonna ask yo' country Bama-ass why you got them drip-drip chemicals in your hair? And then come out in public with a shower cap on!"

After the opposing groups call each other a "bitch," a townsman marks his sense of the immutable condition of race, for black people, that nullifies aspirations for upward mobility and collapses class differences. He says, "Man, I bet you niggas do think y'all white. College don't mean shit. Y'all niggas! And you gon be niggas! Just like us. Niggas!" In the end Dap looks face-to-face with the townsman and tries to transcend the paradoxical moment he faces by saying "You're not niggas!"

Higher Learning in Black and White: Just Different Worlds, I Guess?

If *School Daze* exploited race and class distinctions and tensions *among* blacks in higher education, *Higher Learning* took advantage of relations between black and white/mainstreamers in a similar way. *Higher Learning* comes out of John Singleton's view of a black–white world as much as Spike Lee's film comes out of his. But Singleton's world is an integrated one, where the worlds that are featured are, at least on the surface, very different. Thus, tension and mistrust are present in everything—among blacks, among whites, among and between men and women, and, of course, between blacks and whites. Let us turn to that.

Set at Columbus University in the mid-1990s, *Higher Learning* is a contemporary film that juxtaposes the lives of three first-year college students as the academic year begins. The central characters are: a confident but ambivalent black man (Malik, who has won a track scholarship); an ambivalent and psychologically conflicted white woman (Kristen); and an ambivalent, emergent card-carrying racist white man (Remy). Whereas *School Daze* excluded classroom discourses, *Higher Learning* uses the classroom to highlight different ethics about "making it" and the meanings and purposes of higher education. Whereas *School Daze* occurred in the backdrop of a pulsating R&B beat, *Higher Learning* features a hip-hop beat with accompanying attitudes, clothing styles, and racist police brutality. And whereas *School Daze* opens with portraits of historical black figures, *Higher Learning* opens with the screen covered by the American flag, the mythic symbol of common American-ness.

This film complicates common American-ness, however. It does so by highlighting a multicultural America of people with uncommon interests, revolving mostly around the tension of affirmative action. It spotlights the realities of racial integration amid rekindled spirits of nationalism qua racism with skinheads such as Remy and his crew, and neo-separatists such as Fudge (a popular black student who serves as Dap's counterpart in this film) and his crew.

We begin with the ways in which racial tension takes center stage in the lives of students at Columbus University. However, within these discourses are markings of gender and class as well. In one of the first scenes of the movie, Malik gets on an elevator where Kristen is already a passenger. She steals a glance at him. Seeing that he is black and determining what that means to her, she clutches her purse close to her bosom with both hands. Malik notices and shakes his head in disgust. This is followed by Kristen finding her dorm room and meeting, to her surprise, her black roommate. Gazing at each other in a way that shows their discomfort, Monet, the black student, says to Kristen, "You are not from around here, are you?" Kristen says she is from Orange County (a suburban area of Los Angeles). Monet asks, "Is that near Compton?" Kristen looks at her and gently giggles. Often cited in rap songs and depicted in music videos about gang violence and homies just kickin' it in low-rider cars and the like, Compton is a predominantly black, mixed-income community in Los Angeles.

Such class and racial differences continue in a more pronounced way as we move into other aspects of the social life of students. Here I wish to highlight both the contrasts and tensions between black and white aesthetics in music and other tastes, and the simultaneous reduction or essentializing and homogenization of both black and white tastes and attitudes. In one brief encounter, Fudge, followed by one of his homies, walks into his dorm room, where his two white roommates are studying. He says, "Y'all ain't got no Kool-Aid up in here?" Fudge's homie picks up a bottle of spring water and says, "Y'all got som' Evian in here," and smiles. While Kool-Aid is the quintessential stereotype of black ghetto life, Evian marks middle-class whiteness and upward mobility.

Fudge's dorm room is a popular place for black students to hang out, where hip-hop music blasts in the background. In another scene, Fudge addresses his own crew while the music is playing. He discusses the IMF (International Monetary Fund) and the World Bank and their roles in controlling the students' fate. Then Fudge says to his crew, "Y'all probably don't even have a checkin' account, but y'all got them credit cards." Again, this character is playing with class and racial stereotypes, even if among blacks this time.

Meanwhile, Fudge's two white roommates, who are in the room studying, get frustrated about the loud music. One of them, Remy, goes downstairs to complain to the campus police. He says to a white cop, "They're playing their music . . . It's like fuckin' *Soul Train* up there!" The police go to Fudge's room to confront him. Blasting in the background from an adjacent white dorm room, however, is rock music, but the police ask only Fudge to turn down his music. Fudge says to him, "You don't hear that [referring to the white music], do you?" The cop says, "Naw, 'cause I dig rock and roll." Later, Fudge's white roommates move out.

Equally as explicit as these messages about race and class are those delivered about the role of education and how black students should participate. These themes are highlighted in dialogues between a black professor and Malik. Professor Phipps teaches political science and speaks with a Caribbean accent. Malik is a student in Phipps's class. In this scene, Malik approaches Phipps to discuss a paper he has turned in. As Phipps points out Malik's mistakes, he says, "Perhaps if you could spell as well as you can run, it would be better, Mr. Williams." Malik says, "Sell out," as he walks away. Phipps hears this and takes Malik to his office. Phipps says, "So you think I am an Uncle Tom? What does that have to do with your ability to place a comma in its proper place or put a period at the end of a sentence?" Malik says, "I feel like you trying to use that reverse treatment on me 'cause I'm one of the only black faces in your class." Phipps responds with, "Mr. Williams, I treat everyone in my course exactly the same. And I will continue to give you a difficult time until you have proven you deserve otherwise. Those are the rules of the game." Malik says, "Fucked-up game." The conversation continues with Phipps saying, "Young man, you have to rid yourself of this attitude that the world owes you something. You must strip yourself of that mentality. It breeds laziness. It is laziness that has kept black people down in this country," After telling Malik that he (Phipps, that is) is not the enemy, he says, "I am not in your way. I did not ask you to come to this university. Nor am I here to motivate you. Your own prisons should be motivation enough."

Fudge provides his own version of what Malik should be about as a black student. Fudge's room is littered with posters of black power, Desmond Tutu, African carvings, miscellaneous books, and a computer that he lets other students use. Malik asks Fudge if he has the autobiography of Frederick Douglass. Fudge says, "Yeah." Looking at all of Fudge's books, Malik asks, "You read all these?" Fudge responds, "How you get turned on to Douglass?" Malik says, "A class." Fudge, expressing disappointment, says, "A class? That's the only reason you reading this is for a class?" Malik says, "Yeah. Why else?" Fudge says, "To feed your brain, fool! I thought you were one of the smart [socially and politically enlightened and insightful] ones, but you ain't. So you gotta go." Malik asks if can he borrow the book. Fudge says, "Read for yourself and not for some class."

Before turning to the final excerpt from this film, I have only minimally addressed the place whites see for blacks in higher education at Columbus University, if not in society at large. Relatedly, I have not discussed the parallel battles occurring among white students regarding their own place in an integrated, economically driven world. For example, while Remy gets extreme, claims reverse racism, and with the skinheads, advocates racial separation and purity, Kristen struggles to find tuition money, expresses ambivalence about her sexual identity, and eventually attempts to heal her torn soul by attempting to bring whites and blacks together through a theme of world peace. All of this rises to a climax in the final scene of the film, to which I will turn in a moment.

Returning to the lives of black students, just as Professor Phipps confronts Malik about asserting himself academically, Deja, Malik's girlfriend and a track team member, does likewise. And just as Rachel confronted Dap's racial righteousness in *School Daze*, Deja confronts Malik about his ambivalence regarding race and education in this film. While working out with Deja at the track, Malik says, "I'm tired of running and studying. It's too hard. I feel like a slave." Deja says, "Take advantage of your opportunity." Malik says, "I don't see security stopping you on campus to see your ID . . ." "So you think I got it easy," Deja says. Malik says, "Hell yeah. Easier than me." Deja says, "You know them [white] girls I stay with. Every single time something comes up missing, who do you think they look at? I feel like fightin'! I feel like beatin' people up too! . . . It's a waste of time. Instead, I fight with my head. . . . You gotta stop doing this [pointing to others] and start doing this [pointing to self] . . ." Malik says, "Listen. You're a woman. I'm a black man. I'm a threat, educated or not." Deja does not buy this. She says, "You ain't educated yet!"

In a later conversation on the same theme, Malik appeals to Deja's sense of racial solidarity by pointing out all of the injustices white people have exercised toward Native Americans and others. He finally condemns learning "westernized thought." He says blacks can learn that, but "in their eyes, we ain't nothing but lower-class. Always!" Deja says, "Class is a state of mind." From this point on in the film, the tension shifts to issues of integration, reverse discrimination, and white power. Things culminate with Remy becoming an enraged sniper, shooting several students in the midst of Kristen's peace rally. Deja gets shot and dies. And the film ends with Malik and Kristen discussing the pain and irony of it all as they part on separate paths.

Conclusion

From where the students in both of these films stand, higher education comes with a lot of baggage. Some of the baggage is of their own making, while some is provided by others. But even that of their own making is the result of interactions in a world defined by distinctions such as race, ethnicity, class, and gender. And in examining their baggage from the inside, we may have gotten a glimpse of why affirmative action and the culture wars, as they relate to blacks and higher education, are such contentious matters. Of course, all of this is revealed through the black films I have examined, mediums of black (and American) popular culture.

I cannot help but believe that the nature of the affirmative-action and culture-wars debate would change for the better if a few facts and processes were more widely known and taken more seriously. What would it mean if most Americans knew that education, for example, is as important to black people as it is to anyone else and has been as much a part of black people's history in the United States as it has been for non-blacks? What if they also knew that black (and American) popular culture, such as these films, has sometimes been the most predominant, visible package through which black meanings and values about serious things like education have been delivered? But imagine if they knew that, as black representation and practice, popular culture shows the ways in which black people play with identities (both mythic and real), how others play with the identities of blacks, and how others play with their own identities in relation to and in relationships with blacks?

Unfortunately, most Americans rely on narrow public debates and media for such facts and truths. These forums of information often fall short because "the process of informing" includes all sorts of interactional and cultural politics that dilute and distort the intended messages. More importantly, however, popular culture processes have been given diminished value by many mainstream white and non-white Americans because of a higher, often more aesthetically and rationally appealing Euro-white standard (which I must say, of late, is increasingly eroding among young whites, who are taking up hip-hop influenced clothing and related aesthetics). To the degree that my assertions are true, we have done what George Lipsitz (1990) has argued against. We have relegated (black) popular culture to the status of a sideshow.

Specifically, "sideshow" status for black popular culture contributes to the following: a lack of knowledge about the broad contributions black people make to American culture; our society's difficulty in coming to terms with racism and racism's contribution to an America that is humane less than it can and should be; and the maintenance of longstanding denials and shortsightedness about the prevalence of class relations in American and black life. Indeed, class and race relations permeate popular culture, as we have seen in the films we reviewed.

Moreover, a lack of understanding of the depth and breadth of the social and cultural processes that interact with markets and economies to influence the future is problematic for a fair and productive affirmative action and culture wars debate (Appiah and Gutmann, 1996; Darity and Myers, 1998; Harrison and Huntington, 2000; Loury, 2002; Wilson, 1996). Key players and all audiences in this debate must know that popular culture produces and reproduces images, stereotypes, and forms of relations that reveal and conceal truths about who we are as Americans, whether black or non-black. Consequently, popular culture processes and outcomes must be taken into consideration in our search for understanding. Doing so is necessary for carving an informative public debate and public policy and, thereby, a future of equal opportunity driven by clarity and courage about our realities. This stands in contrast to the other, too-common course that constructs ethnic groups such as blacks as inherently less capable. Herein, individuals and groups who do this constructing profess a cockeyed set of remedies, built on a make-believe hope and faith, that are driven by fear about what the revelation of America's (and the Western world's) distortions, secrets, and misdeeds will mean for the status quo of white over black (Robinson, 2000).

Just so, I have not intended to assert any single truth of fact through my explication of these films. Rather, the point has been to show how these films, as black popular culture mediums, serve as powerful and relevant locations of representation and practice for ferreting out race and class processes among blacks, and between blacks and whites, who participate in higher education. And there is little doubt, at least in my experience and in the world in which I socialize and study, that the points made in these films resonate with the general state of affairs in the United States. Still, it would be appropriate to argue with the intent of the messages I have focused on and interpreted in these films. And I hope such criticism can enrich our understanding of higher education and the multitude of ways it has been influenced by race and class relations.

All things considered, this presentation strengthens and extends theoretical and scholarly engagement around the convergence of race, class, education, and popular culture. May such an engagement enter into the affirmative action and culture wars debate. And may this engagement also raise to awareness the possibilities for undermining the common sense rationalizations in such debates and elsewhere that have been used to justify the unequal distribution of social, economic, and political resources that shape educational enterprises (Giroux, 1992; Tyack and Cuban, 1995).

Notes

1. I use black and African American interchangeably to refer to people of African descent in the United States.

2. The "mainstream" includes persons whose personal and social interests lean toward middle-class, predominantly white, standards, which is why I have in parentheses blacks as well as whites.

References

Allen, W. and Chung, A. "'Your Blues Ain't Like My Blues': Race, Ethnicity, and Social Inequality in America." *Contemporary Sociology* 29(6), 2000: 796–805.

Appiah, K. "Identity, Authenticity, Survival: Multicutural Societies and Social Reproduction." In *Multiculturalism: Examining the Politics of Recognition*, edited by A. Gutmann. Princeton, NJ: Princeton University Press, 1994.

Appiah, K. A. and Gutmann, A. *Color Conscious: The Political Morality of Race*. Princeton, NJ: Princeton University Press, 1996.

Bennett, W., Dilulio, J., and Walters, J. *Body Count: Moral Poverty and How to Win America's War Against Crime and Drugs*. New York: Simon and Schuster, 1996.

Browne, I. "Opportunities Lost?: Race, Industrial Restructuring, and Employment among Young Women Heading Households." *Social Forces* 78 (March 2000): 907–929.

Bullock, H. *A History of Negro Education in the South: From 1619 to the Present*. New York: Praeger Press, 1967.

Cook, P. and Ludwig, J. "The Burden of 'Acting White': Do Black Adolescents Disparage Academic Achievement?" In *The Black–White Test Score Gap*, edited by C. Jencks and M. Phillips. Washington, D.C.: Brooking Institution Press, 1998.

Correspondents of the *New York Times*. *How Race Is Lived in America: Pulling Together, Pulling Apart*. New York: Times Books, 2001.

Cose, E. *The Envy of the World: On Being a Black Man in America*. New York: Washington Square Press, 2002.

Danziger, S. and Lin, A., eds. *Coping with Poverty: The Social Context of Neighborhood, Work, and Family in the African American Community.* Ann Arbor, MI: University of Michigan Press, 2000.

Darity, W. and Myers, Jr., S. *Persistent Disparity: Race and Economic Inequality in the United States since 1945.* Northampton, MA: Edward Elgar Press, 1998.

Dent, G., ed. *Black Popular Culture.* Seattle: Bay Press, 1992.

Early, G. *Lure and Loathing: Essays on Race, Identity, and the Ambivalence of Assimilation.* New York: The Penguin Press, 1993.

Floyd, S. *The Power of Black Music: Interpreting Its History from Africa to the United States.* New York: Oxford University Press, 1995.

Fordham, S. *Blacked Out: Dilemmas of Race, Identity, and Success at Capital High.* Chicago: University of Chicago Press, 1996.

———. "Racelessness as a Factor in Black Students' School Success: Pragmatic Strategy or Pyrrhic Victory?" *Harvard Educational Review* 58(1), 1988: 54–84.

Fordham, S., and Ogbu, J. "Black Students' School Success: Coping with the 'Burden of 'Acting White.'" *Urban Review* 18(3), 1986: 176–206.

Franklin, J. H. and Moss, A. *From Slavery to Freedom: A History of Negro Americans.* New York: McGraw-Hill, 1988.

Gamoran, A. "American Schooling and Educational Inequality: A Forecast for the 21st Century." *Sociology of Education* 74 (2001): 135–153.

Geertz, C. *Local Knowledge: Further Essays in Interpretive Anthropology.* New York, NY: Basic Books, 1983.

Gibson, M. and Ogbu, J., eds. *Minority Status and Schooling: A Comparative Study of Immigrant and Involuntary Minorities.* New York: Garland Publishing, 1991.

Giroux, H. *Border Crossings: Cultural Workers and the Politics of Education.* New York: Routledge, 1992.

Graff, G. *Beyond the Culture Wars: How Teaching the Conflicts Can Revitalize American Education.* New York: W. W. Norton, 1992.

Gutman, H. *The Black Family in Slavery and Freedom, 1750–1925.* New York: Vintage, 1976.

Hall, S. "What Is This 'Black' in Black Popular Culture?" In *Black Popular Culture*, edited by G. Dent. Seattle: Bay Press, 1992.

Hallinan, M. "Sociological Perspectives on Black–White Inequalities in American Schooling." *Sociology of Education* 74 (2001): 50–70.

Harpalani, V. "What Does 'Acting White' Really Mean? Racial Identity Formation and Academic Achievement among Black Youth." *Perspectives on Urban Education* 1(1), 2002: 1–8.

Harrison, F. "The Persistent Power of "Race" in the Cultural and Political Economy of Racism." *Annual Review of Anthropology* 24 (1995): 47–74.

Harrison, L. and Huntington, S. *Culture Matters: How Values Shape Human Progress.* New York: Basic Books, 2000.

Herrnstein, R. and Murray, C. *The Bell Curve: Intelligence and Class Structure in American Life.* New York: Free Press, 1994.

Jacob, E. and Jordan, C., eds. *Minority Education: Anthropological Perspectives.* Norwood, NJ: Ablex Publishing, 1993.

Jencks, C. and Phillips, M., eds. *The Black–White Test Score Gap.* Washington, D.C.: Brookings Institution Press, 1998.

Jewel, S. *From Mammy to Miss America and Beyond: Cultural Images and the Shaping of U.S. Social Policy.* New York: Routledge, 1993.

Katznelson, I. *City Trenches: Urban Politics and the Patterning of Class in the United States.* Chicago: University of Chicago Press, 1981.

Kelley, R. *Yo' Mama's Disfunktional! Fighting the Culture Wars in Urban America.* Boston: Beacon Press, 1997.

Kitwana, B. *The Hip Hop Generation: Young Blacks and the Crisis in African American Culture.* New York: BasicCivitas Books, 2002.

Lee, S. (Writer/Director). *School Daze* [Motion Picture]. United States: Columbia Tri-Star, 1988.

Lemann, N. "The Great Sorting." *The Atlantic Monthly*, September 1995, 84–100.

Levine, L. *Black Culture and Black Consciousness: Afro-American Folk Thought from Slavery to Freedom.* New York: Oxford University Press, 1977.

Lipsitz, G. "Popular Culture: 'This Ain't No Sideshow.'" In *Time Passages: Collective Memory and American Popular Culture.* Minneapolis: University of Minnesota Press, 1990.

————. *The Possessive Investment in Whiteness: How White People Profit from Identity Politics.* Philadelphia, PA: Temple University Press, 1998.

Litwack, L. *North of Slavery: The Negro in the Free States, 1790–1860.* Chicago: University of Chicago Press, 1961.

Loury, G. *The Anatomy of Racial Inequality.* Cambridge, MA: Harvard University Press, 2002.

Lubiano, W. "But Compared to What?: Reading Realism, Representation, and Essentialism in *School Daze, Do the Right Thing,* and the Spike Lee discourse." *Black American Literature Forum* 25 (2), 1991: 253–282.

Lubrano, A. *Limbo: Blue-Collar Roots, White-Collar Dreams.* Hoboken, NJ: John Wiley and Sons, 2004.

Lyne, W. "No Accident: From Black Power to Black Box Office." *African American Review* 34(1), 2000: 39–59.

MacLeod, J. *Ain't No Makin' It: Aspirations and Low Attainment in a Low-Income Neighborhood.* Boulder, CO: Westview Press, 1995.

Malveaux, J. "Popular Culture and the Economics of Alienation." In *Black Popular Culture,* edited by G. Dent. Seattle: Bay Press, 1992.

McCarthy, C. and Crichlow, C., eds. *Race, Identity, and Representation in Education.* New York: Routledge, 1993.

McWhorter, J. *Losing the Race: Self-Sabotage in Black America.* New York: Perennial, 2001.

————. *Authentically Black: Essays for the Black Silent Majority.* New York: Gotham Press, 2003.

Morgan, H. *Historical Perspectives on the Education of Black Children.* Westport, CT: Praeger, 1995.

Murray, C. *Losing Ground: American Social Policy, 1950–1980.* New York: Basic Books, 1984.

Ogbu, J. *Black American Students in an Affluent Suburb: A Study of Academic Disengagement.* Mahwah, NJ: Lawrence Erlbaum and Associates, 2003.

Omi, M. and Winant, H. *Racial Formations in the United States.* New York: Routledge, 1994.

Ortner, S. "Reading America: Preliminary Notes on Class and Culture." In *Recapturing Anthropology: Working in the Present,* edited by R. Fox. Sante Fe, NM: School of American Research Press, 1991.

————. *Making Gender: The Politics and Erotics of Culture.* Boston: Beacon Press, 1996.

Patterson, O. "The Paradox of Integration." *The New Republic,* November 6, 1995: 24–27.

Pattillo-McCoy, M. *Black Picket Fences: Privilege and Peril among the Black Middle Class.* Chicago: The University of Chicago Press, 1999.

Perry, T., Steele, C., and Hilliard, A. *Young, Gifted, and Black: Promoting High Achievement among African American Students.* Boston: Beacon Press, 2003.

Ramsey, G. *Race Music: Black Cultures from Bebop to Hip-Hop.* Berkeley: University of California Press, 2003.

Ravitch, D. "A Different Kind of Education for Black Children." *Journal of Blacks in Higher Education* (Winter 2000): 98–106.

Robinson, R. *The Debt: What America Owes to Blacks.* New York: Dutton, 2000.

Said, E. "The Politics of Knowledge." In *Race, Identity, and Representation in Education,* edited by C. McCarthy and W. Crichlow. New York: Routledge, 1993.

Shanklin, E. *Anthropology and Race.* Belmont, CA: Wadsworth Publishing Company, 1994.

Shapiro, H. and Purpel, D., eds. *Critical Social Issues in American Education: Transformation in a Postmodern World.* Mahwah, NJ: L. Erlbaum Associates, 1998.

Singleton, J. (Producer/Director). *Higher Learning* [Motion Picture]. United States: Sony, 1995.

Spears, A., ed. *Race and Ideology: Language, Symbolism, and Popular Culture.* Detroit, MI: Wayne State University Press, 1999.

Stam, R. and Shohat, E. "Contested Hstories: Eurocentrism, Multiculturalism, and the Media." In *Multiculturalism: A Critical Reader,* edited by D. Golberg. Cambridge, MA: Blackwell, 1994.

Steele, S. "The Age of White Guilt and the Disappearance of the Black Individual." *Harper's Magazine* 305(1830), 2002: 3342.

Thompson, E. P. *The Making of the English Working Class.* New York: Vintage Press, 1966.

Trow, M. "Class, Race, and Higher Education in America." *American Behavioral Scientist* 35 (4/5), 1992: 585–605.

Tyack, D. and L. Cuban. *Tinkering Toward Utopia: A Century of Public School Reform.* Cambridge, MA: Harvard University Press, 1995.

Wallace, M. Review of *She's Gotta Have It, School Daze*, directed by Spike Lee. *Nation* 246 (1988): 800–803.

Weis, L. and Fine, M., eds. *Beyond Silenced Voices: Class, Race, and Gender in United States Schools.* Albany, NY: SUNY Press, 1993.

Wilson, J. Q. *On Character.* Washington, D.C.: The AEI Press, 1995.

Wilson, W. J. *When Work Disappears: The World of the New Urban Poor.* New York: Knopf, 1996.

Wright, E. O. "The Conceptual Status of Class Structure in Class Analysis." In *Bringing Class Back in: Contemporary and Historical Perspectives*, edited by S. McNall, R. Levine, and R. Fantasia. Boulder, CO: Westview Press, 1991.

Contributors

Karen Anijar is an Associate Professor in the Curriculum Studies Program at Arizona State University. Her most recent books were *Science Fiction Curriculum, Cyborg Teachers, and Youth Culture(s)* (coedited with Toby Daspit and John Weaver) and *Teaching Toward the 24th Century: Star Trek as Social Curriculum*. Her forthcoming book, *Culture and the Condom*, will be published this year.

Michele Byers is an Assistant Professor in Sociology & Criminology at Saint Mary's University, Canada. She continues to write about media, popular culture, and youth, especially girls. Currently, she is involved in a major project on the Canadian *Degrassi* series and is increasingly interested in Canadian media, youth culture, and identity. She is also finishing a book about *Buffy the Vampire Slayer* that was once her dissertation.

Linwood H. Cousins is an Associate Professor in and Interim Chair of the Department of Social Work at the University of North Carolina at Charlotte. As a social worker and anthropologist, his research and scholarly interests include the sociocultural dynamics of African-American schooling, the intersection of African-American and American culture, and the sociocultural dynamics of race, ethnicity, and class.

Toby Daspit is an Associate Professor in the College of Education at Western Michigan University. He is the coeditor of *Popular Culture and Critical Pedagogy* (with John Weaver) and *Science Fiction Curriculum, Cyborg Teachers and Youth Culture(s)* (with Karen Anijar and John Weaver), and the co-author of *Talking Gumbo: A Teacher's Guide to Using Oral History in the Classroom* (with Pamela Dean and Petra Munro).

Susan Edgerton is an Associate Professor in the Department of Education at Massachusetts College of Liberal Arts in North Adams. She is the author of *Translating the Curriculum: Multiculturalism into Cultural Studies* and several scholarly book chapters and articles on social studies education, autobiography and education, trauma and schooling, curriculum theory, and the use of literature in teacher education.

Paul Farber is a Professor in the Department of Educational Studies and the Department of Teaching, Learning and Leadership, Western Michigan University. His research and teaching centers on the ethics and politics of teaching and the social-philosophical context of educational practice. He has published in numerous journals including *Educational Theory, Teachers College Record, Studies in Philosophy and Education, Educational Foundations,* and *The Journal of Teacher Education,* among others. He was coeditor, with Eugene Provenzo, of the book series *Education and Culture* for the State University of New York Press, and coeditor, with Eugene Provenzo, Jr. and Gunilla Holm, of the volume *Schooling in the Light of Popular Culture,* State University of New York Press, 1994.

Gunilla Holm is a Professor in the Department of Educational Studies and the Department of Teaching, Learning and Leadership, Western Michigan University. Her interests are focused on race, ethnicity, gender, and social class issues in education as well as the intersection of popular culture and education. She has published in numerous journals including *International Studies in Sociology of Education, Qualitative Studies in Education, Young, International Journal of Educational Reform, Studies in Philosophy and Education, People and Education, Journal of Teacher Education,* and *College Teaching.* She has also coedited, with Paul Farber and Eugene Provenzo, Jr., *Schooling in the Light of Popular Culture,* State University of New York Press, 1994.

Glenn M. Hudak is a Professor and program coordinator of the Ph.D. Program in Cultural Foundation in the Department of Educational Leadership & Cultural Foundations, University of North Carolina-Greensboro. Since 1999, he has been an intern with the Harlem Family Institute, New York City, working with children in economically poor communities, and in 2000, he received a Master of Divinity (M.Div) from Union Theological Seminary, New York City, doing studies in Liberation Theology & Education. He is also coeditor (with Paul Kihn) of the books *Labeling: Politics and Pedagogy* (London: Falmer Press, 2000) and (with Cameron McCarthy, et al.) *Sound Identities* (New York: Peter Lang, 1999).

Susan Ikenberry is a graduate of Vassar and Johns Hopkins University. She teaches Advanced Placement American History, Europe, and Government at Georgetown Day School in Washington, DC. For the school year 1993–94, she received a DeWitt Wallace Teacher-Scholar award to study novels and short stories depicting the college experience from 1880 to 1980 from the National Endowment for the Humanities. She has written the entry on "Eleanor Roosevelt in Fiction" for the Eleanor Roosevelt Encyclopedia, published in 2000. She is a regional consultant for the College Board, a member of the Advisory Board of the Bill of Rights Institute, and received the Bridgebuilder's award in 2002 from the Partnership for Liveble Communities.

Jo Keroes is a Professor of English at San Francisco State University, where she has served as Chair of the English Department and as Coordinator of the M.A. Program in English/Composition. She teaches classes in Stylistics and Jewish Women Writers as well as graduate seminars preparing teachers of college level writing and literature. She is the author of *Tales Out of School: Gender, Longing, and the Teacher in Fiction and Film.*

Morna McDermott is an Assistant Professor in the Elementary Education Department at Towson University in Maryland. She received her Ph.D. from the University of Virginia in May 2001. Her scholarship and work with preservice teachers and practicing educators centers on various relationships between critical aesthetics in education, arts-based inquiry, democracy, and social justice.

Lee Papa is an Assistant Professor of Drama Studies in the Department of English at the College of Staten Island/CUNY. He is working on a forthcoming book on the Double Edge Theatre of Massachusetts. Papa is also a playwright whose works have been performed in California, Chicago, and New York City.

John G. Ramsay is the Hollis L. Caswell Professor of Educational Studies and Associate Dean of the College at Carleton College in Northfield, Minnesota. He is a member of the board of directors of Admission Possible, a Twin Cities nonprofit organization providing tutoring and financial-aid services to low-income students preparing for college. His essays on higher education in the United States have been published in *Change, Liberal Education, Journal of General Education, Review of Higher Education,* and *Ruminator Review.*

Paula M. Salvio is an Associate Professor of Education at the University of New Hampshire where she was the Director of the Doctoral Program in Literacy and Schooling. Salvio's essays on autobiography, performance, and curriculum theory have appeared in such journals as *Curriculum Inquiry, The Journal of Curriculum Theorizing, Cambridge Journal of Education, English Education, Language Arts,* and *The Journal of Teacher Education.* She is currently completing a book on the teaching life of the poet Anne Sexton.

Susan Talburt is the Director of the Women's Studies Institute and Associate Professor of Educational Policy Studies at Georgia State

University in Atlanta. She teaches courses in curriculum, social foundations, and feminist theory. She is the author of *Subject to Identity: Knowledge, Sexuality, and Academic Practices in Higher Education* (Albany: SUNY Press, 2000) and co-editor of *Youth and Sexualities: Pleasure, Subversion, and Insubordination In and Out of Schools* (Palgrave, in press).

John A. Weaver is an Associate Professor in the Department of Curriculum, Foundations, and Reading at Georgia Southern University. His teaching focuses on the culture of technology, popular culture, science, and literature. John is the editor (with Toby Daspit) of *Popular Culture and Critical Pedagogy: Reading, Constructing, Connecting* (1998), editor (with Marla Morris and Peter Appelbaum) of *(Post)Modern Science (Education)* (2001), and the author of *Rethinking Academic Politics in (Re-)Unified Germany and the United States* (2000). His articles and book chapters have focused on the Holocaust, rap, posthuman condition, Neuropolitics, and higher educational reform.

Allison J. Kelaher Young is an Associate Professor in the Department of Teaching, Learning, and Leadership at Western Michigan University, where she coordinates the program in secondary education. She teaches courses in adolescence, educational psychology, and general pedagogical methods. Her research interests include adolescence, motivation, and the social contexts of schooling. Her recent work has centered on the representation of GLBT issues in education, particularly as these issues intersect the context of teacher education programming. She has published in *College Teaching, Journal of Excellence in College Teaching, Encounter: Education for Meaning and Social Justice,* and the *Journal of Learning and Individual Differences.*

Index